Mindfulness-Based Play-Family Therapy

Mindfulness-Based Play-Family Therapy

Theory and Practice

DOTTIE HIGGINS-KLEIN

Foreword by Bonnie Badenoch

W. W. Norton & Company
New York • London

For information about permission to reproduce selections from this book,
write to Permissions, W. W. Norton & Company, Inc.,
500 Fifth Avenue, New York, NY 10110

For information about special discounts for bulk purchases,
please contact W. W. Norton
Special Sales at specialsales@wwnorton.com or 800-233-4830

Manufacturing by Quad Graphics Fairfield
Book design by Bytheway Publishing Services
Production manager: Leeann Graham

Library of Congress Cataloging-in-Publication Data

Higgins-Klein, Dottie.
 Mindfulness-based play-family therapy : theory and practice / Dottie
Higgins-Klein ; foreword by Bonnie Badenoch. — First edition.
  pages cm
"A Norton Professional Book."
 Includes bibliographical references and index.
 ISBN 978-0-393-70863-9 (hardcover)
 1. Play therapy. 2. Family psychotherapy.
 3. Child psychotherapy. 4. Interpersonal psychotherapy.
 I. Title.
 RJ505.P6H54 2013
 618.92'891653—dc23

                          2013003103

                ISBN: 978-0-393-70863-9

W. W. Norton & Company, Inc., 500 Fifth Avenue, New York, N.Y. 10110
                   www.wwnorton.com
 W. W. Norton & Company Ltd., Castle House, 75/76 Wells Street,
                  London W1T 3QT

          1   2   3   4   5   6   7   8   9   0

This book is dedicated to my family, friends, teachers, students, and clients of all ages, and to all sentient beings—present, past, and future.

Inside and Out

This morning you want to curl up
And hide from the world.
All right then, enter into what you want,
And let yourself rest in that cocoon,
Welcome yourself home.
There's nothing you must do,
And nothing you must say.
Only stillness, inhabiting silence.

Soon there is a stirring,
Something bubbling up from below;
A natural urge to reach out,
Only this time, shining
With your own radiance from within.

John Welwood
Poems of Love and Awakening (unpublished)

Contents

Foreword

A T A TIME when so many families are deeply challenged, Dottie Higgins-Klein offers a wise, robust, and beautiful pathway toward healing for all family members in *Mindfulness-Based Play-Family Therapy*. This way of being present to families developed slowly during her 30 years of clinical practice and clinician training at her Family & Play Therapy Center in Philadelphia. For the last 12 years, she has devoted much attention to this manuscript—building, refining, and deepening as she continued her work with children, teens, parents, and others close to the family. At the same time, she was offering trainings to over 2,000 clinicians in the art and science of family healing, raising her children, and engaging in her own healing process as well. These four viewpoints—clinician, mentor, parent, and developing human being—inform every page of this powerful book.

We might ask why it is so needed at this particular juncture. As the demands of our culture push us at ever-increasing speed, secure attachment is in decline because it needs us to be with our children in long, slow moments of warm engagement if it is to develop—something that the acceleration of life doesn't easily afford. As speed increases, so does fear, and this pushes us away from relationships and toward actions to alleviate the pervasive sense of uncertainty. These actions get caught up in the speed—continual texting, hours spent with distractions of all sorts, addictions—anything to try to readjust our out-of-balance systems. When teenagers spend their time together each focusing on his or her own computer, posting on Facebook, it may not be too much to say that we are at a crossroads where relational decline and relational repair are both still possible, and that the health of the nation depends on which road we take.

In a recent editorial, op-ed columnist David Brooks (2012) of the *New*

York Times based his suggestions for broad societal change on the Adverse Childhood Experiences (ACE) study undertaken by Kaiser Permanente and the Centers for Disease Control and Prevention (CDC) in the 1990s. It involved 17,000 participants. The ACE questionnaire offers 10 categories of traumatic experiences endured in childhood, and the researchers found that the higher the score, the greater the likelihood of everything from obesity to alcoholism to attempted suicide to various physical ills. Building on this research, it was also discovered that only 3% of children who scored 0 on the ACE had learning or behavioral problems in school, while 51% of those with a score of 4 or higher had these problems. The study itself delivered these three conclusions:

- Adverse childhood experiences are surprisingly common, although typically concealed and unrecognized.
- Adverse childhood experiences still have a profound effect 50 years later, although now transformed from psychosocial experience into organic disease and mental illness.
- Adverse childhood experiences are the main determinant of the health and social well-being of the nation. (Felitti, 2004, p. 4)

As Brooks concludes, perhaps it is time for all areas of society to realize that we need to focus our efforts on healing the injuries that have already happened and move toward preventing additional wounding if we want to set our feet on a healthy course. Higgins-Klein offers well-grounded, clear, and deeply caring steps along this way.

Dottie Higgins-Klein is a brilliant synthesizer, forming the theoretical base for her unique approach from the traditions of developmental psychology (Margaret Mahler and Allan Schore in particular), family therapy (Boszormenyi-Nagy and Minuchin), mindfulness, interpersonal neurobiology, and play therapy. These strands are woven into a coherent structure that illuminates and holds Mindfulness-Based Play-Family Therapy (MBPFT). At each step, Higgins-Klein blends theory with detailed guidance (including transcripts) that will support both new and seasoned therapists as she accompanies us along a clear trail through repair of the developmental stages of the child, the parents, and the family as a whole. All of her writing is saturated with an interpersonal richness, because the presence and deep seeing of the therapist lie at the core of her work. One aspect of this relational focus can be found in how she moves away from the more usual phrase for the child in trouble, "identified patient," instead substituting the words "child of most concern," or MC child. This shift toward compassion for the whole child and away from a single focus on behavior can be felt throughout the book.

Beginning with a solid summary of Margaret Mahler's developmental theory, supplemented by the groundbreaking work of Allan Schore concerning the centrality of affect regulation, Higgins-Klein moves in the next chapter to the broad outline of how play therapy, family therapy, and parent education are mindfully woven together in single sessions and over multiple sessions. It is like watching an artful tapestry come to life. With unusual clarity and specificity, she charts a well-defined, yet flexible movement through the stages. As always, she is continually reminding us that the self of the therapist—in the richness of communication through body, gaze, prosody, and silence, as well as reflective words—holds the process for the whole family.

In the next five chapters, she takes us on a highly detailed journey from the first four evaluative sessions through the specifics of encounters in the playroom to working with mothers and fathers on mindful parenting. She shares what has gone right and what has been challenging, along with skillful ways to *be* with those challenges. What is most striking is the unique way she weaves work with family into work with the child at many points during each visit—from an initial Talk Time between parent and child, flowing into the child's time for play, moving toward some concluding moments of sharing with the parent. We may be able to imagine the sense of a secure rhythm emerging in these interactions.

It is a particular joy to enter the playroom with Higgins-Klein and a young one. Throughout the book, she draws a parallel between imaginary play and meditation, both of them right-centric experiences of being in the moment with what is. She says, "When a child is ready for the inner freedom that comes with letting the busy mind turn off, he will lead himself to the heart of the matter that needs reworking or healing." And the therapist will be right there, mindfully and with wisdom, accompanying him or her along this healing inward arc.

By the time we reach the last two chapters, we will be ready for the masterful weaving of the beginning with the end. In Chapter 8, Higgins-Klein draws the strands of Mahler's theory together with the actual healing processes she has offered throughout the book. She offers specific guidance for seeing, negotiating, and repairing these stages through moments of meeting in Talk Time, the imaginary freedom of play therapy, and the mindful brainwise space of parent education. The final case study makes it all the more solid and alive, particularly because of Dottie's humility as well as expertise. Oumar, the six-year-old boy who is the child of most concern because of his hallucinations and nightmares, becomes a living presence in the room. After meeting the family and learning the history, we enter the playroom and watch him move through his infant trauma of heart surgery into deeper awareness and release from that trauma, with Dottie's warm, steady support. We walk away with the sense that we can return to any of the chapters for ongoing guidance and nourishment toward flowing with this process in a similar way. Enjoy!

—Bonnie Badenoch

Acknowledgments

As I complete a book that has taken a lifetime to develop and 12 years to write, I am indebted and grateful to many people:

- To my family, my parents who gave me life, and my four siblings. They were my first and constant teachers.
- To my husband, children, grandchildren, in-laws, and nieces and nephews.
- To the hundreds of postgraduate therapists who have attended my trainings over the past 18 years.
- To the children and families who have trusted the therapists at the Family and Play Therapy Center with their healing process. They too have been teachers on this journey.
- To the many pioneers in play therapy, child development, and family therapy, whose work is the foundation of the theory and practice of Mindfulness-Based Play-Family Therapy (MBPFT). To these play therapists in particular: Virginia Axline, Clark Moustakas, Garry Landreth, Eliana Gil, John Allan, Louise Guerney, Byron and Carol Norton, Beverly James, Lenore Terr. To those in sand therapy: Rie Rogers Mitchell, Harriet Friedman, and Linda Homeyer. And to those in child development: Margaret Mahler, Daniel Stern, Allan Schore, and Henri Parens.

I am grateful to Ivan Boszormenyi-Nagy, originator of Contextual Family Therapy (CFT) and a profound teacher for me; and to Margaret Cotroneo, teacher, supervisor, and guide, who for more than a decade mentored me not only in applying CFT in my practice but, more important, in living it in my personal life. For the influence of the pioneers of family therapy, I thank

Murray Bowen, Salvador Minuchin, Virginia Satir, and Carl Whitiker. I particularly acknowledge Eliana Gil, teacher, mentor and friend, for her innovative work in combining family therapy and play therapy.

I am especially grateful to seven therapists who have studied with me continually from the beginning: Tonia Betancourt, Mary Beth Hays, Alyson Nowell, Laurie Parker, Estelle Price, Sue Ryan, and Ann Schneider-Meisel. They are partners in the development of the theory and practice of MBPFT. They have read various versions of the book over the years and implemented it into their own practices covering a wide range of client populations. I appreciate that many of them are now teaching this framework in both graduate and postgraduate settings. For years of dedication to the play-family therapy approach, I thank Jann Stuart Glider, Dorothy Vereen, and Susan White.

I thank Bonnie Badenoch, Daniel Siegel, and Allan Schore for their dedication to making the field of interpersonal neurobiology more accessible to therapists and therefore to families. They have provided an understanding that affirms what play therapists witness, particularly in spontaneous play therapy, and they have given us a language for explaining it to parents. I am most grateful to Bonnie for her encouragement and her belief in this book.

I thank John Welwood, Daniel Siegel, and Jon Kabat-Zinn for their steady, world-expansive contributions to mindfulness mediation. I extend appreciation to my teachers of Tibetan and Zen Buddhism, including John, who influenced me to incorporate deep mindfulness into my life and practice over the past 25 years. I thank 83-year-old Balinese healer Tjokorda Gde Rai for sharing his knowledge of the healing power of energy and his grasp of the connections among the body, mind, and spirit. As my teacher, he imparted his wisdom to me in a very personal way, and allowed me to learn through witnessing his unique healing techniques.

I am grateful to Deborah Malmud at W. W. Norton. In her available and thoughtful way, she helped me to take my unwieldy manuscript and tame it into a reasonably sized book. I thank Sophie Hagen, the managing editor; Rachel Keith, the copy editor; and Jean Blackburn, production editor. I am fortunate to have had good communicators who were able to take the book and make it better while maintaining the integrity of the text.

My writing experience was enriched by many opportunities to work in beautiful environments away from my home and office. The settings included a one-year sabbatical in the woods at a spacious Zen center in New York as I started writing in September 2001; a year at the shore, with the ocean at my doorstep; multiple visits to Bali; the island of Pantelleria in the Mediterranean; a house by the bay in New Jersey; and many enjoyable weekends at Pendle Hill, a Quaker retreat center that offers refuge to writers. I am grateful to the people who made those sensuous places available to me.

Thirty years ago, the two worlds of play therapy and family therapy were much more separate than they are today. I am grateful to the director of my graduate program at Hahnemann University (now Drexel University) in Philadelphia, Robert Garfield, MD, for giving me—the first student to make such a request in the master of family therapy program—permission to have a placement that would allow me to begin to combine family therapy and play therapy. It was up to me to find such a practicum. My first-choice placement was to receive mentoring and supervision from Leslie Pepitone, PhD. Leslie was a professor in our program who was dedicated to helping family therapists appreciate the importance of understanding how to work with the deeper, individual psychodynamic adult issues while appreciating the relational family context. She understood that I was looking for an ethical way in which the family therapist could provide individual play therapy for the child while also offering parent–child meetings and parenting education, as well as multipartial, individual, or couple therapy when clinically advisable. Thanks to Dr. Pepitone, the seeds of this book were planted in 1982. Years later, during the final stage of editing, I asked Leslie to read the family therapy chapters of this book. I did not realize what a skilled and thoughtful editor she would prove to be. She ended up editing almost the entire book, helping us to meet deadlines, and offering insightful suggestions.

I thank my son Luke, who loved words before he could speak, for faithfully editing this book throughout the first nine years, as well as for his scrupulous dedication to the final polishing before going to press. His enormous creative and technical skills have been an indispensable part of the growth of our worldwide training center that has nurtured MBPFT. And I thank Jerry, my husband, for the past three years of constant writing, reorganizing, reading aloud, and editing. He has given me such patient attention to detail that he is like a coauthor!

Finally, I wish to express my gratitude for having been placed on a life path that is beautiful while challenging and richly fulfilling.

Introduction: A Word About Mindfulness and the Zen of Play Therapy

MINDFULNESS-BASED PLAY-FAMILY THERAPY (MBPFT) has developed from the experience and insights of mindfulness meditation. The pivotal element of MBPFT is what happens in the "deeper awareness" stage of play therapy, when the child is offered a space to enjoy predominantly right-brain function and relax his* "busy mind." As his experience reaches a state comparable to mindfulness meditation, profound healing can occur. This book describes what happens in the therapist–child relationship and how to maximize the healing potential of this process.

Meditation teacher, scientist, researcher, and writer Jon Kabat-Zinn offers us a straightforward definition of mindfulness: "Mindfulness means paying attention in a particular way: on purpose, in the present moment, and nonjudgmentally" (1994, p. 4). Through paying attention in this way, we arrive here and now in our lived moments. One benefit of being "awake" to experience living is that we can "realize the richness and the depth of our possibilities for growth and transformation" (1994, p. 4).

There is abundant research on the efficacy of mindfulness, including work led by Kabat-Zinn at the Stress Reduction Clinic at the University of Massachusetts Medical School. His writing has disseminated information about this ancient Buddhist method of meditation to a wide spectrum of people, who are learning to use it to reduce stress in everyday life. Mindful-

---

*Throughout this book, play therapists will be primarily referred to using female pronouns and the children with whom they work using male pronouns. This is meant to reflect the reality that the vast majority of play therapists are female.

ness allows for healthier living in body, mind, and relationships. It is accessible to everyone, not just to those who think of themselves as spiritual.

In *Mindsight: The New Science of Personal Transformation* (2010b), Daniel Siegel gives a masterly presentation on how the body-mind-brain system works in everyday relational living and on the consequent impact that the practice of "mindsight" can have.

> Mindsight is a kind of focused attention that allows us to see the internal workings of our own minds. It helps us to be aware of our mental processes without being swept away by them, enables us to get ourselves off the autopilot of ingrained behaviors and habitual responses, and moves us beyond the reactive emotional loops we all have a tendency to get trapped in. (p. ix)

In the presence of a mindful therapist, a child can achieve this state in play therapy. In *The Mindful Therapist* (2010a), Siegel helps clinicians understand the application of brain science research to psychotherapy by showing how internal attunement promotes neural integration. "The brain continues to develop throughout the life span, and with the proper focus of our minds we can actually strategically change our brains in a helpful way" (p. xiii). The more we develop the presence, empathy, and compassion that come with our own internal attunement, the better we become at helping others develop themselves in similar ways.

In the series editor's foreword to *Trauma and the Body: A Sensorimotor Approach to Psychotherapy*, Daniel Siegel describes the tradition, thousands of years old, of using practices that focus on the body as a means of moving toward mental and emotional well-being:

> Modern neural science clearly points to the central role of the body in the creation of emotion and meaning. The brain is hard-wired to connect to other minds, to create images of others' intentional states, affective expressions, and bodily states of arousal that, through our mirror neuron system's fundamental capacity to create emotional resonance, serve as the gateway of empathy. In this way we see that the body is both relational and embodied. (Ogden, Minton, & Pain, 2006, p. xv)

Referring to research by Richard Davidson and his colleagues, the authors of *Trauma and the Body* state that "the use of mindfulness has been shown to change brain function in positive ways, increasing activity in areas of the brain associated with positive affect" (Ogden et al., 2006, p. 169). They note that the mindful capacity to stay connected to the internal process can help to activate the executive and observing functions of the prefrontal cortex instead of shutting them down, as occurs during posttrauma reactions.

John Welwood is a prolific author and clinical psychologist who has quietly dedicated his life to exploring the interface of psychology and contemplative spirituality. I met John in 1981 while taking one of his courses. Heeding the advice he offered that weekend, I spent the next year noticing the relationship between *doing* and *being*. This was my first step in learning unconditional presence. For six years, beginning in 1987, my training with John included attending his week-long trainings in "Psychotherapy as a Meditative Process" at the Omega Institute in Rhinebeck, New York. He had studied with Eugene Gendlin, developer of Focusing, which is at the root of many of today's body–mind modalities. At the trainings, in addition to teaching mindfulness meditation, John taught us Focusing, both for personal use and for working with therapy clients. A support group grew out of these encounters and met monthly for many years, applying focusing and meditation to our own lives.

In *Awakening the Heart: East/West Approaches to Psychotherapy and the Healing Relationship*, John (Welwood) compiled the "first book to concretely explore how meditative and contemplative practices can inform and provide a larger context for the healing relationship" (1983, p. xiv). In his own contribution (pp. 44–46), he states that for change to occur in psychotherapy, it would seem essential that "clients speak *from* their immediate experience, rather than from familiar thoughts, feelings, beliefs or judgments *about* their experience." He recommends communicating from what Gendlin calls a *felt sense*. "A felt sense is a wider way our body holds or 'knows' many aspects of a situation all at once—subverbally, holistically, intuitively. It is concretely *felt*—in the body—as a *sense*—something not yet cognitively clear or distinct." In exploring the relationship between psychotherapy and meditation, Welwood presents similarities and differences between this "felt sense" way of being with a client and the spiritual process described by Zen writers.

Welwood notes that meditation is not goal oriented, but simply a space for us to be ourselves, in our true nature. This is the same energy that occupies the playroom during the deeper awareness stage of MBPFT. Freed by the language and experience of "pretend" and helped by the therapist's mindful presence, children often enter a meditative state during the fourth stage of therapy. While the child remains in pretend, she is able to create metaphors that mirror the present pain of the traumas or difficulties in her real-life circumstances, casting them naturally into a form safe enough for her to face. Through her own metaphors, she gradually confronts the source of her trauma and life pain. In the safety of the playroom and with the trusted therapist as witness, the child experiences what she has perhaps dissociated from and releases the traumatic effects that have been trapped in her body. It is crucial to her healing that she face her own powerlessness while being supported by the therapist's unconditional presence, and "the most profound of our experiences and our insights come without words. They are unspeakable except as image or pure feeling" (McCarthy, 2007, p. 15).

To communicate how similar this stage of MBPFT is to deep meditation, with all its healing power, this process is described as the "Zen of Play Therapy." The best responses of the therapist are those that support the child in staying as completely in the present moment as possible. When the distractions of the reality-based thinking mind are no longer present, the child is able to stay in a prolonged healing state. During this stillness, she can reach a level of consciousness parallel to the deepened awareness that occurs during mindfulness meditation. After she has experienced this stage in multiple play sessions, reworking some of life's hurts through her play, the therapist and the parents will see a happier child. Eckhart Tolle points out that stillness allows us to experience a tree, a flower, or a sunset, rather than to analyze the tree, flower, or sunset. He notes that while there is a place for analyzing, too much of it interferes with our capacity for stillness.

> Stillness is inseparable from who you are in the depth of your being. One could say everybody is still already. The stillness is already there. . . . The only thing is, you may not notice it. If there is a lot of mental noise, then you don't even notice it is there. (Tolle, 2005)

Healing occurs when the therapist and child together descend into their respective places of inner stillness. Sometimes the child's play looks somewhat mad, foolish, angry, or desperate; but this, too, can arise from the sacred stillness. The child's feelings may reflect the source of the powerlessness at the root of her trauma. The therapist learns just the right moment—not too soon and not too late—to mirror those powerless feelings. The only way out is through.

The therapy model described in this book has been practiced and taught since 1995 at the Family & Play Therapy Center in Philadelphia, where we provide therapy to clients of all ages. Our week-long courses in the summer and our certificate courses, which follow the academic year, offer extensive training for graduate- and postgraduate-level therapists in Mindfulness-Based Play-Family Therapy, Contextual Family Therapy, and Sandtrap Therapy. We also host Advanced Seminars presented by authors in these fields. Students earn credit toward professional credentials and can also fulfill their requirements for continuing education credits. Participants in the courses include therapists at the start of their careers as well as those who have a lifetime of experience. Many therapists continue their study at our Center for over ten years.

The breadth of this community makes the class dialogues richly rewarding, and this community is further enriched by the national and international makeup of the group. The Center's IT department has designed our own state-of-the-art online system, called *iLOC*—"interactive, live online classroom"—which connects the classroom in Philadelphia with therapists anywhere in the world. Participants report an "in the room" feeling, as they see and hear the live presentation and are able to join into the class dialogue as it is happening. Our classes have included participants from across the United States—including Alaska and Hawaii—and from around the world, including Mexico, Ireland, the U.K., the Netherlands, Russia, India, Japan, Australia, and New Zealand. In order to foster this multicultural element, and in an effort to extend economic fairness to all, we have a directory of geographical discounts that range from 20% to 75%, depending on the full-time residence of a student whose professional credentials meet the requirements of his or her country. (See Appendix B.)

Mindfulness-Based Play-Family Therapy

1

Early Childhood Development and Interpersonal Neurobiology

> Each individual starts and develops and becomes mature; there is not adult
> maturity apart from the previous development. This development is extremely
> complex, and it is continuous from birth or earlier right up to and through
> adulthood to old age. We cannot afford to leave anything out, not even the
> happenings of infancy, not even those of very early infancy.
>
> —D. W. Winnicott (1965, p. 21)

THIS BOOK IS about helping children to heal from emotional suffering
and to change the behavioral problems that accompany that suffering.
It is also about the collateral healing that can occur in the family system of
the child in treatment. These healing events arise from techniques derived
from the rich fields of early child development theory, play therapy, family
therapy, and interpersonal neurobiology, all combined within a framework
grounded in mindfulness. This framework is what we call Mindfulness-
Based Play-Family Therapy (MBPFT).

When a child comes for therapy, his current situation is the product of
his experience of life to that point. His development has been influenced by
the reverberations between his changing developmental needs at each stage
and the assets and deficits of his caregivers' responses, all evolving within
the long-established emotional climate of the family. Because treatment
starts with exploring the causes of the child's current problems, we begin

our elucidation of MBPFT with an overview of early childhood development.[1]

The foundation of early child development theory, and the basis for early intervention work, is Margaret Mahler's theoretical framework of separation and individuation.[2] This has been expanded and enriched by Allan Schore's exploration of affect regulation theory and the interpersonal neurobiology of emotional development; Schore's studies address the workings of attachment and the roots of shame. Daniel Stern has shown us how and when the core sense of self-awareness is established, and Henri Parens has tracked the development of aggression.

When therapists have an adequate grasp of theory, they sense where, in the child's past, the necessary stages of growth were complicated by neglect, abuse, medical trauma, genetics, ignorance, or untimely family circumstances, resulting in the child's emotional or behavioral problems. The therapist forms a treatment plan based on an understanding of how essential needs that were unmet earlier may be revisited and satisfied well enough to reestablish true developmental balance. It is equally important to acknowledge how family members have nurtured healthy development in their children. An additional goal for the therapist is to give parents explicit information that will help them understand the connections between a child's early history, past family pain and traumas, and the present situation.

The Background of Early Child Development Study

Development is not a succession of events left behind in history. It is a continuous process constantly updated.

—Daniel Stern (1985, p. 260)

Over a 20-year period of research, Margaret Mahler and her team invited mothers and children to attend a group that met regularly so they could focus on the emotional growth and development of each child and on his

---

[1] The word "mother" is used to indicate the primary attachment figure. In various family situations, this figure may be the father, grandparent, or another main caregiver.

[2] This chapter is intended only to highlight the importance of locating the sources of current symptoms in a child's early history, and it is recommended that clinicians read Mahler's work directly.

or her relationship with the mother. The mothers came to the groups with newborn babies and stayed until their youngest child was three years old, and thus the research team was able to view children and sometimes siblings with their mothers over an extended period. From this research, Mahler and her team demonstrated that the first three years of life, through a process of separation and individuation, are a gestation period for the psychological birth of the child, which occurs at approximately age three. Margaret Mahler, Fred Pine, and Anni Bergman describe their work with the mothers, babies, and toddlers in their classic text, *The Psychological Birth of the Human Infant* (1975). A few years later, Louise Kaplan elaborated on Mahler's theory of separation and individuation in the very accessible book *Oneness and Separateness* (1978), a somewhat poetic introduction to Mahler's research and its application to clinical practice, whose information is appreciated by many new parents.

In his landmark book *Affect Regulation and the Origin of the Self: The Neurobiology of Emotional Development* (1994), Allan Schore uses Mahler's stages of development as a framework for discussing the parallel processes of brain development, affect regulation, and attachment formation. Schore states,

> In agreement with the concept of sequential stages of early development propounded in current neurobiological, neurochemical, ethological, embryological, psychological, and biological theory, Mahler (Mahler, Pine, & Bergman, 1975) has proposed specific phases of socioemotional development. As a result of her observational and clinical studies with infants and toddlers, Mahler—who is perhaps the most important impetus to the inception of a program of rigorous developmental, psychoanalytic research—characterizes a sequence of universal sequential stages of socioaffective ontogeny. (p. 23)

Mahler's more than 20 years of research and her consequent conceptualization of the psychological birth of the human infant have provided an essential basis for learning about the first three years of life. Until Mahler's work of directly observing infants and toddlers—considered the most groundbreaking contribution to psychology since Freud's development of psychoanalysis—knowledge of what happens in a young child's life was based primarily on retrieved memories, dream analysis, and transferential relationships in work with adults. Now, through Mahler's work, we understand in detail the process of attachment in a child's first relationship.

Mahler's Phases of Separation and Individuation

Mahler considers "separation" and "individuation" to be two complementary and interwoven aspects of development. *Separation* is the baby's intrapsychic achievement of a sense of differentiation from the mother and, through that, from the world at large: a sense of boundaries. Starting from a symbiotic-like body connection with the mother, which peaks at four to five months, the baby gently relaxes toward this sense of difference. In Stern's view, this is happening all along: "The infant begins to experience a sense of an emergent self from birth" (1985, p. 10). Mahler sees the primary achievement of a major leap in separation of the child from the mother ideally occurring at about the 30th to the 36th month. One might say that a child's third birthday is the celebration of his psychological birth.

Mahler's *individuation* is concerned with the actual achievements that the child makes toward establishing his own personal characteristics and affective and cognitive skills. It is the felt sense of being a separate self, a little boy or little girl different from his mother, that the child holds inside. Mahler would say that the child gradually gains a conscious *awareness* "that I am," and this is followed by "who I am" (1975, p. 8). Stern emphasizes that emergent infants are "pre-designed to be aware of self-organizing processes" (1985, p. 10). In normal growth and development of the emotional social self, similar to physical development, he notes that "between periods of rapid change there are periods of relative quiescence, when the new integration appears to consolidate" (p. 8).

The Awakening Phase (Birth to Two Months)

Mahler considers the Awakening Phase (formerly called the Normal Autistic Phase) to be the forerunner of the separation and individuation process. Although an infant's eyes may wobble in the first month, often enough his first attempts at eye contact may be quite direct. As he is able to gaze more competently into his parents' eyes, he begins to respond to a smile. First, we see an unspecific, social smile, followed by the preferential smile for the mother. John Bowlby (1966) regarded this as an indicator of a special bond developing between infant and mother.

By the second month, the infant is gradually experiencing a symbiotic-like relationship between himself and his mother, described by Mahler and her colleagues as a boundless, oceanic feeling. They found that symbiosis was optimal when the mother naturally sustained gazing eye contact with her baby, especially while nursing or bottle feeding or talking or singing to him. Some babies, toddlers, and children who enter the family through adoption may struggle to make eye contact. In many cultures, these little ones benefit greatly when the new family is coached to play games to engage eye contact. This early connecting to the infant's inner sensations is important as a way of reaching the core of the self, which will give rise to a sense of identity (Mahler et al., 1975, pp. 46–47).

What the Mahler team knew, perhaps more intuitively than scientifically, was that the baby's brain is affected by the pleasure that builds up inside the right brains of both mother and infant, and that the very growth of the baby's brain is dependent on contact with an adult brain, as is the development of his structure of behavior. Schore highlights the important work of Colwyn Trevarthen, who found that

> the affective regulations of brain growth are embedded in the context of an intimate relationship, and that they promote the development of cerebral circuits. This interactive mechanism requires older brains to engage with mental states of awareness, emotion, and interest in younger brains, and involves a coordination between the motivations of the infant and the feelings of adults. (Schore, 1994, p. 9)

When a baby coos with his mother or father in the sweetness of the mutual gaze, he moves his body in a pattern that matches his vocalization. This is a whole body experience of love! "It is now well established both that it is the affective state that underlies and motivates attachment behavior and that the combination of joy and interest motivates attachment bond formation" (Schore, 2003a, p. 10).

The First Subphase: Differentiation and Development of a Body Image (Two to Seven Months)

From the Awakening Phase, the baby enters the Normal Symbiotic Phase. This begins the process that leads to his differentiation. During symbiosis, the baby's primary psychological achievement is his growing attachment with his mother, peaking at about four to five months. Mahler's use of the word *symbiosis* fits with recent neurological discoveries; although the baby is now more aware of his mother, his psychological separateness from her is growing. Baby and mother really do need one another in order to flourish. Mahler uses the term *hatching* to describe the period where the baby becomes more permanently alert, persistent, and goal directed. Stern accurately refers to the very early formation of a sense of core self and core other as "active acts of integration," assuming that the sense of self is integrating from the beginning (1985, p. 101).

We know that children who are abused and neglected during these early months grow up with challenges in the area of trust. A healthy child learns how the mother plays and coos and delights in him. She is predictable, reliable, and trustworthy. Soon, he starts to more overtly initiate reaching out for this person, as he wants his "appetites" to be engaged. The fulfillment of his desire for maternal presence and empathy gives him a primary sense of relational, unconditional love. This conceptualization concurs with the observation of developmental neuroscientists "that the early critical period growth of structures which subserve self-regulatory functions is profoundly influenced by postnatal social environmental forces" (Schore, 1994, p. 27). Schore elaborates that the neurological maturation noted at 15 months—particularly in the limbic system, which is responsible for emotions—appears to correlate directly with the actions of affectionate caregiving at these earlier stages (p. 30).

Schore asserts that "the most basic level of regulatory processes is the regulation of arousal" and traces this back to the early months when the mother provides internal regulation for the infant. There is a bodily experienced dyadic "dance" that promotes development of the infant's synaptic connections, or, in other words, "drives brain development[,] and in human beings where the post natal development of the brain is so extensive, . . . the relationship between the caregiver and the child . . . directly [impacts] brain development" (2009). A disturbance in the relational experience results in dysregulation for the infant, who is more dependent developmentally on the mother than she is on him. Mindfulness-based, existential, and spontaneous child-centered play therapy methods simulate this implicit, nonverbal early experience, and offer effective healing in a way that left-brain therapies may not.

When a mother experiences postpartum depression, or is too unpredictable or ambivalent, too restrained or too "smothering," or when the child is the victim of neglect or abuse, there is interference of the bonding process. The child's attachment needs may be compromised, and though this may or may not show up in the present, the body will remember. There are preventive measures that can help the mother and baby through these difficult times, and when symptoms appear in an older child, there are healing measures that can be built into the play therapy, family therapy, and mindful parenting experience. The child may be feel separation anxiety, have difficulty connecting to adults or making friends with other children, or have low self-esteem. Such issues can often be traced back to the early months of his life. Early abuse and neglect may correlate with difficulties in affect regulation and with more disturbing antisocial, oppositional, or destructive behavior. Without intervention, the child may display levels of anger, rage, and aggression as he gets older that are out of proportion to his current stage of development. A consequence of neglect can be hopelessness and despair. Bruce Perry emphasizes the importance of having a community of caring, loving people of all ages to rework the impact of early abuse and neglect (Perry & Szalavitz, 2006, p. 231).

Offering hope for healing, Norman Doidge (2007) reassures us that the brain has much more neuroplasticity than was formerly believed. The overall conditions of the time from conception to the first three years of life are of fundamental importance in the child's development, but they are not the final determination in the potential of mental abilities.

> The damaged brain can often reorganize itself so that when one part fails, another can often substitute; that if brain cells die, they can at times be replaced; that many "circuits", and even basic reflexes that we think are hardwired are not. One of these scientists showed that thinking, learning, and acting can turn our genes on or off, thus shaping our brain anatomy and behavior—surely one of the most extraordinary discoveries of the twentieth century. (p. xix)

This hope illuminates the value of the steady experience of play therapy, even for children who have been severely abused or neglected.

The Second Subphase: Practicing (7 to 18 months)

The *early practicing period* (7 to 10 months) is the phase of object constancy, when the child gradually grows to understand that his mother has a separate identity and is truly a separate individual. When the mother leaves the room, the child has a newfound awareness: She didn't just disappear;

she exists. Out of sight no longer means out of mind. This leads to *internalization*, or the formation of an internal representation of the mother. This internalization provides children with an image that helps supply them with an unconscious level of guiding support and comfort from their parents. Deficiencies in positive internalization may lead to a sense of insecurity, low self-esteem, and a range of attachment issues even in adults.

> The central feature of this subphase is the elated investment in the exercise of the autonomous functions, especially motility, to the noted exclusion of apparent interest in the mother at times. It is the relationship, and not the development of motor skills *per se*, that characterizes the normal practicing subphase. (Mahler et al., 1975, p. 69)

What needs to be negotiated with the parents during this age-sensitive socioemotional practicing phase is greatly impacted by the success of earlier attachment and "affect amplification experiences" during the symbiotic phase. Ideally, the earlier mother–infant relationship has developed connection through nonverbal methods, and visual cuing is now particularly important for "refueling" behaviors as the baby moves away and returns to the parent (Schore, 1994, p. 97).

This emotional refueling allows the baby to extend more into his world and to move farther away and for longer periods. Thus, it is essential for the parenting figure to be reliably available when he does crawl away. The parent waits, without disappearing, and knows that she is needed for this emotional development to succeed. This is not a time to tease the baby or to be preoccupied by phone texting. Neither does she hover. The baby needs availability without smothering. The refueling hug affirms their connection, thus giving confidence to the little one that he can go back out and stretch even farther this time. Stern adds an important insight to the significance of refueling:

> [Refueling] is a reaffirmation that the infant and mother (as separate entities) are sharing in what the infant experiences. For instance, an infant experiencing fear after wandering too far needs to know that his or her state of fear has been heard. It is more than a need to be held or soothed; it is also an intersubjective need to be understood. (1985, p. 270)

During the actual refueling, the parent and baby may, in an attuned manner, share delight in a toy or in the ability of the baby to navigate unknown territory. "The creation of intersubjective sharing permits the exploration and pursuit of curiosity" (Stern, 1985, p. 270). It is easy to see how refueling is related to the development of connection, and thus of attachment. To the degree that the parent offers constancy of physical and emotional presence, the baby learns to feel attached and connected. The constancy of the caregiver aids in this bonding. Through repetitively controlling the moving away and returning to the parent, the baby solidifies the existence of the parent even when they are apart. Prolonged separations at this stage can cause depression for the baby and problems later on. Often the problems of children in therapy at an older age can be traced back to a challenging practicing period.

Schore, appreciating both Mahler's and Stern's contributions to the development of affective experiences in early development, adds essential information from more recent brain research (2009). The brain is lateralized into the left brain and right brain, with most people having very specific functions assigned to each side. The left-brain hemisphere is rational, verbal, conscious, serial, analytical, and logical, the place where we process information. The right-brain hemisphere, which is more connected to the limbic system, is concerned with emotions, the unconscious, and processing of nonverbal and emotional information. Schore notes that a cognitive left-brain perspective is giving way to a focus on the emotionally driven right brain, challenging some of the tenets of cognitive behavioral therapy. He states,

> One manifestation of the paradigm shift is that we are not talking about two halves of one brain but rather two separate cortical/sub cortical systems, each with its own unique structure, each processing different types of information in different ways. This dichotomy allows for a left brain and a right brain, and it splits evenly into a left conscious mind, a right unconscious mind, a right implicit self, and a left explicit self.

Schore notes that this information about the importance of what is happening in the separate right brain is shifting the limelight of attention from a cognitive behavioral left-brain perspective to understanding of emotionally driven right-brain focus. He notes that it is challenging some of the tenets of cognitive behavioral therapy (2009).

The mother's responses of attunement, misattunement, or reattunement help to modulate the activity-passivity cycle in the infant, which will in turn affect the cycles of social engagement or disengagement. Whatever happens or does not happen during this sensitive period has impact on later development.

We can see how the death of a parent is a serious loss for a young child. A parent's failure to return as expected challenges the child's secure knowledge that the parent who loves him will always be there and that love is constant. It can also be disturbing to the grounding of the child's development if his parents separate when he is at a young age, especially if he must adapt to living in two separate households. Spontaneous, mindfulness-based, and existentially rooted play therapy offer the child a quiet, nonintrusive experience that will allow him to express those losses in his own deep way, providing the optimal potential for healing. Children who have been separated from their birth family or orphanage during this developmental period similarly benefit from having families who are aware of the impact of the separation.

The practicing subphase proper (10 to 12 months to 16 to 17 months) is primarily characterized by the baby's capacity to walk. (Mahler calls upright locomotion "the greatest step in human individuation" [1975, p. 70].) Not only can the toddler see the world from a higher vantage point, but he also has access to a whole new range of objects in his environment. He begins exploring people and things with greater curiosity and delight, and healthy self-love is evident.

Regarding affect regulation and socioemotional development at this stage, Schore notes, "according to Mahler, *et al.*, the chief characteristic of the practicing period is the child's great narcissistic investment in his own functions and in 'the objects and objectives of his expanding reality'" (1994, p. 108). It is a time when we can observe more clearly the uniqueness of the baby in the forming of his personality.

> These dramatic affective transformations are critical to the establishment of permanent characteristics of the emerging personality. Perhaps more than any other time in the lifespan, the individual's internal state is externally observable and susceptible to socio-environmental influences. (Schore, 1994, p. 93)

Quoting Mahler, Schore notes that the baby experiences exhilaration and narcissistic elation more at this time than at any other time in development. The "world is my oyster" feeling and boundless energy are "associated with heightened activation of the sympathetic component of the autonomic nervous system" (1994, p. 94). Mahler gives us a warning about the importance of this emotional development: "It is precisely at this point at which the child is at the peak of his delusion of omnipotence—at the height of the practicing period—that his narcissism is particularly vulnerable to the danger of deflation" (Mahler et al., 1975, p. 228). Trauma that occurs during this stage may have long-term consequences in the development of personality.

When the toddler moves away from his mother, he initially keeps his eyes on her while exploring his new world. Schore calls this event "synchronized mutual gaze transactions" (1994, p. 105). During this time the baby's affect may be toned down. It is through the visual sense that he keeps emotionally connected; this allows him the confidence to conquer new feats and to begin the important task of pre-playing activities. When he returns, he "perks up" and the reunion "literally occurs in the form of her triggering infant cardiac acceleration and elation" (p. 104). This in turn may activate "the attachment and thereby the exploratory motivational systems" (p. 104). The baby's awareness of closeness parallels these increased sensorimotor skills. Being at ease with exploration promotes healthy individuation.

Thus, "the self-organization of the developing brain occurs in context of a relationship with another self, another brain" (Schore, 2003a, p. xv). The caregiver tactically helps the baby to regulate his "arousal, affective and attentional state" (Schore, 1994, p. 100). Schore notes that as the baby moves away from his mother, he tends to notice more subtle expressions on her face. "The child thereby uses the mother's affective expression as a signal, an indicator of her appraisal of danger or safety in a particular environmental circumstance" (p. 102). This includes using her cues as an "amplifier of positive arousal" (p. 102), helping him to decide how far to wander. Such sensitivity on the child's part involves "not just an orientation but also a recalibration of the arousal level produced by the toddler's plastic, developing nervous system against the reference standard of the mother's, which is reflected in her visually communicated facial signals" (1994, p. 102). In healthy development, the baby receives nonverbal, right-brain-to-right-brain permission to hug, laugh, connect, and then go back into the world. *What happens during this sensitive time period has long-term consequences for life span development.* When the relationship does not assist—but rather harms—affect regulation without the parent providing repair, there are long-term consequences for the baby. Early attachments, whether healthy or difficult, are recorded in the right brain with such enduring strength that they affect its lifelong capacity to cope with interpersonal stressors.

The roots of bullying may be traced to abusive behavior by a sibling, parent, or caregiver during the first years of the child's life when his brain was adapting itself to the environment. It is valuable when schools are aware of the consequences on children who have been raised in aggressive or neglectful environments.

> Amazingly and tragically, the brain of the bullied child can start to actually alter itself to be more suited to living in a bullying world. This can result in hypervigilance, reptilian brain fight-or-flight defense mechanisms, and either overactive or underactive RAGE or FEAR systems in the mammalian part of the brain (limbic system). (Sunderland, 2006, pp. 234–235)

Repeated bullying can alter the amygdala in the brain and the child will "overreact to minor stressors as if they are big threats," and this can cause fear to "become an ingrained part of the child's personality" (pp. 234–235).

The later part of the practicing subphase, from about a year onward, is an especially important time for the toddler to begin to extend trust to adults other than the parents for brief periods. In addition to needing the parent's availability for repeatedly playing out the important dynamics of this stage, the baby—by the nature of his exploration—is open to getting closer to other adults and children. This autonomy can be noted by his expression of whom he prefers to hold him or play with him.

If the parent is overprotective, fearful, or impatient, she may prevent the toddler from even attempting to master age-appropriate skills. Sensory integration issues can develop, such as difficulty with modulation or low muscle tone. Children coming to therapy, who are demanding and very self-centered, may not have had enough experience with frustration tolerance during their practicing stage, and may therefore have missed development of affect regulation. Distracting a child who cannot have what he wants is sometimes an adequate way to respond, but it is healthy for the little one to experience his anger when he is not getting his way. The adult kindly soothes the unhappy toddler but does not always give in or constantly divert his requests. Henri Parens, child psychiatrist and researcher, used to say, in his classroom teaching, that the parent does not have to create scenarios that help the toddler to develop normal frustration tolerance; life naturally provides many opportunities.

When a parent distracts the practicing baby too often away from what is frustrating, the baby does not experience a range of feeling. Schore points out the importance of shifting our thinking about the first year from an emphasis on cognitive development to a focus on affect regulation. We may find that the seemingly "good" baby may not be having *enough* experiences of a range of affective responses. Experiencing *manageable* frustration during the practicing stage benefits the next stage of development.

> The practicing phase in which the infant truly becomes a behaviorally and socially dynamic organism represents a critical period for the formation of enduring attachment bonds to the primary caregiver. The nature of the attachment to the mother influences all later socio-emotional transactions. (Schore, 1994, p. 98)

Speaking at the 2009 conference of the EMDR International Association, Schore stated that attention in the field of neurobiology has shifted from a predominantly cognitive view of development, which held that the purpose of the child's first year is "to create more and more complex cognitions," to an emphasis on emotional development "as an expansion of affect array." That is, an emotionally secure baby will have a continually developing capacity to experience feeling across expanding ranges of variety and intensity.

> The positively secure infant is not one who is always in the happy state. It is somebody who can feel it and can communicate it, and it is easy to read it. When you look at insecure, avoidant infants, with that flat face, they are hard to read. It's hard to pick up their emotions, et cetera. The child who is securely attached has this broad range. (Schore, 2009)

In normal development, the refueling process becomes more efficient as the toddler moves out to trust the world and returns to a "secure base." How this stage is negotiated with the parent will affect similar dynamics of oneness and separateness in relationships later in childhood and as an adult, including the ability to be connected intimately and to extend into the world socially. Most of the communication during this stage is nonverbal, involving the baby's learning to read body language, facial cues, sign language, and emotive sounds; this skill is essential for future mental health. Schore hypothesizes that "practicing phase refueling reunion transactions involving a pattern of energy transmissions between the mother and the infant may represent the fundamental core of the attachment dynamic" (1994, pp. 103–104). "These events may represent the dialectical psychoneurobiological imprinting process by which the mother critically influences the permanent 'hard-wiring' of brain regions in human infancy" (p. 104).

In *Affect Regulation and the Repair of the Self* (2003b), Schore has integrated multiple disciplines. He considers the methodology of his research to be not merely a review of the literature of socioemotional development, but the articulation of a conceptual model confirmed by reliable cross referencing (p. 152). Schore tracks how shame develops during the practicing phase and the impact it has on attachment. During this essentially preverbal time, the 7- to 17-month-old baby, at the peak of healthy self-love, is vulnerable to the dysregulation of affect. Self-consciousness and the first nonverbal cues for embarrassment can be observed as the baby learns to modulate the natural hyperarousal of this stage. It is not the separating, as baby crawls away, that initiates the shame, but suboptimal quality of the refueling connection, which ideally is not too loose and not too tight. The mother wants to engage the elation fully by mirroring the baby's tone, but not overdo the response and lead the baby to feel overwhelmed. Nor does she want to underrespond by ignoring the baby's excited affect. The apathy of a drug-addicted mother or the inconstancy of caregiving in an overcrowded orphanage or day care will induce hopelessness in the ignored baby.

The practicing subphase goes on daily for months, offering many opportunities for the "good-enough" parent to meet the baby's affective needs as he learns to tolerate the normal frustrations of life. Negotiating with his available parents, the toddler learns to regulate his emotions, including disappointment, anger, and shame as well as joy, delight, and exuberance. The parent's goal is not to keep these feelings from surfacing but rather to comfort and rework painful feelings that are healthy to experience in moderate doses. The securely attached baby is met by a parent who helps to modulate these responses. Ideally, if the parent has been insensitive, she offers to repair the baby's confused and hurt feelings with verbal and nonverbal soothing.

The maternal response to the reengaging toddler at reunion after an attachment break is critical to the reparable process of affect regulation. If she is responsive and approachable, the object relations link is reconnected, the infant's attachment system is reactivated, the arousal deceleration is inhibited, and shame is metabolized. As a result, the child recovers from the injury to narcissism and recovers from shame. (Schore, 2003b, p. 166)

However, when a parent is abusive or neglectful during the practicing stages, the baby is more prone to experiencing extreme levels of arousal, especially shame. A major consequence, in addition to attachment problems, may be that the toddler does not learn to modulate his affective responses with others. This can have long-lasting impact on the child's ability to meet the socialization requirements of living in the world. When the underground reactions resurface it can be confusing that the source of this older child's pain is rooted in the original experience of early shame. Shame "is felt as an inner torment, a sickness of the soul. It does not matter whether the humiliated one has been shamed by derisive laughter or whether he mocks himself. In either event he feels himself naked, defeated, alienated, lacking in dignity or worth" (Tomkins, 1963, p. 118). Could this be, at least in part, at the root of what may later be labeled "bipolar"?

In *The Science of Parenting* (2006), Margot Sunderland cautions that high cortisol levels can be associated with babies, particularly those who are cared for in day care for more than 20 hours per week in the first year of life. The consequences can include "difficult relationships between parent and child and more aggression and noncompliance in the children. It starts showing up at age two" (p. 54). This may be confusing to parents, who generally do not make connections between what may have happened in infancy with behaviors that show up two or more years later. Sunderland also quotes research with children five years old and younger showing an association between elevated cortisol levels and day care:

In one study for 91 percent of children, cortisol rose at daycare, and for 75% of the children, it dropped when they returned home. This research is worrisome because a key stress response system in the brain can become wired for hypersensitivity early in life. (p. 54)

In short, destructive experiences during a baby's practicing stages can have devastating impact on the child, teen, and adult that he becomes. When the parent is experienced as both protector and perpetrator, the child, perhaps because of his innate loyalty, will assume that something is wrong with *him*. In *Psychotherapy with Infants and Young Children*, Alicia Lieberman and Patricia Van Horn note that children will perceive that "only their own behavior or intrinsic badness could explain the parent's punitive or violent behaviors" (2008, p. 23). They begin to internalize a negative self-esteem, which impacts normal development.

However, when the baby learns to regulate extreme levels of affect in relationship with his caregivers, it paves the way for a more successful transition into the next, very challenging developmental stage: rapprochement. In summary, "the necessity for a psychic structural system to autoregulate affect, shame, and self-esteem is required from toddlerhood through adulthood, and its existence and availability depends on early object-relations experiences in the practicing-critical period" (Schore, 2003b, p. 181).

The energy that we see in the toddler in the practicing stage can seem hyperactive. Mahler attributes this to the child's defense against his sadness over the loss of the earlier symbiotic union (Mahler et al., 1975, p. 66). Not until the end of the practicing phase do we begin to see hints of the more subdued rapprochement subphase, where the child develops a new cognitive awareness that he must become a more separate self.

The Third Subphase: Rapprochement (18 to 36 Months)

In this stage of development, the infant once again becomes more dependent on the mother. The child realizes that his physical mobility demonstrates psychic separateness from his mother and may become tentative, wanting her to be in sight so that he can read her nonverbal cues as he explores his world. At the same time, he clings and exhibits more neediness than he did during the practicing stage. The risk is that the mother will misread his neediness and respond with impatience or unavailability. This can lead to an anxious fear of abandonment in the toddler. In the development of personality, a basic "mood predisposition" may be established.

Since we often think of growth as occurring in a linear fashion, the apparent regression that parents observe in their toddler as he moves into rapprochement can be quite confusing. However, rapprochement initiates regressive behavior as part of the course of normal development. Mahler's team found that "separation reactions occurred with varying intensity in all children during the *rapprochement* struggle" (Mahler et al., 1975, p. 211). After a toddler has explored his world for a while, his cognitive development makes a leap forward and, as he begins to grasp the reality of his situation, fear mingles with his excitement. Ambivalence becomes his normal state of being in the world. In the progression of the "refueling" ritual, there comes a "deliberate search for, or avoidance of, intimate bodily contact" (p. 77). A child in the rapprochement subphase is a challenge as he deals with the inevitable "longings and losses" of his young life (p. 230). Often the problems of children who arrive for play therapy at an older age can be traced back to a challenging rapprochement period.

The onset of rapprochement represents a transition in areas of the brain where social and emotional development occur. Orbitofrontal growth had been especially active during the dyadic relationship with the mother; now begins the critical period for growth of the dorsolateral system. This development seems to occur parallel to, and be influenced by, a deepening father-toddler relationship. Whereas until now the baby has bonded primarily with the mother, rapprochement tends to begin a more triadic relationship, drawing the father or secondary parent more actively into the circle. Schore notes that for the child, this relationship to an available father is on par emotionally with the maternal relationship. Interestingly, Schore points out that

> the orbital prefrontal cortex performs an executive control function in the right hemisphere, while the dorsolateral cortex performs such a role in the left hemisphere. The unique anatomical and functional properties of the two prefrontal systems account for the hemispheric differences in the lateralization of emotions. (1994, p. 239)

Thus, the executive function in the right hemisphere develops parallel to the baby's relationship to the mother, and the left hemisphere develops a similar function parallel to the intensification of the toddler's relating to the father.

Mahler notes that it is the mother's love of the toddler and her acceptance of his ambivalence and his sometimes sad mood that allow for healthy development to progress. "Predictable emotional involvement on the part of the mother seems to facilitate the rich unfolding of the toddler's thought processes, reality testing, and coping behavior by the end of the second or the beginning of the third year" (Mahler et al., 1975, p. 79). Mahler's team also learned the value of the mother's emotional willingness to let go of the toddler, rather than staying overprotective and enmeshed—"to give him, as the mother bird does, a gentle push, and encouragement toward independence. . . . It may even be the *sine qua non* of normal (healthy) individuation" (p. 79). This major leap in individuation begins with the toddler's concept of a self that is so separate that, by 20 to 22 months, he starts to understand and even to say "mine." Individuation culminates by age three, after the parents have been patiently available for the intense, often irrational ambivalence of the rapprochement phase.

One of the major emotional tasks for the parent–child relationship is resolution of "splitting" behaviors that normally intensify during the rapprochement subphase. The split is between pleasure and pain, or "good" and "bad." Constancy, the resolution of the split, is attained when the child begins to experience *emotionally*—not merely by cognitive awareness—that anger and love can coexist in the parent–child relationship. When splitting is not resolved, optimally by the Fourth Subphase, a child fears that when he gets mad at his mother or father or his parent gets mad at him, then the parent will stop loving him. This unresolved dilemma is at the root of many issues, including attachment and separation problems such as school phobia, that we see later in children coming for play-family therapy. Splitting issues can also be at the root of the problems of teens and even adults, including oppositional or passive-aggressive behaviors and bullying. Henri Parens's *Taming Aggression in Your Child: How to Avoid Raising Bullies, Delinquents, or Trouble-Makers* (2011) is dedicated to understanding this complex dynamic in order to prevent children from developing habits that not only hurt others but also hurt themselves.

In an earlier book, *Aggression in Our Children: Coping With It Constructively* (1987), Parens writes that dealing with our own and our child's hostility is among the top challenges of raising healthy children. He addresses the role of aggression during the rapprochement stage as well as feelings of aversion throughout childhood. Children of all ages feel hate for their parents from time to time. The children carry regret for that feeling, whereas parents prefer to deny it. Parens also notes,

> It is equally unavoidable that we, as parents, will at times be furious with our children and, because we love them, feel terrible about it afterward. Few experiences produce more guilt and shame in good parents than those moments when we feel, "I would like to be rid of that little . . . " (pp. 1–2)

Parens helps us to realize that it is part of normal development for these strong feelings to exist in both child and parent.

Parens (1987) describes two major forms of aggression: nondestructive aggression, which is present at birth, and hostile destructiveness, which is not present at birth per se, although the mechanism to generate it is present. Nondestructive aggression is seen as a positive innate energy that shows itself when we are assertive, autonomous, trying to reach goals, or protecting ourselves. Hostile aggression is brought on by experiencing excessive displeasure, pain, or distress. Hostile destructiveness can be seen in "angry, nasty, hurtful behaviors: hate, rage, bullying, torturing, vengefulness, and the like. Although it is also self-protective, it causes many individual and collective problems and suffering for humans" (p. 7). It is the parents' job to protect their children from the excessive displeasure that generates hostility and manifests at the root of attachment problems.

The low mood that the baby shows in the rapprochement stage may have to do with increased levels of corticoids, which alter mood states, and decreased levels of endogenous endorphins and adrenocorticotropic hormone (ACTH). Schore notes that this gradual increase in corticoids occurs as the baby moves from the earlier exciting practicing stage toward the later practicing stage, and then on to the rapprochement stage. He goes on to say that these changes in brain chemistry occur during shifts of arousal in the sensitive phases (1994, pp. 226–227). "The mother, the primary provider of affective socialization experiences to the child, thus directly influences the growth of prefrontal axons back down the neuraxis onto subcortical targets. These connections complete the organization of the lateral tegmental forebrain-midbrain limbic circuit" (p. 230). What is important to convey here is that there is a reciprocal relationship between the growth and development of the brain and the important attachment relationships in the first three years of life. Good-enough parenting includes the consistent repair of the inevitable mistakes that parents make. When life circumstances fracture the care and attachment, the brain map shows physical evidence of the not-good-enough relationships. Schore (2009) states that

> it will compromise such functions as the capacity to play. Also compromised is the capacity for attachment—meaning also the capacity for intimacy and the ability to read the emotional states of human beings. . . . This severe attachment trauma leaves behind a permanent physiological reactivity in the limbic areas of the right brain, thereby inhibiting its capacity to cope with future stresses and also to

develop into more complexity. Most of the stressors therefore are interpersonal stressors.

The Fourth Subphase: Consolidation of Individuality (36 Months On)

The consolidation subphase exhibits a wider range of variations of behavior than the previous three years. There is no "single definite permanent terminal point" (Mahler et al., 1975, p. 227). The child's self-esteem continues to develop, and a growing ability to carry the internal mother inside manifests itself in the generally delightful three-year-old. "The intrapsychic processes are now mediated by verbal and other forms of symbolic expression and have to be inferred from them—very much like in clinical child psychoanalysis" (p. 40). The Mahler team did use symbolic play sessions to try to understand what was happening in the separation and individuation process, but minor attention was given to this segment of the project.

Variations among individual children in the consolidation subphase are partly the result of how the first three years have progressed. Although many of the children in Mahler's study developed transient problems along the way, they were able to resolve the rapprochement crisis and, thereby, to arrive at emotional integration. They were able to achieve the early phase of healthy attachment, namely the ability to hold the parent's love inside even when the parent was not physically with them. They resolved the emotional love-anger split. Part of the complexity of this stage is that the child's individuation occurs as he realizes that his dependency on his parents will continue for some years to come. In the consolidation stage, the child begins to develop a conscience, including the experience of guilt.

Acknowledging what might be called "normal trauma," Mahler confronts the reality that we cannot be perfect parents. It is inevitable within the first three years that there will be difficulties that both directly and indirectly affect the child.

> It seems to be inherent in the human condition that not even the most normally endowed child, with the most optimally available mother, is able to weather the separation-individuation process without crises, come out unscathed by the rapprochement struggle, and enter the oedipal phase without developmental difficulty. (Mahler et al., 1975 p. 227)

How is the understanding of early child development relevant to the child and family who seek play-family therapy? How does the clinician formulate the treatment plan using this early history, and how does she explain the interconnections to the family? The following chapters address these questions.

2

Background and Overview of Mindfulness-Based Play-Family Therapy

MINDFULNESS-BASED PLAY-FAMILY THERAPY (MBPFT) is a method of working therapeutically with children, using play to promote healing of emotional and somatic problems, correction of behavioral issues, and repair of developmental deficits. The healing process addresses traumatic events that may be part of the child's history. Key to MBPFT is the therapist's attunement with the child, which is based on establishing a space of unconditional presence where the emotional and somatic conditions of the child are free to unfold from their confinement and be transformed. Ideally, this joint experience nurtures the growth of trust, allowing the child to feel, "I am okay for being me, as I am in my core self." There is an appreciation of the crucial value of allowing silence to be interspersed with mindful speech, as well as an awareness of nonverbal body cues.

MBPFT is rooted in early play therapy teachings (see Allan & Hillman, 1988; Axline, 1964, 1969; Gil, 1991, 1994, 1996; Guerney, 1978; James, 1994; Landreth, 2002; Moustakas, 1959; Norton & Norton, 1997; O'Connor & Schaefer, 1994; Schaefer, 1993; Terr, 1990; Webb, 1991) as well as systemic and relational family therapy (see chapter 6). It can include a wide range of directed and spontaneous play therapy modalities, in which the therapist may use receptive silence and nonverbal communication along with reflective responses. One goal of this book is to formulate a unified system derived from conscious integration of a range of therapeutic frameworks. Play therapy and family therapy have been slowly gaining an appreciation of each other over the past 30 years, and these fields are combined with the wisdom of interpersonal neurobiology (IPNB) and mindfulness practice into a rich system of treatment for children and families. The above-mentioned fields offer an evidence-supported framework for Mind-fulness-Based Play-Family Therapy that is rooted in the wisdom of the fundamental principles of early child development, play therapy, family therapy, and interpersonal neurobiology. Nine identifying characteristics of MBPFT are detailed below.

Nine Characteristics of MBPFT

1. An Evaluation Precedes the Treatment Phase

Generally lasting four sessions, a four-segment evaluation gives the therapist time to become familiar with present problems and concerns, the relational strengths of family members, the developmental history of the child for whom there is the most concern (MC), and the family histories of both parents.

2. The Parent Is Present With the Child for Discussion of Life Circumstances

Talk Time is a fifteen- or twenty-minute meeting prior to each play therapy session to develop inter-subjective communication. During this time, parent and child together address both what is going well for the child and family, and one or two of the specific symptoms or behaviors that are motivating the therapy. It can be conducted using various clinical approaches such as family therapy, behavior therapy, and cognitive therapy. It may include role playing, advocating for the child, or reframing negative behaviors. MBPFT does not focus solely on the child's problems but also attends directly to the family relationships.

Parents take turns bringing the child to discuss the "hard-to-talk-about" things. Once treatment begins, all information concerning the child's current issues and past history is discussed within the shared domain of Talk Time. There is no traditional "confidentiality contract" with the child; that is, the therapist does not promise to keep confidences with the child. With few exceptions, such confidentiality is unnecessary, because appropriate parent–child issues are discussed by the child, parent, and therapist together. This arrangement meets requirements that an agency or insurance company may have in order to allow parents to be more included in the child's treatment. In this way, the parents learn tools for attaining an emotional intimacy with their child that continues after therapy ends. An added benefit is that discussions often enrich the pretend play that follows.

3. The Child's Play Is Kept in the Imaginary Realm

An essential principle of MBPFT philosophy is that—as much as clinically possible—the playroom is preserved as a "pretend" space during play therapy time. (Most references to family circumstances and the child's real life are kept for Talk Time, as stated above.) The therapist takes the lead in setting the tone for playtime, encouraging imagination, mindful speech, and an appreciation of silence; this invites the child more deeply into the healing process. A parent may or may not be part of the ongoing playroom sessions, depending on the best clinical recommendation. If a parent is present, then he may sit quietly, witnessing the child's play, or he may be included while being coached by the therapist to keep the play in the imaginary realm. Spontaneous play in the presence of a mindful therapist is optimal, if the child is able to do it.

The therapist often engages in subtle reflection of the child's words and experiences. This sensitive skill is a crucial element in the practice. The play-family therapist also allows for natural moments of silence, knowing that profound healing can occur in the meditative gaps within the play. This is the Zen of Play Therapy, and it allows the implicit right-brain experience to facilitate the child's healing without the intrusion of left-brain questions or interpretations. Adaptations of MBPFT are made for children who, for various reasons, are not able to initiate spontaneous play. The less intrusive the therapist can be, even with directed play therapy, the more opportunity the child will have to lead her own play.

4. Play Therapy Is Versatile

The play therapy element of MBPFT is informed by a wide range of play therapy styles, both spontaneous and structured. There are many kinds of play therapies, and Mindfulness-Based Play-Family Therapy can usually be adapted to the therapist's own framework. Master's and doctoral level thera-pists and child psychiatrists can bring the richness of their own training to the practice of MBPFT, and those trained more in play therapy than in family therapy, or vice versa, can enhance the effectiveness of their work by exploring the less familiar path.

MBPFT's broad contextual basis makes it suitable to a variety of set-tings: private practice, inpatient and outpatient clinics, schools, home vis-its, hospitals, and shelters. It is effective in treating a wide range of issues and in working with both individual children and their families.

5. A Multicultural, Multiethnic Perspective Is Valued

Awareness of the child's racial and ethnic heritage is a core value of MBPFT. The genogram, an assessment tool, is used to invite family mem-bers to recount their family histories, providing an approachable means of uncovering the attachment and trauma backgrounds of the parents' lives. These backgrounds, which have served as a template for raising the child, offer a starting map for the journey toward family healing. The process also enables the therapist to assess the parents' strengths and to empathize with their life pain. Included is an appreciation of every family member's class, race, ethnicity, gender and sexual orientation, and religion or spiritu-ality.

6. Family Therapy Is Based Mainly on the Contextual Family Therapy Model

The family therapy component of MBPFT is based primarily on Contex-tual Family Therapy (CFT) as developed by Ivan Boszormenyi-Nagy. Train-ing in the ethics-based relational model of CFT gives the therapist skill in using the concepts of empathy, loyalty and fairness, split loyalty, positive and negative parentification, acknowledgment, constructive and destruc-tive entitlement, dialogue, exoneration, and, importantly, multidirected partiality. CFT is particularly known for its value in working with families who feel very stuck, and the skills that this framework cultivates in the therapist are especially applicable to the dyadic parent–child dialogue at Talk Time.

Three primary values inspired by Contextual Family Therapy provide a basis for the therapist to offer therapy to both the child and the adults in her life, either sequentially or in parallel:

1. The therapist maintains a multipartial stance toward all family members during the family therapy portions of MBPFT.
2. Behavioral and emotional problems are openly addressed in the shared family therapy venue of Talk Time; the play can then be kept in the child's imaginary world, and the therapist remains free to communicate in an appropriate way with the parents about the progress of the child's play therapy without violating any confidentiality agreement between him and the child.
3. Healing is most effectively accomplished and most enduring when there is awareness and exploration of the intergenerational resonance of issues.

Several other major schools of family therapy are appreciated in MBPFT, including Minuchin's Structural Family Therapy and Monica McGoldrick's contributions to the family therapy field.

7. Regular Mindful Parenting Meetings Are Held

Dialogue and feedback meetings with parents, without the child present, are required after every fourth play-family therapy session. Extensive parent education and coaching are included in these meetings, as is discussion of issues at home, at school, and with the outside world. This discussion may focus on the problems and resources of the parents and all of their children, as well as those of the MC child. The parents and the therapist raise issues that have come up in Talk Time during the previous four weeks.

The therapist's basic understanding of interpersonal neurobiology enables him to explain to the parents, when applicable, the present impact on their child of implicit body memories from earlier traumatic experiences. IPNB can help by offering the realization that, when it comes to behavioral change and healing, the body–mind system has its own inexorable pathways and timetables. Knowledge of this reality makes it easier for parents to extend—to their child and to each other—understanding and help rather than blame.

8. *Multiple Family Members Are Included*

During family therapy meetings, the play-family therapist is sensitive when identifying and discussing parents' personal issues in front of their children. He may be quite skilled in addressing mindful parenting issues when alone with the parents, and these issues may lead to an awareness that the parents have unworked life pain that may benefit from therapy. A parent's decision to initiate his own therapy is a personal decision. The therapist is sensitive to this boundary and avoids plowing ahead, uninvited, in the role of a parent's therapist.

However, particularly when parents exhibit recurrent patterns of "stuck" or even harmful responses, the therapist may recommend individual or couple therapy. The MBPFT framework frees the therapist, when clinically appropriate, to serve multiple family members, whether simultaneously or sequentially. Parents may request therapy parallel to the child's sessions. Conducting individual or couples therapy with the parent(s) assumes the appropriate clinical training and supervision.

9. *Treatment Often Involves Cooperation With Other Professionals*

When appropriate, the play-family therapist cooperates with other professionals concerned about the child and her family members. After obtaining informed consent, the therapist is willing to work directly with school personnel, such as teachers, administrators, and school counselors, as part of a team focusing on problems that have arisen in the school setting. Other professionals who may be consulted or invited to collaborate include family or pediatric practitioners, psychiatrists, physical therapists, and occupational therapists trained in sensory integration.

The MBPFT Mandala and a Word About Working Within the Broader Social System

The MBPFT mandala provides a visual representation of Mindfulness-Based Play-Family Therapy, illustrating the importance and interconnectedness of each element. Before we begin our detailed journey through the phases and stages of MBPFT in the following chapters, we would do well

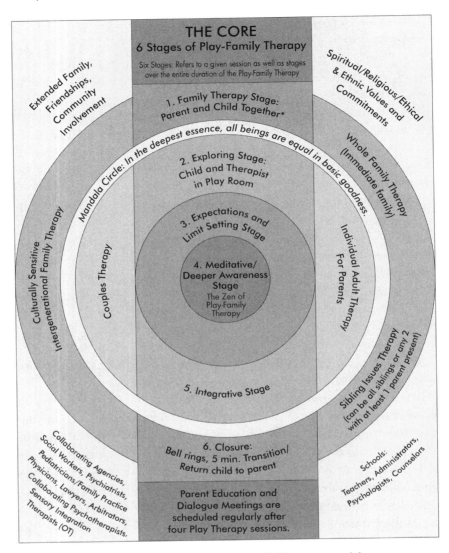

THE CORE
6 Stages of Play-Family Therapy
Six Stages: Refers to a given session as well as stages over the entire duration of the Play-Family Therapy

Extended Family, Friendships, Community Involvement

Spiritual/Religious/Ethical & Ethnic Values and Commitments

1. Family Therapy Stage: Parent and Child Together*

Mandala Circle: In the deepest essence, all beings are equal in basic goodness.

2. Exploring Stage: Child and Therapist in Play Room

Whole Family Therapy (Immediate family)

3. Expectations and Limit Setting Stage

Culturally Sensitive Intergenerational Family Therapy

Couples Therapy

4. Meditative/ Deeper Awareness Stage
The Zen of Play-Family Therapy

Individual Adult Therapy For Parents

5. Integrative Stage

Sibling Issues Therapy (can be all siblings or any 2 with at least 1 parent present)

6. Closure: Bell rings, 5 min. Transition/ Return child to parent

Collaborating Agencies, Social Workers, Psychiatrists, Pediatricians/Family Practice Physicians, Lawyers, Arbitrators, Collaborating Psychotherapists, Sensory Integration Therapists (OT)

Parent Education and Dialogue Meetings are scheduled regularly after four Play Therapy sessions.

Schools: Teachers, Administrators, Psychologists, Counselors

FIGURE 2.1. The Mindfulness-Based Play-Family Therapy mandala.

to take a look at the four corners of the mandala, which depict structures beyond the nuclear and intergenerational family that are integral to the child's life and healing and thus relevant to therapy. The extended social system is a major emotional domain and a significant resource for healing. It is important that the therapist maintain an attitude of cooperation and respect, rather than being competitive or working in isolation.

Corners I and II: Extended Family and Friendships, the Community, and Family Values

When families come to us for Mindfulness-Based Play-Family Therapy, they show both their strengths and their incongruities. How family members relate to their life values, their friends, their extended neighborhood, and the global community are all relevant to the well-being of the next generation: the family's children. As a child grows and develops, she witnesses how her parents and grandparents live. For example, observing and experiencing her parents' friendships is an important part of her growth and development; when her parents lack friendships, it is difficult for her to develop her own trustworthy friends. The child takes in more from what she sees than from what she is told, clearly noticing whether the behaviors of her primary role models match the values they espouse. If not, she will inevitably, and often in very unpleasant ways, let her parents know that she sees discrepancies. She may challenge them to live as consciously as possible, or she may give up and abandon that self-appointed mission. If a child stops confronting her parents, her own destructive entitlement may surface even more than previously.

Over time, the therapist gradually becomes more attuned to the ethnic, religious, spiritual, and ethical values of family members. Healing is dependent on the willingness of the family to be aware of this larger environment. Parents may already want help with more conscious living, or they may need some time to move in that direction. Therapy may include discussions of how the values of the grandparent generation serve as resources, as well as ways in which those values are not consistent with how the parents and other younger family members want to be. Sometimes there are serious intergenerational differences. A parent, as an adult child, may not be loyally following the ethnic or religious values expected by the grandparents—for example, in regard to the race or religion of his life partner, his relationship to a formal religion, his gender or sexual orientation, or his manner of having children, as in the case of a single parent choosing to have a child by adoption or artificial insemination. Sometimes the parent may be confused and angry about his own parents' lifestyle and values. For instance, an adult child whose parents were immigrants may feel that his parents did not appropriately adapt to the cultural norms of their new country. Or he may have rejected behaviors of his parents that he perceived to be greedy or materialistic. He may be frustrated with a parent who has been trapped in addiction. The senior parents may have harmed this adult child during his childhood and may never have asked their now grown-up offspring for forgiveness. Trust may be broken and close connections may be severed.

These attitudes, undertones, and clashes between parents and grandparents are an important part of the child's environment. How can such differences exist without fracturing the family? How are these issues impacting the MC child, who is experiencing depression or anxiety? The family that comes for therapy often wants the therapist to see the problems of their child without reference to the larger family context. Sometimes therapists are not trained to ask questions that bring the focus to this larger picture. MBPFT, however, invites culturally and ethnically conscious intergenerational therapy. Are deeply rooted tribal values being questioned by the second or third generation? Can the child's parents and grandparents and even friends dialogue about current differences or past hurts? Can they work through intense feelings and find solutions to problems? Can they stay connected and forgive or exonerate one another?

Each family has conscious and unconscious beliefs about the meaning and value of life. It is wise for the therapist to be aware of these and to respect the belief systems that flow across the family life cycle. Discussing beliefs can be a valuable part of therapy. How do members relate personally to family-held religious or spiritual ideas, ethical principles, and cultural rituals? Or how does the lack of these things affect the lives of family members? The therapy process may include helping families create formal or informal expressions of their life events. Belief systems may offer help when feelings of depression arise. Collaboration with a minister, rabbi, or spiritual leader, when appropriate, can provide a supporting alliance during times of stress or significant life transition.

Corners III and IV: Collaborating With School Personnel and Other Professionals

When therapists work with children, it is important that they realize the potential benefit of involving other professionals and that they are willing to collaborate with a range of people in the wider community. He welcomes a team approach and, knowing that everyone has a separate role to perform, he may ask the school counselor for help. He may also attend meetings at the child's school or be available to help the teacher or counselor when the child has a particularly difficult day. Parent education meetings can include coaching parents in seeing the links between what is happening at school and at home. The child will benefit from seeing that the caring people in her life are united. Conversely, she suffers split loyalty when the school, home, and therapy environments seem incompatible with one another.

The child may be taking medications prescribed by a psychiatrist or medical practitioner, and the play-family therapist's input may be valuable in medication management. Although it is not the therapist's job to recommend medications, his informed questions and insights into the meaning of the child's behaviors can help the prescribing clinician choose the best course of action. Medication without therapy is not advisable for a struggling child. Today, most physicians, psychiatrists, and nurse practitioners recommend or require psychotherapy in combination with taking medication for behavior or mood; when the therapy process reaches the root issues, children are often able to reduce or stop the medication. Sometimes, the therapist may believe that a particular medication is not well matched to the child's symptoms or not optimal for her well-being. Collaboration with the parents and the prescribing practitioner is important so that decisions are made in the best interests of the child. Research into the use of alternative or complementary treatments such as homeopathy and aromatherapy may make it possible to help symptomatic children by reducing or eliminating medication.

A child who comes for therapy may have a court-appointed guardian *ad litem* or a case manager, a social worker dedicated to helping the family in myriad ways and often intimately involved in the details of family life. Particularly when a child is in crisis or in long-term care outside her family, the social worker may be a very important person in her life. It is essential that the play-family therapist offer the case manager or guardian *ad litem* his respect and cooperation.

Therapists are trained to recognize the issues of sensory integration (SI), a field of occupational therapy, and to refer children who are having such symptoms for an SI evaluation. Many children with sensory integration problems have difficulty relating and socializing. When there is a strong SI profile, as often happens with children on the autism spectrum, the effectiveness of play therapy is diminished if SI treatment is not included. Occasionally, the SI issue is so overwhelming that the play-family therapist will recommend including both play therapy and sensory integration in the treatment plan from the beginning. At other times, it is helpful to start with play-family therapy to work on behavioral and social issues and address how the family is handling parenting concerns. This creates a foundation that will allow the child to receive more benefit from the SI treatment, which may be initiated during the integration stage of play therapy. The play-family therapist is primarily concerned about the emotional growth and development of the child and all family members. The sensory integration therapist cares about emotional issues, but is trained mainly to offer a wide range of physical activities that help the child to cope better in her world and to heal. However, it is beneficial that the SI therapist understand how the collaboration with with play-family therapy can enrich his therapeutic relationship with the child.

Finally, it is important for any clinician to cooperate with the legal system, and it is equally important that he understand the expectations for his role as he works with children and families. Play-family therapists are clinicians trained to help children with the process of healing their inner and outer worlds. They do not combine therapy with investigative inquiry. Even if a therapist has been trained to do investigative work, he does not mix roles. When parents call seeking help, indicating that there is a possible legal problem, the therapist can make it clear that his work is to help the child and the family with their emotional healing. He can let them know that, although there are times when a therapist may be required to go to court, he is not trained to do so, and that it may be appropriate and sufficient for him to write reports that can be used in the legal process.

Even when there are extensive legal issues, it may be the family's—as well as the therapist's—priority to help the child heal. In this case, the family may be asked to pledge that they will hire a separate social worker trained to collaborate with the courts, leaving the therapist free to work with the child and her family for healing. Families seeking legal services may be referred to appropriate investigative agencies or arbitrators.

Despite this stance, the therapist may be subpoenaed to attend a court hearing, and it may be important for him to share his perceptions in order for the court to facilitate the best resolution for the child.

3

Intake, Four-Segment Evaluation, and Special Considerations

THIS CHAPTER DESCRIBES the intake procedure and what happens during each segment of the evaluation that constitutes the first phase of Mindfulness-Based Play-Family Therapy (MBPFT). The four-segment evaluation generally takes four sessions to complete and is intended to familiarize the therapist with present problems and concerns, the developmental history of the child for whom there is the most concern (the MC child), and the family histories of both parents; it is described here as it applies to working with an MC child between 3 and 12 years of age. (See the relevant section of the case study in chapter 9 for an example of what this evaluation might look like.) The last section of the chapter explains adaptations that may be made to the evaluation process in certain circumstances and how the plan of therapy may be adjusted to meet specific needs.

The Intake Procedure

Connection with the new family starts when the first call is made to a therapist or an agency by someone seeking help. This call generally takes about 20 minutes. First, the intake interviewer gives the potential client a brief introduction to the agency. (For example, our interviewers at the Family & Play Therapy Center might say, "We have a network of experienced therapists in the greater Philadelphia area who are qualified to see adults, teens, and children. They have all received extensive training in child development and play-family therapy, here at the center.") She notes that the information from the interview is confidential and will be used only for the purposes of the referral. After the caller's information is gathered, the agency's director is consulted to decide on an appropriate therapist for the family.

The people who call need understanding and patience. We want to make the best match of therapist and client, suiting the particular needs of the family and meeting scheduling and insurance requirements. Attending to these issues from the start helps the caller avoid the frustration of contacting multiple professionals and revealing personal imformation unnecessarily.

The list below provides a description of the intake information collected for a child as it appears on the form we use at the Family Center; the same process can be used by an agency or an individual clinician in private practice. However, during the actual conversation with someone seeking therapy for a child, the interviewer may find that a different sequence of information gathering makes more sense. (Note: Most of our therapists at the Center have extensive training in working with adults and older teens as well as children, and this requires a different process.)

Sample intake information

- Names of parents. Place an asterisk next to the parent who initiated the call. Note if a parent is deceased or living at another location.
- Telephone numbers: home, work, cell. Note with an asterisk the number that should be called first, if the caller relates a preference. Is it appropriate to leave a message there?
- Place of employment and position held, for both parents.
- First and last names, ages, and dates of birth of all children. Place an asterisk next to the child or children for whom there is the most concern, the MC.
- Anyone else living in the home? Names, dates of birth, relationship to family.
- Insurance information. Is insurance compatible with the agency or the therapists? Is the family willing to pay out of pocket if the insurance company will not cover therapy? (It is often helpful to ask this information early in the conversation, to save the caller from giving out a lot of information only to find that the agency cannot work with the family's insurance. When appropriate, we let callers know that many states have a victim compensation fund that may cover the cost of therapy for a person who has been a victim of, or witness to, a crime

that has been reported to the police. We provide contact information and assist families in this process as necessary.)

- Referral source.
- Description and duration of issues. (During the initial call, the intake interviewer asks for a brief description of the problems, noting that the caller will be able to discuss more details with the recommended therapist. The interviewer's skill lies in helping the caller to say enough but not too much.)
- Previous therapy MC child or children have received. Make sure to record duration and outcome, including why the therapy ended. (This is important for many reasons. Much can be learned about a family from their past experiences, and this information may help the therapist determine if this is a suitable referral. Sometimes family members are still in therapy with another therapist, and it is important not to get inappropriately triangulated. In such a case, the director talks to the parent. She may recommend that the family go to the existing therapist and talk very directly with her about why they are considering a change. Such honesty often opens the door for the family to get their needs met through the original therapy.)

After obtaining this information, the intake interviewer briefly describes the four-segment process:

1. *First parent meeting.* The parents come to the first session without the child.
2. *Full family meeting.* Next is the full family session, attended by parents, children, and teens.
3. *Introduction to play therapy.* One parent comes with the MC child. The child plays in the playroom with the therapist, with or without the parent present, depending on the specific emotional situation of the child and parent.
4. *Family history meeting.* Parents come without the child. They review, with the therapist, their family history. Then the therapist and parents engage in a dialogue about how they each understand the issues and about the therapist's recommendations on how to proceed.

The interviewer then explains that this four-segment evaluation is generally followed by weekly therapy sessions with the child and a parent. It is ideal if parents are able to alternate accompanying the child for these weekly sessions. After every fourth session, there is a meeting without the child for the purpose of feedback and dialogue between the therapist and both parents.

It is helpful for the interviewer to get an idea of the preferred times for therapy as well as constraints in the parents' and children's schedules. It is generally best that the appointment time be the same every week. The therapist may be able to schedule the child's appointments in the afternoon and parents' appointments, for feedback sessions or adult therapy, in the evening. A therapist with limited hours can have scheduling information obtained early in the interview so that the client can be given a different referral if needed.

At our Center, the intake interviewer discusses all the information she has gathered with the clinical director. Once an appropriate referral match has been determined, the interviewer or the director returns a call to inform the family. The intake information is faxed to the referral therapist, who then makes direct contact with the family and schedules the first meeting with the parents.

This first call by the referral therapist to the parent is best limited to a few minutes. Although the potential client may wish to say more when the therapist calls to set up the appointment, it is generally recommended that the initial connection not resemble a therapy session and that the therapist avoid giving advice without a more thorough mutual evaluation. In our private practice model, the therapists are not employees, and they and clients are then responsible to set up the appointment, discuss fees, and work out the parameters of their relationship.

MBPFT is not a short-term model. It normally requires from 20 sessions to three years. The evaluation alone, with its four weekly meetings, takes at least a month. Families sometimes push for the therapist to skip the evaluation and begin the clinical work immediately, but these four segments provide a firm grounding conducive to long-term healing. If parents prefer to begin the treatment sooner and their schedules permit, the evaluation process can be done in two weeks by having two sessions each week.

Clinicians cannot afford to be rigidly stuck to any one model of intervention. If a family has an emergency situation, it may be imperative that the therapist attend immediately to the crisis, giving several sessions per week, if needed. Meanwhile, she explains that the evaluation should be started as soon as possible after attending to the emergency.

Segment I: The First Parent Meeting

Segment I of the evaluation normally requires an hour to an hour and a quarter, during which the therapist and the parents meet without the child present. There are several reasons for this. At this point, the parents need to be free to discuss the problems, including any frustration, distress, or anger, without exposing the child to the rawness and complexity of these details. Some of the information presented may be confidential and inappropriate for the child to hear. Also, this first session allows the parents to join with, and ideally to become comfortable with the therapist before introducing the child.

As described below, there are three major goals for the first segment of the evaluation, and, with practice, it is generally possible to achieve all three goals within the first meeting with the parents. Certain circumstances, including complex family structures, may warrant an additional session to complete this first segment of the evaluation. If the presenting problem is emotionally charged, it is especially important to respond compassionately to the parents' feelings in the moment. When there has been a recent crime or exposure to violence, or when a family has a child who has already had multiple physical or emotional issues, the therapist remains present to the parents, and they complete the developmental history at a subsequent session.

The First Goal: Joining Empathically

To start the session, the therapist prompts the parents to take turns describing the situation, including its present form, its history, and its family context, as well as their sense of contributing factors. The parents may have valuable insights into the reasons that the problems are occurring at this particular time. The therapist listens empathically while asking clarifying questions. This can generally be completed in about 20 minutes, although in exceptional cases it may take the whole hour.

The Second Goal: Taking a Developmental and Social History

The next step is to start to assemble a developmental and social history of the MC child (see the Developmental and Social History Questionnaire in

Appendix A for a sample form). This history will be helpful in pinpointing early events, particularly in the first three to six years of life, that may have interfered with the child's expected development. The child may have had a traumatic experience during a particular stage of development, such as early abuse or neglect. He may have been affected by chronic negative family dynamics or by events in the lives of any of the family members, such as an untimely death, postpartum depression of the mother, or a traumatic relocation of the household. A clear grasp of all of this information will help the therapist to better understand the child's play themes as well as to gain a sense of the anticipated course of therapy. Occasionally, there is nothing remarkable reported in the developmental history. This may predict shorter-term therapy.

It is strongly recommended that the history be recorded by the therapist in person rather than being completed by the parents at home. The intention is not only to get an accurate image of the child's early development but also to get a feeling for the parents' experience during that time. An organic response from a parent may trigger a question that is not on the form, and spontaneous recollections that parents relate while recounting the child's history are a rich source of information about his life.

It is a priority to complete the fifth section of the history form ("Habits") during the first session, as it establishes a mutually understood baseline appraisal of the child's current behaviors and symptoms. Sometimes, there is significant symptom relief within the first month or two, and it is helpful to be able to refer to this initial information to contrast how conditions were at the beginning of the therapy.

In examining the developmental history, it is important for the therapist to ask about toilet training (see the "Developmental Milestones" section of the form). During rapprochement, the parent–child relationship shifts as the parent engages the child with an often challenging set of expectations, such as that the little one learns to become aware of bodily sensations so that he can use a potty instead of diapers. Body awareness increases at this time, and the toddler can feel internal stirrings that naturally lead toward using the toilet. How toilet training is managed by parents and caregivers can have sig-nificant impact on growth and development. Most children succeed in urinary and bowel training by age three or soon after, and continuing problems in this area are frequently an indicator of emotional difficulties. The roots of a child's shame can often be traced back to the rapprochement period.

Another very important aspect of the child's development is his ethnic and cultural background. We want to encourage the family to engage the resources of the family's roots as part of their child rearing, and of the child's own roots if they are different from those of the family. Even though it is a sad reality that our contemporary mobile culture makes it more difficult to provide children a grounding in their heritage, most families today are conscious of how important it is to allow children to maintain a connection to their past.

While MBPFT deeply respects the parents' viewpoints, it also recognizes that the MC child's presenting problems are related to the larger context. Therefore, it is made clear to the parents that this child's developmental and social history are part of a larger evaluation that will include a meeting with all the family members living in the household, as well as another meeting with both parents where they will each explore their own family histories. The evaluation sets the tone for the family, allowing them to understand that, even though attention may initially center on the pain, trauma, or behaviors of one child, this child's problems are occurring within the larger family system. With the clear intention of avoiding making the MC child a scapegoat, it is acknowledged that this child's personality has developed within, and been influenced by, the family system. While his issues do affect the whole, this child is not responsible for the family's systemic difficulties. Likewise, although parents are primarily accountable for their child's development, there is a deliberate effort made to avoid blaming them. Parents generally do the best they can, and the therapist respects their request for help. Healing in the family system will occur parallel to the healing of the child.

The Third Goal: Showing the Mandala

In the last part of the first session with the parents, the therapist explains the MBPFT mandala, a colorful chart illustrating the various elements that make up Mindfulness-Based Play-Family Therapy (see figure 2.1). Because the parents usually get just a quick glimpse of the mandala during the meeting, they are invited to take it home for later perusal. Many referred families already trust the process and need only a brief introduction to the work, but this is a good time to answer questions for parents who are skeptical or want more information.

Note: You may want to read the segment of the case study that applies to Segment I, which is found on p. 226.

Segment II: The Full Family Meeting

In Segment II of the evaluation, the therapist meets the entire family, including all the members living in the household. This meeting has three parts: a *group talk*, about 20 minutes long, identifying the resources and problems for each child in the family; a *group playroom activity* for the whole family, which takes about 30 to 35 minutes; and *closure*, consisting of saying good-bye and preparing for the next session, which lasts about 5 minutes.

The therapist's goals for this session are:

1. To initiate her connection to the whole family. She provides space for the expression of each family member's positive qualities.
2. To invite the parents to explain to the children why they have decided to initiate therapy and identify concrete areas for each child to work on.
3. To experience how all the family members relate to one another as a group. This helps the therapist to develop intuitive knowledge even if she is not working directly with all of the children.

When parents show a positive attitude and play in the playroom with the children, the children are powerfully imprinted with the message that the playroom is a safe place. Therefore, the therapist usually includes the parents in the playroom for this first family session. (Exceptions will be explained later in the chapter.)

The First Part: Group Talk

For the first part of the session, I may use the waiting room, if it is private at the time, and we change environments for the second part, which has a different tone. In addition, it helps to do this initial group meeting without the distraction of a room full of toys. The waiting room contains only a few toys, such as a puzzle, a couple of stuffed animals and dolls, a visual oil-

and-water toy, and some drawing materials and modeling clay. Children may use the toys during this group talk, and young or anxious children may actually be able to listen more attentively when occupied with a simple activity. When there is one room, children learn to hold a toy and to wait until it is time for the group activity.

First, the therapist introduces herself to each child, making eye contact and shaking hands. She makes sure they know that she has already met their parents, helping to build a bridge that will allow them to be at ease and join in. She also tells the family, "After our talk, we will all go to the playroom and play a game together."

The parents are asked to describe three things that they appreciate about *each* child. (See the Family Evaluation Session form in Appendix A.) The therapist suggests that they address each child directly and use vocabulary that the child can grasp. This gives the therapist data to begin planning the treatment. During this exercise, she is careful to steer the parents away from saying anything negative. She often nods, and she repeats each affirmation, making eye contact with the appropriate child. Children often respond to this acknowledgment with appreciation and pride. It may be the first time that family members have had such an experience.

The therapist then asks each parent to list, for *each* child, two or three problems that the parent would like that particular child to work on. She suggests that they select challenges that the children can accomplish within three to six months. This becomes the basis of communicating the initial treatment plan to the MC child. (If mentioning a specific problem will cause the child undue shame, then that issue can be held back until the next meeting, when the siblings are not present. Issues related to bowel control or sexual abuse are examples of what may be omitted from discussion at this first meeting, although it is important that the MC child know that the therapist has been told about these issues. A parent can discretely let the child know that the parents talked about this the week before.)

Through this process of mentioning strengths and problems, the parents let the children know that this is a trustworthy place to bring their issues, even though the therapist is presently a stranger. If there is an MC child, he is not singled out from the other children at this point. The other children are usually aware of their sibling's problems, and it can be some relief for them to know that their parents are asking for help. This is especially true for siblings who tend to be overresponsible.

Children often respond spontaneously to discussion of their problems.

The therapist may give some space for their comments, while still containing this part of the session to 20 minutes. If time permits, she may ask the children what activities they like to do with each parent. It is important at this time to honor the family's hierarchical structure, so the therapist does not ask children how they would like their parents to change. Instead, she may ask what changes they would like to see in their family. Occasionally, a child may say, "Do I get to say what I want to change about my parents?" The therapist may respond playfully, "What *would* you like to change about your parents or your family?" Later in the work, she will address the child's grievances as they come up naturally in family interactions.

The Second Part: Group Activity

After concluding the first part of the evaluation session, the therapist invites the family into the play therapy room and describes an activity that they will do as a group. There are a variety of possible activities that are simple, yet can provide significant information about how the family functions.

The sand game, which uses a sandtray and an assortment of miniatures, is a favorite choice for this activity. Each child and adult is given a basket and asked to pick out three objects. During the course of the game, they will make a pretend story, so their selections should represent the imaginary realm. Children are usually able to do this more readily than adults, so the therapist may need to "check in" with the parents as they pick their pieces, encouraging them not to think too hard. She may suggest that they select objects that make them curious, as if they were in a gift shop. She asks the MC child to select either the moist sandtray or the dry one, and she places the stools around the one he chooses. She steps back to observe the selection process, then guides all of the family members to take a stool and hold the objects in their basket until everyone has sat down. She takes note of each person's objects and of where they sit.

When everyone is ready, the therapist explains to the family that their next job is to make a picture together. She says, "You can put in your own objects one at a time, and watch the others put their pieces in too, as you make a family picture. Eventually we're going to tell a pretend story together." The therapist remains present and observes family dynamics as she negotiates questions and process, respectfully taking in the gestalt of the family. She helps to settle boundary issues as they come up; for example, when pieces are being placed, any family member may speak up if they feel someone is placing a miniature in a way that is intrusive.

After all of the pieces have been put in the tray, the therapist notices how they are arranged. Have the family members simply set their own pieces down in clusters, in front of themselves, or have they placed their pieces in relation to other members' pieces some of the time? Once the story begins, each person can narrate their turn in their own way. The therapist lets the family know that anyone can add a piece if they need to as they tell the story. Many things may happen, or not; it does not really matter what happens, and there is no particular agenda. In the storytelling, when does the sequence of the story continue with the next person? When does it abruptly change? The therapist notices how the participants use the pieces when they tell their stories. Do they refer only to their own pieces, or do they include others' pieces as well? When there is time at the end, the therapist may ask for each person to give the story a title. She may also ask what each person liked or did not like about the story.

The Third Part: Closure

While saying good-bye to the family in the waiting room, the therapist makes sure to prepare the MC child for what will happen at the next session by saying something like this: "Next week we're going to talk here with your parent for a little bit, and then you and I will go to the playroom. In the playroom, you can play with whatever toys you would like. Your mom will be in the waiting room while we play." With an anxious child the therapist can assure the child that parent and child may go to the playroom together.

Note: You may want to read the segment of the case study that applies to Segment II, which is found on p. 231.

Segment III: Introduction to Play Therapy

The goal of segment III of the evaluation is to give individual attention to the MC child, who, for the first time, usually plays alone in the playroom with the therapist. Only one parent needs to accompany the child, which begins the pattern of parents taking turns to come to the sessions with the MC child.

When the child and parent arrive, the therapist repeats to the child her preparation statement from the end of the previous session. Most children will have remembered that they will be with the therapist in the playroom while the parent remains in the waiting room, and they are generally comfortable enough to be alone with the therapist at this point. The experience of having used the playroom and toys during the previous session with the entire family has communicated a message of safety, trust, and familiarity. However, circumstances such as attachment disturbances, separation anxiety, death of a significant person, or past abuse may mean that the child will feel safer if the parent accompanies him into the playroom for this session.

Before going to the playroom, the therapist asks the child and his parent what they enjoyed about their previous week. This question, which she will repeat every week, provides a way to connect to the child around something that is fun for him and to explore what is positive in family life. This practice helps cultivate the dialogic, inter-subjective engagement between therapist and child that is a crucial aspect of the MBPFT therapy experience.

At this evaluation play session, the parent may mention an incident of concern regarding the child: for example, "He hit another child at school today." The therapist listens and acknowledges the problem. She avoids the in-depth discussion that such an occurrence would receive later on, after the initial evaluation segments have been completed. She may attend briefly to the problem; for instance, she may say to the child, "This is a really hard problem, and I bet you want help so you don't keep getting in trouble for this. I hope that by coming here we can all figure this out together." On occasion, there is a crisis of such intensity in the family that the therapist may decide that this whole appointment should address it immediately. She will communicate this assessment before starting playtime, letting the parent know that the child will need to return for another evaluation session in the playroom.

When they are ready, the therapist leads the child to the playroom. At the beginning of the session, she warns the child that there is a bell or a beeper to signal the end of playtime, which will last about 35 minutes. She watches how the child engages with her and with the toys. If the child is comfortable, then she simply follows his lead. If the child hesitates or is shy, then she may introduce him to the different areas of the playroom, thereby inviting exploration.

The toys are geared toward communication through play. Children often sense this right away, providing an avenue for the therapist to obtain very helpful information from this first play session. How does the child relate to the therapist? Does he explore many areas and never settle into one area? Does he explore and then choose something to play with for a longer time? Does the child play with just one area, excluding the other toys? Children who are anxious may play much of the time with wet sand, which can have a calming effect.

What metaphors are beginning to surface in the child's play? Does he tend to be verbal or nonverbal? Is he able to engage in imaginative play? Is the child at first disappointed at the lack of electronic toys? Does he push against limits at this first session? How does he respond to limits imposed by the therapist? Many children request to use the bathroom at some point; it is important for them to know that they can have some control over leaving the playroom. On the way, they invariably glance into the waiting room to check on their parent.

The ringing of the timer signals that there are five minutes left until cleanup time, which, in itself, is an important part of the play therapy experience. (See chapter 4 for more on limit setting and cleaning up.)

After the child and therapist clean up together, they leave the playroom and rejoin the waiting parent for a five-minute transition. The parent will be curious. The child may comment about the experience, if he wants to. The therapist may educate the parent about the guidelines for the play: "The child's play is considered private but not secret. A child is welcome to say anything about the experience." However, she does ask the parent not to interrogate the child about his time in the playroom and warns the parent that a lighter touch is appropriate.

Since the way a child plays is considered private, the therapist does not discuss what the child chose to play with in the playroom. She may say, for example, after this first playroom session or at the next parents-only meeting, "Isaac explored three or four areas in the room before settling in and playing in one area for 20 minutes. He used his imagination in such a way that I think that this will be a good method to help him to deal with the issues that are of concern to him and to you."

At the end of the Segment III session, the therapist shakes the child's hand, if the child permits, and makes direct eye contact while saying, "For the next meeting, I will see your mom and dad without you. I hope to see you again in about two weeks. Your mom and dad will tell you more about that." It is good for children to know that sometimes their parents will have a turn to come without them, and it is a valuable part of the process to have parents communicate to their child their decision regarding whether or not to continue therapy. The four evaluation meetings are intended to help parents make this decision. Occasionally, the therapist may recommend seeing the child for two play therapy sessions prior to the fourth segment of the evaluation. This is particularly helpful when working with children who have developmental delays, post-traumatic stress, or separation or attachment issues. In such cases, it may be valuable to have the parent present in the playroom for one or both sessions.

Note: You may want to read the segment of the case study that applies to Segment III, which is found on p. 241.

Segment IV: The Family History Meeting

The final segment of the evaluation has two main goals. The first goal is to gather the family history of each parent, recorded in the form of a genogram. The genogram process has multiple levels of value:

- It helps the therapist to become grounded in the larger cultural and ethnic context of the family.
- It invites the therapist to have compassion for the couple's life narratives as well as for their current circumstances.
- It is a primary early tool for beginning to understand attachment relationships within the family.
- It gives the message that a parent's history can be important to the child's issues. Parents are thus not surprised during the course of the therapy when the therapist asks about parental behaviors that surface around the child's problems.
- It promotes deeper personal and relational awareness.
- It invites the parents to better understand present problems set within the context of three or four generations.
- As couples listen together, it can engender mutual compassion for their shared challenges and appreciation for each other's strengths.
- It can shed light on the presenting problems, and as time goes on and trust develops, parents may be more willing to share stories that lead to deeper healing.

- The process of hearing the family history with compassion and "caring observation" enriches "right brain to right brain communication" and therefore enhances neural integration (Badenoch, 2008, p. 164).

The second goal of the evaluation, which may take only 5 or 10 minutes at the end of the session, is to give feedback about what has been learned so far and to make a recommendation about how to structure the treatment. Treatment plans contain variables such as how often to have mindful parenting meetings, whether to give play therapy sessions to siblings, whether to refer the child for another modality such as sensory integration work, and so on. If there is more than one household, the treatment plan may include another set of relationships.

The Segment IV session generally takes from an hour to an hour and a quarter. It can be a powerful, empathic right-brain-to-right-brain connection with clients; the therapist is not merely gathering information, but also offering presence. Occasionally, there is not enough time to complete genograms for both sides of the family and a future time is set to finish up, either an additional session or part of the first parenting meeting. When the parents are separated, divorced, or remarried, there will need to be a separate family history meeting with each parent household. If one parent has died, I ask the surviving parent to provide as much information as available. The format for the family history session, as described here, is applicable to families across the spectrum of gender orientations, ethnicities, and cultural backgrounds.

In taking the family history early on, the therapist tries to be simultaneously compassionate, present, comprehensive, and succinct, facilitating a caring experience while gathering information that is highly relevant to the family treatment. This is challenging! Although this is apparently a primarily verbal exchange, with the therapist taking the lead by asking questions, she also takes note of what the client's body language is communicating. When is the body relaxed or tight? Does the voice fluctuate? She may occasionally comment about this, if it is helpful. At the same time, she stays present and in touch with her own internal responses. She expresses compassion, largely nonverbally, as she gathers family information from each parent for about 25 minutes. This session sets the tone for an intimate experience among the adults, serving as a model for a deeper connection to develop between therapist and family over time. A most helpful tool is the theory and format developed by Monica McGoldrick, and explained in

Genograms: Assessment and Intervention (McGoldrick, Gerson, & Petry, 2008).

Many therapists use the valuable sandtray genogram, as developed by Eliana Gil. However, unless they have family systems training, they may not have learned to use the format described above. For therapists who are not yet using the three-generational genogram, learning to create them is one of the most pivotal skills to add to their evaluation framework. A recent survey notes that this is changing. The December 2012 *Play Therapy* magazine includes a survey, "What Play Therapists Need to Know About a Child to Develop an Individualized Treatment Plan," by Schaefer and Gilbert (2012). They interviewed 50 registered play therapy supervisors and asked about essential initial intake information. The second category of feedback was "Top Things to Know About the Client." The number one most frequently mentioned variable was that the therapist collect a family history, and they specifically recommended a multigenerational genogram.

Genograms give access to valuable information regarding parents' early histories of attachment and trauma and help parents gain more awareness about how they were parented, which in turn helps them reflect on how they could parent more mindfully than they are currently. In *Being a Brain-Wise Therapist: A Practical Guide to Interpersonal Neurobiology* (2008), Bonnie Badenoch poetically calls the genogram process "listening to family histories" and recommends that it be done early on. She also recommends that the therapist take time to understand her own genogram in a deeper way:

> Taking time to sit with your own intergenerational history can be a first step. Bringing what you know about the power of early neural patterning and cultural pressures to your family's story may make room for compassion even in the midst of acknowledging your own sorrow. (p. 165)

In connecting the genogram process with the whole duration of therapy, Badenoch writes,

> The beautiful thing about laying groundwork for visceral, multigenerational empathy is that eventually people are able to compassionately release—in essence forgive—their parents and others in a way

that deeply frees them from ties of anger, resentment, and hatred, all of which impede brain integration and subtract from well-being. This act of acceptance often also brings them relief from their own shame. All of this is a long process, with the fullness of it usually unfolding near the end of therapy. However, being conscious of it during the first few sessions can give us a running start. (p. 165)

The simple, initial gathering of family histories gives the parents the message that the therapist will include this level of inquiry into the treatment of the child. This can be useful later on, especially if the parents' behaviors are blocking their child's healing process. Asking these questions can open painful places. When spontaneous emotions appear, the therapist may slow down the process and give space; staying with the client's feelings supersedes the need to gather more information at that moment.

Therapists have various styles for eliciting family history information. Following is a description of my own style, developed over many years of practice and teaching. I first gather the full family history of one parent and then I go through the same process with the other. I begin by asking about the parent's relationships with his or her own siblings. This is an easy way to begin drawing the genogram, and it can also be relevant to the presenting problems. In addition, this process provides a more gradual entry into an exploration of the parents' relationships with their own parents, which is often a sensitive topic.

I next ask about the children of the parent's siblings, which may reveal whether the children of the client family play with their cousins or are isolated from their extended family. This can also be revealing about the parents' current relations with their families of origin. I also ask about any pregnancies in the families of origin that did not come to term.

Other relatives may have had problems similar to those of the MC child. A common issue is that a parent feels that the child is "just like my sister"— or brother, or father, or mother—and this can carry with it a confusion of identities. The parent's feelings about this relative can be carried over into a positive or negative relationship with the child. Therapy allows the parent to see how painful relationships, past or present, can be harming the current parent–child relationship, and offers healing.

Next, I ask about the parent's relationship to his or her own parents— that is, to each one separately, not the parents fused together as a unit— including what she appreciates as well as dislikes about her parents or stepparents. I am seeking a perspective about the quality of these relationships from young childhood, through adolescence, and into adulthood. I want to know what she liked and did not like about how she was parented. The short narratives that the parent relates in response to my prompting help me to begin to understand the nature of her attachments with her own parents.

Thus, an MBPFT therapist begins to reference the intergenerational attachment history as part of her work with the child. The genogram inquiry can reveal which values parents may be incorporating, both consciously and unconsciously, into their relationships with their own children, as well as which behaviors they may wish to eliminate. John Bowlby, known for his pioneering work on attachment, points out that the deeply emotional rooting of child rearing in the parents' family histories is relevant to understanding attachment. "There is strong evidence that how attachment behavior comes to be organized within an individual turns in high degree on the kinds of experience he has had in his family of origin" (1988, pp. 4–5).

Next, I ask about the client parent's ancestry. I want to know when, and under what circumstances, the families migrated to the United States. Although this may not at first seem relevant to the presenting problems, one frequently discovers, when working with genograms, that the current family entrenchment has roots in previous generations. This may be a pattern of behaviors or a medical history. I ask if there is anyone in the genogram who reminds her of her child. I ask about the parent's own history of therapy. It may be that a temperament or personality similar to that of the MC child can be identified in each generation on the mother's or father's genogram picture. One can sometimes see an intergenerational issue attributable to how things were in their country of origin. Is a family history of famine related to current weight and body image issues? Are present anxiety and trauma symptoms related to fear stemming from past or present immigration or forced migration issues?

I especially want to know about the parent's individual, familial, and societal trauma background, such as a challenging immigration history or a holocaust history. I am also interested in learning about the present degree of connection to, or disconnection from, the family's racial, ethnic, religious, and spiritual roots. This includes how this person was raised as well as present affiliations, if any. If the parent has a stepparent or other parental guardians, those relationships are addressed here. I ask the parent to describe traumas or serious difficulties that she has experienced, or witnessed, at any point during her life. An understanding of how a traumatic event was addressed at the time of its occurrence may help to clarify the origin of some part of the family's current problems. I inquire about family responses to additions and losses within the group, such as birth, marriage, serious illness, loss of employment, divorce, and death.

Looking at the genogram as a whole, I now ask about any issues within the extended family of which I should be aware. Are there present or past estrangements from parents, siblings, or children? I am particularly interested in voluntary cutoffs due to relational difficulties. Are there any accounts of alcohol or drug addiction, eating disorders, mental illness, trauma, untimely death, suicide, witnessing of violent crime, criminal activity, or physical, emotional, or sexual abuse? Any family secrets? Anything that might be helpful for me to know? The final question I pose to the first parent before interviewing the next parent is, "How is your relationship going as a couple?" Then I begin the second parent's genogram process with the same question that ended the first parent's: "How is your relationship going as a couple? There may be some things you agree with, and some you disagree with, concerning what your partner said. It's normal to have some differences in how you view things."

For the second parent, I then use the same format as above, starting with his sibling relationships. One useful thing about having the parents participate in the genogram session together is that partners occasionally emphasize or highlight relevant information that the other may be omitting. Sometimes a response brings out information that the partner was not aware of in the other's family history. I often ask each partner how he or she gets along with the other's family. I note the dynamics when one member of the couple continually answers for the other, saying, for instance, "I know more about his family than he does." However, I continue to address the questions to the person whose family is being discussed and encourage him to respond. The family history process is a valuable experience in its own right, often eliciting facts and feelings that connect people to hidden vulnerabilities.

At times, the therapist needs to slow the pace in order to be present and empathic. Such open presence assists people when they are feeling uncomfortable or searching for understanding. The speaker feels securely grounded when the therapist humbly understands the larger context of his family life. Sometimes truths arise from this open presence that could otherwise remain hidden for months. For example, one family omitted to tell me at first that the MC's grandmother was dying of cancer. At the family history session, I learned that the mother was her mother-in-law's primary caregiver and so was not home many evenings. With this new information, the complaints about her child took on a new perspective. Another parent whose child was playing with matches neglected, for some time, to tell her son's therapist, "Oh, I never told you that I was burned in a fire when I was a little girl and have always had a fear that my children would get burned, too." The therapist worked separately with the parent to address this early trauma. Eventually, the mother was helped to find a developmentally appropriate way to share her concern with her son, and his destructive tendencies greatly diminished.

Mindfulness-Based Play-Family Therapy works at the root level. It is beneficial to nurture, from the start, an environment that encourages buried facts to surface. The genogram process itself can help to put the parents at ease. As the therapist draws out their information in a concise and accurate manner, clients may feel that she really cares about their life context. It is crucial, however, that the therapist have the experience of doing in-depth work on her own genogram. Supervisees lacking this personal experience have reported that they felt intrusive asking the necessary questions. It is also important to take into account the cultural background of the therapist. For example, Asian and Asian American students have said that it can be challenging to do a genogram because, in their own families, asking such questions would be impolite. *Ethnicity and Family Therapy* (McGoldrick, Giordano, & Garcia-Preto, 2005) is an exceptional resource for understanding a wide range of family mores and values. I recommend reading, prior to gathering genogram information, the chapter that matches the client family's ethnicity to help find approaches that may be respectful to family values.

A more recent work, *Re-Visioning Family Therapy: Race, Culture, and Gender in Clinical Practice* (McGoldrick & Hardy, 2008), extends further the application of a multicultural viewpoint to family history experience, providing a deliberate, insightful focus on race, class, gender, sexual orientation, religion, and spirituality. It offers a wholly inclusive cultural perspective, one formerly marginalized in family therapy training programs as well as in clinical practice. The narratives are deep, honest, and revealing of many of the authors' heartfelt and vulnerable life experiences. This body of work has offered a major contribution to the formation of the values of Mindfulness-Based Play-Family Therapy, which itself requires an appreciation of the multiple cultural, social, and individual factors that have accumulated over the generations of every family—and that form every individual.

Developmental History and Family History Feedback

Upon completing the second genogram, I move into a brief feedback segment, weaving what I have learned in the course of these interviews into the experiences of the prior meetings, including the developmental history. I ask questions that help me to clarify the family's values. I want to hear responses from the parents about what this process has been like for them and address any of their own questions. Sometimes parents begin to see the interconnectedness between adults and children, between past and present, and they share these insights; this sharing is very helpful to me.

The genogram process brings to the surface the dynamics of how the parents were raised. For better or for worse, this is the primary template of their own parenting. MBPFT follows a continual process of threading reflections from the past into the family's present parenting practices. For example, one father stated that he was the youngest of three children, and that his two older siblings had problems that warranted more attention from his parents: one had emotional difficulties and undiagnosed ADHD, and the other had severe asthma. Because his mother gave what he felt to be excessive attention to his siblings, he felt ignored. This man explained that he still had trouble expressing his own needs to his wife. He realized that he identified with their second child, who was having behavior difficulties.

The evaluation helped this father to see that his older child had been a demanding child since birth, and that the second child had suppressed his needs until recently. The father felt conflicted. On the one hand, he thought, "Why can't the younger son be like me and stay 'low maintenance'?" On the other hand, because he identified with his second son, he was glad to see him being the "squeaky wheel" for a change. His insights were discussed at length during parent feedback sessions and helped the therapy progress more quickly.

Duration of Treatment: Qualifying Factors

As the Segment IV session of the evaluation comes to an end, a parent may ask how long the treatment will take. Although there are always areas of the unknown, the therapist can learn, with experience, to give an estimate of duration, based on consideration of the information discovered so far: the causes, duration, and intensity of the presenting issues. What has the therapist learned from the developmental history? Was there medical trauma or separation in the early years? Have there been multiple traumas? How have the adults in the child's life been responding to normal developmental stages and problems, as well as to traumatic experiences? Sometimes misdirected efforts to help trauma lead to more trauma.

How many "moderate" or "serious" problems were checked in the behavioral section of the developmental history? Some families seem to be strict in areas where the child's development indicates that they should be more lenient, and overly permissive on issues where the child might benefit from more limit setting. This indicates that the process will take longer.

How did the child use the playtime? Are the issues repressed, denied, or accessible? What has been learned from the family histories? How are current issues rooted in the problems of earlier generations? Children exposed to split loyalty can experience much pain and confusion and often feel self-hatred. This may occur if the child feels pulled by one or both parents to take sides against the other parent, such as when parents behave oppositionally or talk disparagingly about one another. Shifting a dynamic that is very entrenched in the family relationships will take time.

What is the parents' physical and emotional availability to work with the therapeutic process? Have they had their own therapy? Has it been helpful? Are they willing to enter into their own therapy, if recommended? Is there a good rapport between the therapist and the family? The parents' capacity to be caring and supportive of one another, whether they are living together or apart, impacts the length of the treatment.

When giving an estimate of how long play-family therapy may last, the therapist clearly explains that it is approximate, since it can be based only on currently understood factors. New issues or new difficult experiences may arise, requiring more time. Although there are a few exceptions, 20 sessions seems to be the minimum time period required to work through issues. When families have lived with problems for years, therapy often takes a year or two. On the high end, the reworking of entrenched issues of abuse or neglect may require three years of family and play therapy. If parents have committed to their own deeper therapy work, either previously or simultaneously to the child's, the time needed for the child's therapy may be reduced.

Trauma and loss that continue in a child's life may indicate that the child will need play-family therapy for quite a while. Such issues include severe trauma, early abuse or neglect, chronic trauma, multiple traumas, ritualized abuse, children who have emotional issues overlapping learning problems, or parents who have had their own difficult parenting experiences, particularly if they have not had successful therapy and have avoided doing their own work. A long history and high intensity of the presenting problems, especially where there have been previous unsuccessful attempts at resolution, may mean long-term treatment.

Note: You may want to read the segment of the case study that applies to Segment IV, which is found on p. 246.

Adapting the Four-Segment Evaluation and MBPFT to a Variety of Settings

Each child and family has unique qualities and needs. Sometimes the differences require adaptation of the MBPFT model. For example, the evaluation generally takes four sessions, but in the interest of clinical effectiveness, the therapist may expand one or more segments into a two-hour meeting or have the sessions closer together so that all four are completed within two weeks. Or a two-family household may require extra sessions to accommodate each family group. Following is a list of some of the exceptional situations that benefit from adaptation:

- Babies from crawling age to three years may be excluded from the four-segment evaluation. It will be valuable to meet them later.
- If the parents confidently predict that a teenage sibling of the MC child would bring a spirit of harmful criticism (e.g., by saying, "This place is for babies"), then it may be best to postpone meeting that teen with the parent(s) to the not-too-distant future.
- Grandparents who live in the household may or may not be included in the evaluation. It would be valuable to bring them in later if they are part of the parenting team.

- If the parents live separately and only one of them is seeking therapy for the family issues, the therapist may ask to meet the other parent during the evaluation. This may help the therapist understand the child, and it can be important if issues of shared parenting arise later. Working together tends to help family life in both households, as long as boundaries are honored concerning issues specific to each household.
- Consultations by telephone or by videoconferencing may be appropriate for a parent who lives at a distance. The therapist needs to be clear on ethical and legal issues that arise with the use of these technologies.
- If a parent is deceased or otherwise absent from a child's life, the remaining parent narrates the history of the absent one. Grandparents may also be a resource for providing family history for a deceased parent.

While adaptability can be very beneficial, I have occasionally skipped a part of the usual evaluation process only to regret it later. An MBPFT therapist confronts a wide range of family situations, and it is important that she develop her own reliable intuition regarding adaptations.

During one of our Center's MBPFT training classes, one of the teaching assistants who had been practicing this modality for years spoke up, saying that she often put Segment II after Segment III. My first response was to review the theory, namely, that by being in the context of the whole family for the first meeting, the MC child is not uncomfortably spotlighted. He is also familiarized with the playroom and may be more at ease for the next meeting alone with the therapist. However, I found myself curious and, respecting this therapist, asked more about her experience with the switch. Upon reflection, she acknowledged that she inverted the sequence of the segments when she herself felt intimidated by parents. As she continued to look at her own method in class, she began to feel that the recommended order was better. She decided to strengthen her grasp of the family therapy component in order to become more comfortable working with parents.

Children Experiencing Separation or Divorce

Segment I: For a family that has experienced separation or divorce, each parent can be invited separately to an initial Segment I meeting. Occasionally, parents prefer to attend the first meeting together. Their judgment can most often be trusted in this matter, provided the therapist senses a good-enough level of accord between the two of them.

If the children are caught in a split-loyalty situation, with parents overtly or subtly denigrating one another, it is more beneficial to have two separate meetings. Each parent can meet the therapist alone to discuss the child's early development and current concerns. The therapist is interested in concerns peculiar to each household as well as in matters of shared parenting. The issue of split loyalty is important to assess in all families and particularly when parents are hostile with one another. (For more information about this very important dynamic, see chapter 6.)

Segment II: It is recommended that there be a separate meeting for each household, with all children in each household attending each respective meeting. The parents and stepparents join their family of residence.

Segment III: In situations of separation or divorce, it frequently happens that the parents are equally concerned about all of the children and are requesting family therapy without play therapy. In this case, the therapist may skip Segment III, since she has already met all of the family members. She moves on to Segment IV to complete the evaluation with the intention of pursuing family therapy instead of play therapy.

On the other hand, there are some situations in which the therapist may recommend having two family play sessions in Segment III.

Segment IV: I recommend seeing each parent separately to complete the family histories. Parents appreciate this time alone with the therapist, and it gives each one of them the chance to talk about his or her version of what happened in the marriage. If the parents are cooperative, I may ask them to attend another session together, following the genogram sessions, to give feedback and discuss treatment. If there is hostility, or if one parent prefers it, I usually meet with them separately.

Children in Stepfamilies

It benefits the child most when both of his primary parent(s) and stepparent(s) offer support for therapy. This can be complicated if the therapy has been court mandated. If one parent or stepparent is against it, treatment may be difficult or even impossible, especially if the child feels the split. It is highly recommended that parents have "uncoupling" sessions, if that is possible.

The goal is to minimize or eliminate the potential for a split. The notes above for divorced families also apply for stepfamilies.

I suggest seven or eight sessions for the evaluation process, as follows:

Segment I: The default for stepfamilies is that there be two separate first meetings with the therapist, one for each set of parents.

Segment II: I recommend that all the children participate, each with his or her respective family group. Again, there are two separate meetings.

Segment III: Only one parent accompanies the MC child. If the parents are equally concerned about all the children, as might be the case with death of a grandparent or a traumatic car accident that everyone has experienced, the therapist may choose to skip Segment III altogether and move on to Segment IV, since she has already met all the family members. In such a case, the best clinical choice may be family play therapy for everyone.

Segment IV: When the parent is in a new relationship and the new partner is taking a stepparenting role with the child, I recommend that the partner join the parent genogram session and provide his or her own family history.

Children Who Have Entered the Family Through Adoption

For a child who joined his adoptive family at birth, the four-segment evaluation is similar to the default process outlined earlier in the chapter. There is usually basic information available about the child's birth parents and family history as well as the mother's pregnancy, and access to these records has become a more common option in recent years. However, laws vary, and there are circumstances where teens or young adults may still suffer from closed records.

When a child enters the family at a later age, it may be more complex to gather relevant information. In some cases, there can be a trail of temporary surrogate family arrangements in the child's background.

Segment I: In collecting the developmental history, the therapist gathers as much information as possible from the adoptive parents regarding the first three years of life and on up to the child's present age. Sometimes this history is part of the child's file, and at other times there is little information about the child's early development. (See the Adoption supplement to the Developmental and Social History Questionnaire in Appendix A.)

Segment III: If the child was adopted at an older age, I sometimes keep the parent and child together in the playroom for the third session, as well as for a number of sessions following completion of the four-segment evaluation. This is especially appropriate when there are issues of bonding and attachment.

Segment IV: In addition to obtaining the adoptive parents' histories, it is valuable for the therapist to gather as much of the history of the birth family as possible.

It is usually beneficial for children who are adopted at an older age to have long-term therapy. Under the best of circumstances, the process of parent–child bonding takes time and patience. When there has been abuse, neglect, or political trauma in the child's past, this bonding may be especially difficult as well as especially necessary. It is highly beneficial for both parents to take turns bringing the child to play-family therapy as normally recommended. When there are attachment issues, engaging the parent in the playroom for at least part of the session can help to facilitate a more intimate connection. The therapist may choose to coach the parent in the Floortime method, as described in Stanley Greenspan's book *Infancy and Early Childhood: The Practice of Clinical Assessment and Intervention With Emotional and Developmental Challenges*, or in filial-like therapy. At first the parent may mostly observe while the therapist demonstrates giving responses suitable for play therapy. If the child chooses to engage the parent immediately, the therapist can prompt her as needed (Greenspan, 1992). Sometimes it is most beneficial to divide the playtime in two halves: one directed, with the parent in the room, and one spontaneous, with the parent in the waiting room.

Children who have entered the family through adoption can express play themes that are quite profound, and they usually reveal the child's way of grasping the complexities of his life. I recommend providing at least six months of play therapy for all children who have the task of integrating this complex reality. Deep healing needs time and inner space.

Children Who Have Entered the Family Through Foster Care

A recently placed foster child is called on to make challenging adjustments. Play therapy with the foster parent present in the room can offer the child caring support for his effort to form a healthy filial attachment. A child in the foster care system may never have been afforded such comfort. He may have suffered early abuse or neglect and multiple losses, followed by stays with temporary caregivers. Long-term play therapy offers him a place where he can start to sort out the enormous challenges of his life situation and renew his ability to trust, especially if there is possibility for a loving relationship with the foster parent. *Attachment Theory in Clinical Work With Children: Bridging the Gap Between Research and Practice* (Oppenheim & Goldsmith, 2007) offers research and practical application for working with children who have had disorganized beginnings. The authors recommend providing specialized training and support for the foster caregivers so that love can conquer the resistance that arises in many children in foster care.

Thus, for the child's optimal growth and development, it is important that the foster parents be involved in his treatment. The system is sometimes set up so that their participation is not required; the child may be provided transportation by social services or may be accompanied to therapy by his social worker. The therapist may have no other option, but I recommend letting the foster parents know that their lack of participation handicaps the child's potential therapeutic benefit. It is ideal for the child to experience lasting attachment in the same foster care home, with parents who are willing to attend therapy sessions. Providing some of the family sessions in the home can also be valuable. Given the availability of video-conferencing options, I recommend their use for the 20-minute weekly Talk Time if the foster parent cannot attend in person.

Sometimes, the social worker may be the person most connected with a child who has been moved repeatedly. If the child is in transition, his social worker may be invited to take the parent's role in Talk Time until the child's new foster placement is achieved. The therapist may need to adjust her approach and demeanor during Talk Time in order to compensate when a constant caregiver is not available or when the child is in transition between caregivers.

Segment I: In addition to understanding the presenting issues, the therapist attempts to elicit an accurate accounting of the child's early development and determine when he reached his developmental milestones during the first three years. Gathering the developmental history of a child who has joined a family through the foster care system can be very complex, especially when there has been a rupture in the birth family and multiple home settings. Learning about these disconcerting experiences offers a small glimpse into the repetitive losses that may be suffered by a child in the foster care system. Valuable data include causes of disruptions and dates of traumatic events. (See the Foster Care supplement to the Developmental and Social History Questionnaire in Appendix A.)

Segment II: At the second session, it can be helpful to meet all of the biological and foster children who are living in the household.

Segment III: I recommend that one parent stay with the child for the first individual play session, even if the child is willing to accompany the therapist without the parent. If the child is comfortable with the therapist during this session, then she may conduct another play session without the parent in the room. This will allow her to observe how the child uses the playroom without a parent present.

Segment IV: The therapist gathers the foster parents' histories and as much of the child's birth family history as possible. What were the circumstances and qualities of his birth family, including their resources as well as problems? Who provided care? At what ages did the disruptions occur in the child's birth home? Can the foster parents make contact with original family members or with former foster parents to gather information on the child's early history?

Children Who Have Witnessed Domestic Violence or Have Experienced Physical or Sexual Abuse

When children have witnessed violence or they, their parent, or a family member has been a victim of abuse or violence, I am sensitive to the possibility that the parent and child may need to stay together for a more extended evaluation. These children tend to be very fearful and may not easily trust the therapist. When multiple relatives have been been victims or witnesses of domestic abuse, it may be wise to prepare to see all of the family members during the treatment time.

Segment I: It is very important that perpetrator and victim not be together at the evaluation meetings. When a parent is party to the abuse or domestic violence, it is best to interview each parent separately. A team of two therapists, one working with each parent, may be established at the onset. If there is a concern about safety with one of the parents, both therapists can participate in the first meeting. During the first session, the therapist needs to begin some assessment of whether a parent is too toxic at the present time to be in the playroom with the child, or indeed is too dangerous to be seen as a client.

Segment II: At the first meeting with a child who has been abused or has witnessed violence, it is important that he not be required to discuss the difficult events with the play-family therapist, who is still a stranger. After telling the therapist what they love about their child and what they see as his strengths, the parents can address the abuse. Speaking briefly and simply, in the therapist's presence, they can let the child know that they shared the information about the abuse at a prior meeting. For example, they may say that last week, when they met with the therapist, they told the therapist the difficult thing that happened to the child at camp. Although I invite the child to say something at this point, most of the time there is embarrassment, and I assure him, "Today is our first meeting and we don't have to talk more about what happened." However, it is important that the child know that his parents have told me details about what happened, and I reiterate to the child that I know about the problem. For the therapy to be effective, the child needs to know that the therapist is aware of the situation and is available to discuss it openly and directly. Discussion of topics that evoke shame can be built gradually into the therapy.

Segment III and further sessions with the child: If the child has been abused by a parent, I include a nonoffending, safe parent in the room for the Segment III evaluation. Therapy can involve the other parent only if the situation can become safe enough. I also recommend that the child have supervised visitation with an offending parent when there is concern about safety. The offending parent needs to be pursuing his own treatment.

I may also keep the safe parent in the playroom for some initial sessions as the child grows to trust me. This allows the child, and also the parent, time to gradually develop trust and let go of their fear of violation. I may do more directed play in these early sessions.

If the child has otherwise witnessed domestic violence or is a victim of abuse and there is one parent who helps the child feel safe, I prefer to keep that parent present to ground the traumatized child. However, I have learned from some of my supervisees, who see clients in shelters and work with domestic violence cases, that it is better to use a different space if the parent seems too toxic to be in the playroom. This can be a friendly auxiliary space with just a few toys.

At the beginning of the relationship, the therapist helps prepare the parent with behaviors that make it safer for the child to engage. For some children, it may work to have the parent be a completely quiet witness while the therapist models being accepting and not critical. Other children may be too self-conscious or fearful to play in the parent's presence.

Children may be very loyal to the perpetrating parent, and they may not want to talk about the trauma of their lives upon meeting a new therapist. The therapist can handle this by having the other parent tell the child that she has shared the difficult experiences with the therapist. Keeping the play therapy in the pretend realm can allow the child to play out feelings without being disloyal. Talk Time will include the "hard to talk about" realities. The long-range goal is for the child to begin to feel safe with both the therapist and the parent. Generally, a child who has been a victim of sexual abuse gradually learns to talk about the abuse in small doses during Talk Time.

The therapist must to be able to listen to her intuition when she thinks that a child needs to talk to her alone. This may not happen until after she has developed a relationship with him. The child is more likely to want to discuss painful experiences without the parent present if he is caught in a familial loyalty conflict or has trouble trusting the parent. If the therapist suspects abuse by the accompanying parent, it is important for her to give the child a chance to tell her.

Trust building may be impossible if the parents are so toxic that they openly criticize a child or are negative about the playroom. Since the dysfunction is part of the family lifestyle, it is inevitable that the therapist will be exposed to some of these dynamics. In such cases, there may be a need for more parent education followed by directed Family Play Therapy techniques. These activities should be done in a neutral space until it becomes safe to bring parents and children together in the playroom. The therapist's sensitivity to these issues helps keep the playroom a safe space for the child's individual play sessions. Resources that may provide ideas include *Play in Family Therapy* by Eliana Gil (1994); *Family Play Therapy*, edited by Charles Schaefer and Lois Carey (1997); and *Creative Family Therapy Techniques: Play, Art, and Expressive Activities to Engage Children in Family Sessions* by Liana Lowenstein (2010).

Couples involved in domestic violence usually require supplemental individual therapy, generally with separate therapists. The couple benefits when the therapists share compatible frameworks and work well as a team. Eventually, after individual and separate group therapy, some couples can safely have some joint parenting sessions. When it is deemed clinically advisable for both parties to dialogue, I recommend that the two therapists join as a team to bring the couple together, being as multipartial as possible. A multipartial stance does not mean approving of abusive behavior. Goals of parenting sessions include helping the parents to become more accepting and verbally affirming of the child and to understand the consequences of parentification, destructive entitlement, and split loyalty (see chapter 6).

I do not recommend that parents witness the play therapy of children who have been sexually abused, once the initial sessions to develop trust have been completed. The nature of both the verbal and nonverbal play can be very disturbing. Even experienced therapists who are parents of an abused child usually prefer not to witness the deeper reworking of their own child's sexual abuse trauma enacted in pretend play.

It is essential to remember that play therapy is concerned with the whole child, not just the traumatic event. A child will rework other issues during playtime, and it is important for the therapist to follow his direction. As he learns to feel safe in the therapy relationship, he will, in the pretend realm, face the powerlessness brought by the traumatic events and release the trauma from his physical body.

One final note is that the play-family therapist is not an investigator and should not take the roles of both investigor and therapist. If a therapist is professionally qualified in both areas, she may serve the family only in one capacity or the other. When a family calls our Center with suspected sexual abuse, I recommend that it be reported to the care clinic of our area children's hospital, which has a compassionate and experienced staff. The law requires that the family, hospital, or therapist report abuse to the appropriate children's protective service, which will carry out an official investigation.

The above suggestions primarily address how to plan therapy and proceed with the four-segment evaluation. There will be cases not covered by this general information, and it is always important for the therapist to have a solid framework for complex circumstances and to think clinically when adapting generic information to specific situations. It is an ethical requirement that a therapist have supervision when working within a clinical area that is new to her.

Children in Bereaved Families

Segment I: For a parent seeking play-family therapy due to the death of the other parent, I suggest that he or she invite a close friend or relative to attend at least part of our first meeting as an emotional support. I trust the parent's judgment on this option.

Segment III: I often include a parent in the room for this segment of the evaluation, as the child may not yet be ready to separate from the parent. When one parent has died, children often experience separation anxiety with the remaining parent.

Segment IV: If one parent has died, I usually ask the other parent to provide the family genogram history for the deceased spouse. Another option is to have the deceased spouse's parents provide the family history.

Here are a few things to keep in mind when working with bereaved families:

- Therapy with children experiencing the death of a close person, or even a loved pet, may bring very deep issues into the playroom.
- Loss of a parent under any circumstances deeply affects the root identity issues that children naturally bring to play therapy. Play therapy has the potential to offer a profound healing experience.
- It is important for the therapist to track normal development for children who are experiencing major loss. Trauma can disturb the path of healthy social, emotional, and cognitive growth.
- There may be serious difficulties that were present prior to the loss. Understanding the history will help not only with compassion, but with formulation of an inclusive treatment plan.
- Children may prefer to work on issues other than bereavement before they feel safe and comfortable enough to deal with serious loss.

Children With Attention-Deficit Disorder (ADD) and Attention-Deficit Hyperactivity Disorder (ADHD)

Segment III: During the third segment of the evaluation, I generally see a child who has been diagnosed with ADD or ADHD alone, but only if the child is comfortable with this.

If I become concerned about ADHD early on in the treatment process because of a child's continuously distracted or unfocused play, I ask the parent to attend a session, where I invite the child to make a sand story. I like the parent to see the development of this story because it often reveals the nature of the difficulty with attention, control, focusing, and sequencing, which the parent may not have have consciously noted. It can be helpful to tape a story early on so that there is a baseline of the child's skill.

When the evaluation indicates that this is an ADD or ADHD child who would benefit from play therapy, I may devote half of the session to directed therapy, using storytelling with a beginning, middle, and end. The parent or the therapist can tell a rotating story with the child using sandtray miniatures, puppets, the dollhouse, and so forth. This repetitive process helps the child to organize his mind. For the remainder of the session, the parent can move to the waiting room, and the child can have a period of nondirected play.

Some children who are suffering primarily from anxiety or trauma exhibit symptoms that appear similar to those of ADHD. This misdiagnosis is confusing. Such a child may be able to move earlier toward spontaneous, child-directed play. When the child has arrived at the integration stage of MBPFT, his symptoms may diminish as the traumatic effects receive healing.

Children With Autism and Developmental Delays

Segment I: When a child is on the autism spectrum or experiencing developmental delays, there may be so much information that the first segment requires two sessions. The therapist may need to review with the parents an extensive medical history.

Segment III: I usually include the parent in the room for the third segment. I may recommend doing two sessions with the child in the playroom, the first with the parent and, if the child is comfortable, the second with the child alone. In addition to the child's social, emotional, and relational functioning, I want to understand the developmental level of his play.

Segment IV: While relating the family history, the parents can express their feelings about having a child with special needs. This may help reduce the projection of these feelings into the family dynamic. When a child's problems appear to be more medical than emotional, it is often challenging for the therapist to help the parents understand the importance of parental self-inquiry.

I offer the following suggestions for working with special-needs children and their families:

- Many children on the high end of the spectrum, such as those diagnosed with Asperger's syndrome, benefit from spontaneous play therapy. It offers the most direct path to organizing their minds through the play therapy experience.
- The therapist decides whether the child should start in a playroom with fewer toys. Would the regular playroom cause sensory overload for the child?
- Parents can help to translate for the therapist when the child's language is unclear. The therapist can signal with a finger when she needs the parent to repeat what the child is saying.
- Many children on the autism spectrum need a more directed developmental play therapy approach. This approach is explained in Viola Brody's book *The Dialogue of Touch: Developmental Play Therapy* (1997). It includes, of course, development of a close relationship with the therapist.
- Developing or enhancing parental connection is a very important goal. It may be helpful for the therapist to teach parents and children Greenspan's Floortime modality, or for parents and their young children to become involved in Theraplay, developed by Phyllis Booth and Ann Jernberg and described in *Theraplay: Helping Parents and Children Build Better Relationships Through Attachment-Based Play* (2010).
- Mindful, conscious parenting is very beneficial for all parents, including those whose children are on the autism spectrum.

Counseling: MBPFT in a School Setting

A school counselor employing MBPFT in the school setting needs signed permission before she can talk with teachers and administrators. Parental involvement is beneficial, and she may meet with the parents without the child present to gather a developmental history and description of the concerns. Basic information about the child's trauma history should be included. If the school allows the counselor to record a brief family history, this is often quite helpful. It prevents the appropriate school staff from remaining ignorant of important issues that are impacting the child's well-being. In a school setting, the written history need not include details of the parents' individual problems, and school counselors keep parental information confidential.

In schools where the program allows for long-term therapy, the four-segment evaluation may be used in its full form. Where only short-term therapy is possible, the counselor can adapt the evaluation process as constructively as she is able, according to the unique situation. When parents are active in a child's counseling, the counselor needs to exercise discretion regarding what is appropriate to share with teachers and administrators. On the one hand, the counselor extends confidentiality to the parents where it is appropriate. On the other hand, she knows what may be shared with teachers to aid their efforts at helping the child in the classroom.

It is generally recommended that the school counselor and parents stay connected regarding the child's problems. Therapists have found it valuable to build in regular meetings with parents when a child is suffering at school. Since children benefit from experiencing everyone working together, it can be helpful for the child to attend a team meeting that includes his teacher, parent(s), the school counselor, and, when applicable, his off-site therapist. At times, it may be best for the child to join the team toward the end of a meeting.

Given the constraints of time scheduling, the counselor may not be able to provide weekly or bimonthly sessions to more than a handful of children, and the child and family may benefit from regular meetings with an outside therapist. In this case, the counselor and the outside therapist may confer from time to time, as benefits the child. It is important for counselors and administrators to refer to therapists who will work cooperatively with the school when the problems are school related.

Use of a sandtray and art are highly recommended modalities for children's expression. A portable sandtray collection can fit into a school counselor's setting, and a child may express feelings with greater ease through imaginary play than through direct speech. The witnessing presence of the counselor can be reassuring and healing. Sandtray materials can also be used for problem solving. A child who knows he can have a session at school each week with the counselor may be able to cope better in school, especially during a difficult time.

4

The Six Stages of Mindfulness-Based Play-Family Therapy

Aᴛᴛᴇʀ ᴛʜᴇ ꜰᴏᴜʀ-ꜱᴇɢᴍᴇɴᴛ evaluation is completed and the decision is made that the child and family will receive Mindfulness-Based Play-Family Therapy (MBPFT), the child and a parent may begin the treatment phase. A parent dialogue and feedback meeting follows every fourth play session (see chapter 7 for details).

The six stages of MBPFT are as follows:

Stage I: Talk Time

Stage II: Exploring the playroom

Stage III: Expectations and setting limits

Stage IV: Deeper awareness

Stage V: Integration

Stage VI: Closure

Micro View: Each daily play-family therapy session as a unit comprises the six stages as noted above. In Stage I, the parent accompanies the child for Talk Time, and Stages II through VI occur in the play therapy room.

Macro View: An overview of the entire course of treatment is also best understood by these same six stages—whether the duration is twenty weeks or three years. After initially exploring his environment, the child moves gradually into more sustained and focused play. As the course of therapy progresses from early stages toward integration and closure, the structure of each session gradually shifts its emphasis toward deeper awareness and integration.

This chapter explores the six stages mainly as they pertain to a typical play-family therapy session.

Stage I: Talk Time—Family Therapy/ Parent–Child Dialogue

Talk Time is a 15- to 20-minute meeting prior to each play therapy session. Together with the therapist, the parent and child address what is going well for the child and the family as well as one or two of the specific symptoms or behaviors motivating the therapy. It can be conducted using any of various clinical approaches, such as family therapy, behavior therapy, or cognitive therapy. It may include role playing, advocating for the child, or reframing negative behaviors. Sibling sessions or parenting support in context may also play a part.

Although both parents are welcome to accompany the child to Talk Time, most of the time it suffices for one parent to attend each session. It is ideal that parents take turns bringing their child to the sessions; over time, the child's relationship with each parent is thus enriched. If taking turns is not possible, the less available parent should come to at least one of the four sessions in each cycle. If parents who live in the same household do not have this minimum of participation, the therapy may begin to parallel the household problem of one parent being overresponsible for child rearing and the other being too disconnected. This can significantly reduce the effectiveness of the MBPFT approach.

Although introducing the use of technology for Talk Time can be complicated, it can sometimes provide a solution when parents are otherwise unavailable. Recently, in the case of a foster parent who needed to stay at home with three other children, face-to-face interaction via a secure Internet connection allowed her to participate in real time and to discuss the resources and problems prior to the play session.

Upon arriving five minutes prior to the session, the parent and child enter the waiting room, where they can "settle in," maybe get a healthy snack and water or juice, and prepare for the hour. The parent and child are then greeted and invited into the room where Talk Time will be carried out. Although it is not always possible, it is preferable to have a family talking room, ideally separate from the playroom. When the waiting room is empty, it can serve as the space for Talk Time. If the only option is for Talk Time to be held in the same room that will also be used for play, the child learns to sit with the parent holding toys set aside for Talk Time. Another option is to gate off one section of the playroom for use as the meeting space. Wherever the space, it should be a comfortable room, possibly with a futon, a folding chair for the therapist, and a few toys, for example, puzzles and building toys, drawing paper and markers or crayons, oil-and-water toys, and a couple of puppets. One very helpful item is a doll with various facial expressions—happy, sad, angry, scared, and surprised.

One goal of every Talk Time meeting is to help children and parents increase their competence in intersubjective relating; this emerges through intentional efforts at honest verbal expression of feelings and thoughts. The parent acts as a model in constructive communication by using empathic "I" messages and avoiding judgmental "you" messages. The child learns to express herself in an authentic way and gains the benefit of feeling understood by her parents. Of most importance, this experience focuses not only on the child's problems but also on the parent's behaviors and responses. The mindful parenting approach means that the parents discuss with the child insights about how they are sometimes disappointed with their own parenting actions. Such efforts at communication by both children and parents make the intersubjective experience reciprocal. As parents and children use these skills more regularly, a major change may occur within the parent–child relationship.

Daniel Stern (2004) points out that recounting past events or anticipating future ones can have all the benefits of a "present moment" experience. "If the present moment is not well anchored in a past and future it would float off as a meaningless speck" (p. 28).

> Even the telling of something that happened is actually happening now. Telling is a now experience, even though it refers to a present moment that occurred in the past. We also have anticipations about the future, but these too are being experienced now. (p. 23)

Weekly scheduled talk times, "moments of meeting" where parent and child share the joys and pains of life, occur in the verbal and nonverbal power of the felt present moment. This creates the possibility of a powerful intimacy with each parent separately. Stern asserts that this intersubjective connection is more than increasing attachment between parents and children.

> The attachment system is designed for physical closeness and group bonding, rather than for psychological intimacy. Many people who are "strongly" attached do not share psychological closeness or intimacy (in fact, it's the opposite). The system of intersubjectivity is needed for that. (p. 101)

Talk Time is a mini-session and consists of three parts:

Part A: Checking in, focusing on what is going well (5 minutes)

Part B: Discussion of reality, including therapeutic intervention for problems (10 to 14 minutes)

Part C: Transition to playtime (1 minute)

Stage I, Part A: Checking In

The overarching goal of Talk Time is for the child and family members to enrich their capacity to express their thoughts and feelings in words; this increases intimacy and neural integration. Because concentrating on the resource side of family life reinforces the habit of positive dialogue within the household, the first five minutes of Talk Time are focused on the satisfactions and joys of living. The therapist may ask what good things have been happening, and everyone listens to the responses. How does the family enjoy life? How do they spend their weekends? Are the children developing friendships? What is going well at school? Have the child and parents spent any time together doing something fun? The therapist addresses the child directly or invites the parent to respond first. If the child wants to answer first, that is fine. If the child really does not want to answer yet, the therapist encourages the parent to model. This allows the therapist and parent to connect and provides a good communication example for the child.

These conversations develop valuable skills in children as they learn, over time, to select something that was enjoyable and special about their week. It is generally important that the parent not answer for the child, even though the child may not remember the weekend or have other events to discuss. In that case, the parent can give the child a clue without actually answering and then permit him to elaborate if he is so inclined. When a child is too self-conscious or uncomfortable, the therapist may ask the parent, "What did Jacob and the family do over the weekend?"

The parent speaks from her own viewpoint; the child is not allowed to control whether or not his mother responds. Often I ask the parent what she did without the child over the weekend. As parent and therapist talk, the child may feel drawn into the discussion and, over time, he develops valuable conversational skills.

Talk Time can also include discussion of practices aimed at the development of mindfulness through body awareness. The therapist can demonstrate simple exercises with the child and parent; the parent can then invite the child to "play these games" at home. A timer or a little bell can be used to pace the games, and to invite quiet and being in touch with inner feelings. Appropriate activities include the following:

1. The child pretends to be a turtle with his head tucked. After 15 seconds, the turtle brings his head up and moves it from side to side, and then he puts his head back down for 15 more seconds. This can connect to a child's awareness of energy in his throat.

2. The child closes his eyes and pretends for 20 seconds that he is a log. Then he keeps his eyes closed and imagines that the log is floating down the river on a sunny (or rainy) day. This lasts for another 20 seconds. After the quiet exercise, the therapist can ask the "log" if it has agitation or grumbles inside and to point out where it might be feeling that, for example, in the chest or stomach. Or if the log is angry, what part of the log feels it?

3. The parent can ring a bell, chime, or a crystal or Tibetan bowl, having instructed the child to stay completely still and listen to the sound resonate until it stops completely. Children also like to tap the bowl and listen.

4. Sitting in meditation position, the child can quietly gaze at the movement in a colorful oil-and-water dropper (one minute, building to three minutes).

5. In a cross-leg sitting position, the child can clench his fists lightly and close his eyes (building from 15 seconds to three minutes). I saw a classroom of six-year-olds do this five-minute mediation in India. In a lying-down position, the child can clench his fists tightly for five

seconds and then release. After repeating this a few times, he can observe whether his body feels different.

Books that inculcate mindfulness in children can be at hand for parents and children to look at in the waiting room, such as *Planting Seeds: Practicing Mindfulness with Children* by Thich Nhat Hanh (2011) and books by Kerry Lee MacLean, like *Peaceful Piggy Meditation* (2004) and *Moody Cow Meditation* (2009). Also, a simple book addressing parents, *The Mindful Child* by Susan Kaiser Greenland (2010), is full of concrete exercises. One of my favorites is "rocking a stuffed animal to sleep with your breath" (p. 77).

Another element worth discussing is yoga, which is a wonderful way to use the body to invite mindfulness. The parent can join the child in doing some suitably accessible and playful yoga positions, and they can also look at books like *Peaceful Piggy Yoga* (MacLean, 2008).

The practices described above are aimed at helping children experience how awareness of their bodies can help them be comfortable with their mindfulness. It is important that all these efforts be done with a light and playful attitude. Jon Kabat-Zinn, author of *Wherever You Go, There You Are: Mindfulness Meditation in Everyday Life* (1994), makes this clear. He cautions against teaching children meditation if they feel coerced in any way. He recommends instead that parents model the value of meditating, which may pique the child's curiosity.

> If you are devoted to your own meditation practice, they will come to know it and see it, and accept it matter of factly, as part of life, a normal activity. The point is, the motivation to learn meditation and to practice should for the most part originate with them, and be pursued only to the degree that their interest is maintained. (pp. 257–258)

Throughout all the Talk Time exchanges described above, the therapist is learning what the child likes to do and how this family has fun together—or not. The child often begins to appreciate the focus on positive life experiences, and he may especially enjoy his parent's affirming acknowledgments of him. He understands that the therapist is not only interested in hearing about problems, but that she also wants to encourage a connection between him and his parent over positive events. In order to foster this connection, the therapist may lead awareness exercises that help family members to be mindfully present. He becomes accustomed to including the therapist in what happens in the family in a way that facilitates Part B.

Stage I, Part B: Discussion of Real-Life Problems

In Part B, the therapist and the parent–child dyad engage in discussion of real-life problems and in the therapeutic interventions used to address them. This flows naturally from Part A. Both child and parent have time here for what we call "talking about the hard-to-talk-about things," which is part of the philosophy of Contextual Family Therapy. They address the concrete problems and concerns that brought the family to seek therapy as well as issues that have arisen in the daily lives of the child and family, particularly among those who are present.

Since each parent–child relationship is unique, the therapist is particularly interested in how issues have manifested recently with the parent who is present, rather than in discussing problems that involve the absent parent. Since parents take turns bringing the MC child, each develops the skill of talking about these hard-to-talk-about things. The conversation often centers on the particular symptoms and problems that the parents described during the evaluation period. Humor, spontaneity, and authenticity are qualities of engagement that the therapist brings to this often serious discussion.

At his conference on attachment at the Family & Play Therapy Center in Philadelphia in 2012, Daniel Hughes pointed out that informally talking with the child before confronting the more difficult topics may relax the child. Sometimes in this transition, the child will divert the focus away from the content to be discussed. He may try to engage the therapist's attention. Hughes cited the example of a child who notices a bird outside the window and suggested that the therapist and child take turns with this one distraction, with the child going first. After giving full attention to the child's interest, the therapist then makes a nonnegotiable claim on being second. This appeals to the child's sense of fairness. The therapist then returns to the original hard-to-talk-about issue.

In *Awakening the Heart: East/West Approaches to Psychotherapy and the Healing Relationship* (1983), John Welwood highlights the value of talking about challenging topics:

> If a client can stay with and unfold his negative feelings, he will eventually yield or point to some more positive, wholesome direction underneath them. In meditation, the practice of being with parts of ourselves that we would rather not look at builds confidence as we realize that nothing inside is as bad as our avoidance or rejection of

it. By not running away from our experience, but staying with ourselves through thick and thin, we begin to accept ourselves in a new
way and appreciate the basic openness and sensitivity at the root of
our being. (p. 52)

Most children can learn to manage about 15 minutes of deeper focus on
one problem; then they communicate their readiness for play to begin.
Once the child and therapist enter the playroom to start Stage II, the focus
opens into "the pretend" and imagination. With only a few exceptions, the
reality discussion ends as the child transitions into play therapy, whether
the parent is present or not. This sequence often leads to deeper imaginative
play therapy, as described later.

Therapy Modalities Useful in Stage I, Part B

While many therapeutic modalities and techniques can be used for the discussion of reality topics, in Stage I these actions are based on the fundamental principle of Contextual Family Therapy: that every individual's life
problems have been formed from ancestral material. Healing is to be found
in the context of the individual's current relationships, the family of origin,
and the earlier generations. This includes an understanding of issues of
early attachment, the impact of traumatic experiences, and affect regulation. All techniques that help this inquiry to bring healing in the present
moment are welcome additions to the therapist's repertoire. Regardless of
the methods used during Talk Time, a primary focus is the verbal and nonverbal expression of thoughts and feelings that may sometimes be challenging to put into words. "Linking language to emotions is an inherently
integrating activity for the brain" (Badenoch, 2008, p. 184). Parents become attuned to their child week after week through meaningful conversation. The therapist is an active participant, asking questions, initiating role
play, and modeling intimacy by responding from an authentic, accepting
place. His constant sensitivity is necessary to enhance the development of
two important ingredients:

1. Intersubjective dialogue: The enrichment of the feelings of love and
   attachment in the development of an intimate, honest relationship
   between child and parent that can continue beyond the therapy expe-

rience. The parent is willing to share his own challenges and can sometimes be vulnerable with his child.

2. Affect regulation: The development of modulated control of a wide range of emotions. Talking about difficult things can bring up strong emotions, and the weekly dialogues nurture the development of competence in this area in both parent and child.

Behavior Therapy

Behavior therapy may include the use of charts with stickers to track positive behaviors, such as success in toilet training stages, doing chores, completing homework, behaving appropriately at school, or practicing a musical instrument. For some children, behavior charts provide an initial motivator to attain symptom relief, while other children may simply not respond to these behavior modification methods. For example, some very oppositional children may be hard to engage in a reward system.

Mindfulness-Based Play-Family Therapy has the goal of going beyond symptom relief. It is therefore important to communicate to parents that success with behavioral methods may not mean that the problems being addressed will be deeply resolved. In fact, they may surface again. Using these external techniques can be considered stimulation to progressing toward a deeper transformation. If there is some symptom relief for families in the beginning weeks and months of therapy, they can be encouraged to persevere in the long-range goal of MBPFT, which is to understand root causes and to help develop the child's internal motivation.

Cognitive Therapy

Cognitive therapy is frequently used during the parent–child discussion of real-time events. It is particularly valuable when children have concrete fears or vague anxieties, including obsessive thoughts and compulsive behaviors. During Talk Time, I use and adapt many of the ideas from the framework of Family Play Therapy as described by Eliana Gil (1994) and Charles Schaefer and Lois Carey (1997). In this model, when therapist, child, and parent discuss reality together, they can use props to help the child experience and articulate concepts that are painful or difficult to grasp. I also recommend the many creative ideas described in *Blending Play Therapy With Cognitive Behavioral Therapy: Evidence Based and Other Effective Treatment Techniques*, edited by Athena Drewes (2009).

It is important to note that there are many children who refuse to use words to talk about their problems. But whether the child joins verbally or merely witnesses the parent and therapist, the discussion that goes on in Talk Time helps prepare the child to address his fears and anxieties at a safer, deeper level. This is noticeable when he goes into the playroom and enters the safety of the imaginary realm.

Awareness of Contextual Elements

Events that occur in the larger societal context are frequently discussed during Talk Time. A common topic is fairness, as exemplified by issues of bullying or being bullied, at school or on the school bus, or by disparaging, mean things that peers say about a child or his parents because of differences in class, ethnicity, race, or sexual orientation. Boys and girls of middle school age are particularly prone to experiencing these behaviors (Parens, 2011). It is suggested that the therapist address them in depth, and, additionally, it is helpful that she be aware of the power of peer interaction. Contextual Family Therapy (see chapter 6) offers a solid basis for the therapist's parent education skills and facilitates her competence in addressing relational problems with the adults, teens, and children in the family.

Role Playing

Role playing is a powerful tool for helping children and parents to change "stuck" patterns of behavior, allowing for left–right brain integration. Therapist, parent, and child may take part in these role plays, with the therapist suggesting the "choreography." Although the child's actions are of concern to the parents, the role plays are enacted with their acceptance of the child's core sense of self. This communicates to the child that, while his behavior is unacceptable or would benefit from a shift, he himself is loved. Role playing can be a playful and gentle way to offer a vision of new possibilities. It is particularly useful when adults have tried unsuccessfully to help the child restrain inappropriate behavior.

Sibling Sessions

A sibling session may be requested by the parents, the child, or the therapist in the hope of improving family dynamics when there are repetitive conflicts among siblings. If a sibling has accompanied the parent and the MC child to Talk Time and such issues arise there, it is good to work directly with both children at that moment. This requires that the therapist listen and offer partiality to each sibling's side. The therapist asks many questions until she understands both the difficulty of the sibling issues and the parent's perspective on the rivalry. She states her understanding of what each child is saying, and adjusts her paraphrasing until both children agree that the therapist's statement fairly represents each position. If there is time, the therapist may encourage the siblings to role play their dilemma, thus bringing the energy of the sibling issues into the present moment. Depending on the clinical issues, the therapist may suggest that there be a sibling play session, either directive or nondirective, for the remainder of the hour. One activity that can be helpful is to invite the siblings to divide a sandtray in half and to each make an imaginative picture using about 10 or 15 objects. After each has had a turn to talk about her own picture, the therapist invites them to create one "pretend" story together, mixing the two sides. The metaphors that develop during this process can be very revealing and point to a direction for healing.

It is not possible to resolve entrenched sibling issues at one meeting. Over time, the therapist explores the truest feelings of each sibling, including envy and jealousy. It is helpful for the parent and the therapist to convey an attitude of acceptance of all of the child's feelings, although not necessarily of all his consequent behaviors. For example, they can say, "I understand that you feel jealous of your brother and I'm glad you can tell me." After the therapist and parent explore and understand this better, they might add, "However, it is not OK to knock over his Lego building." Reading fairy tales can be an avenue for experiencing the complex feelings of sibling rivalry in a safe and healing way.

These concerns need to be worked on in parenting and family therapy sessions and can become part of mindful parenting. It can be helpful to invite the parents to recall how they dealt with their own sibling issues growing up, and compare that with how their children do. How did the parents of each generation address the rivalry? What are the similarities and differences? Are the parents modeling rivalry by overtly fighting each other when they have a disagreement? We recommend a family therapy session where each of the various possible pairs—the two parents, each parent and each child, each set of two children—describes their styles of expressing anger to one another. This discussion may include the use of sandtray objects to describe how each person feels his own anger and the anger of other family members.

Parenting Support in Context

"Parenting support in context" means that the parent–child dialogue addresses parenting concerns prompted by the child's behavior in the moment or by behaviors that have only recently surfaced. This is an opportunity for the therapist to witness parent–child interactions that are similar to those that occur at home. He can note whether the parent's response is too harsh or too lenient for the issue at hand. Except in situations of danger, does the parent try to understand the problem and then empathize before addressing the boundary? The therapist can coach the parent on skills he is working on in the parent dialogue and feedback meetings, including affirming how well the parent is doing. Sometimes, out of discomfort or habit, a parent may laugh while setting a limit with the child. This is confusing to a child. The therapist will explain this at a parent meeting and patiently help the parent incorporate a change, generally avoiding discussing this with the parent in front of the child.

Advocating for the Child

If a parent responds too harshly to a behavior that is considered part of normal development, or if the punishment is disproportionate to the undesirable behavior, the therapist can decide when to intervene. She can do so in the moment by taking the parent aside and discussing it, or she can wait until the next parent meeting. For example, if a child rolls his eyes in response to a parent's remark, it may not be helpful for the parent to let this evoke a reactive response. The parent may simply want to say, "Your eyes are letting me know how you feel about . . . Are your eyes telling me that you're mad about what I just said?" A general rule for all parents is not to take the child's behaviors personally. This can be difficult to do, but practice will allow the parent to respond in a variety of more constructive, compassionate ways. It is, however, important for the therapist to realize that the child's familial culture may have its own meaning for a behavior such as eye rolling.

Reframing Negative Behaviors

The therapist can also reframe obvious negative behaviors by including possible interpretations of body language. The therapist may say, for example, "When Jacob hits you, it seems to me that he is really telling you he is mad and wants your attention. However, I agree that he has to learn another way to let you know what he's feeling." It is valuable for the therapist and parent to ask nonjudgmental questions to try to understand the message behind the hitting. If the therapist or parent feels she has some insight into the meaning of the behavior, she may ask the child if her observation is accurate. For example, the mother might say, "I think that you were mad at me because, just before Dottie came in, you asked me if we could get ice cream cones on the way home, and I said, 'Not today. We have to pick up your brother.'" This may lead to a discussion of the child's desire for more maternal attention. Spending some time affirming this feeling is important. It is also important to address the hitting behavior. The mother may address her son in her "I-mean-what-I-say" voice. This is not an out-of-control, angry voice meant to scare the child, but it gives a clear message about unacceptable behaviors. The mother can say, "Jacob, hitting me is not okay." The therapist may say, "How else can you let your mom know you are mad?" This can turn into a role play.

The families of children whose behaviors are primarily oppositional may initially benefit from family therapy and parenting sessions for a month or two prior to beginning the play therapy sessions. The goal of the therapy then becomes an increased understanding of the ways in which the child has commanded too much power in the family. A concurrent goal is the shifting of the hierarchical structure so that the parents have more appropriate power. Their first task is often just getting the child to the office for a family session.

Sometimes after the four-session evaluation, it is necessary to begin with a series of parenting sessions. This is especially true when the parents are so angry at one another that is not safe enough to bring the family together. If children are suffering from severe split loyalty, helping the parents to be more kind to each other may be necessary before starting regular family or play therapy sessions.

Mindsight

Daniel Siegel has coined the term *Mindsight*, the capacity to observe our own minds, as the "seventh sense."

> [Mindsight] enables us to get ourselves off the autopilot of ingrained behaviors and habitual responses and moves us beyond the reactive emotional loops we all have a tendency to get trapped in. It lets us "name and tame" the emotions we are experiencing, rather than being overwhelmed by them. (2010b, pp. ix–x)

All of the above ways of working in Talk Time month after month can slow down mental and emotional processes and help both the child and her parents gain Mindsight. Siegel uses the hand as a way to demonstrate in simple language how the brain is connected to places that the child and parent feel stuck (2010b, p. 15). With fingers wrapped around the thumb, parts of the hand can represent the basic anatomy of one lobe of the brain. Explaining the "hand brain" to children can help them avoid taking behaviors personally and at the same time gain awareness and accountability.

Perhaps one of the most valuable uses of Talk Time comes into play when parents humbly admit their own experience of what Siegel says is normal: losing our mind. A mother recently came in with her six-year-old daughter, who among other things is a very anxious child. After I heard what went well about the week, the mother affirmed some wonderful things about her daughter. She said that there had been nothing challenging that week in regard to the daughter, but she initiated a story about an event that had just happened. "You know how I have been working to not lose it when *I* am anxious," she began. "Well, I just lost it in the car." She had been using her GPS to guide her to my office as they were coming from a new direction and she did not want to be late. As the daughter listened wide-eyed, the mother reported how she could not get the GPS to direct her to her destination. "I had a full-blown tantrum, yelling at it, and I finally threw the GPS against the steering wheel." Her awareness came when she realized that her daughter had witnessed the incident, and she was more aware than usual that it was scary for her. In the past she would not have thought about the impact that her little GPS meltdown was having on her daughter.

Parents cannot help but have moments like this when they are upset. *Noticing* what is happening is Mindsight. Siegel's idea is that we can learn to have fewer of these moments when we bring our awareness to the situation. So the bigger picture here is the mother's honesty in telling the story, being aware of her daughter's distress, and apologizing to her, while trusting her relationship with me as the witness.

> In our shame, we often try to ignore that a meltdown has occurred. But if we own the truth of what has happened, not only can we begin to repair the damage—which can be quite toxic to ourselves as well as to others—we can also actually decrease the intensity of such events and the frequency with which they occur. (2010b, p. 25)

When the mother asked the daughter directly, the daughter admitted that she had been scared and quickly excused her mom. As the mother acknowledged the daughter's feelings and they hugged, I privately reflected that the daughter had experienced more to heal her own anxieties that day than most other interventions could have taught her.

Stage I, Part C: Transitioning From Talk Time to Play Therapy

About one minute before bringing the child to the playroom, the therapist gives a warning that it is almost time for play therapy. If there is a separate room for the play, then the natural transition is that the therapist, child, and parent leave the meeting room, the parent goes to the waiting room, and the child and therapist go to the playroom. If the check-in and discussion are done in the playroom, then it helps if there is some way of creating a sense of the two separate events, one being in the "real" world and the other in the imaginary realm. Some therapists use a tunnel for younger children to crawl through each week, giving the feeling of transition. Another concrete boundary closing the Talk Time can be established simply by the action of the therapist. She sets the timer to start the 30-minute playtime as the parent returns to the waiting room.

We now leave the real-world version of the parent–child dialogue and become immersed in the pretend realm of play, where the hurts and joys of life will be translated into imaginary form. In that form, the issues will gradually emerge and be reworked as the child heals.

Stages II and III: Exploring the Playroom and Expectations and Setting Limits

Stages II and III are woven together and, for some children, may initially occupy the main body of the play therapy. Since most of the session is based on the therapist following the child, her relationship with the child is balanced by her taking responsibility for structure and safety in the play room. Parents appreciate that, although there is an emphasis on the amount of freedom a child has in the playroom, the therapist is setting limits when needed. Two basic safety rules, traditional for the play therapy room, are that the child may not hurt himself or the therapist and that he may not break the toys deliberately. There are other basic rules as well, such as that the dry sandtray needs to stay dry so that other children will have the choice between a wet and a dry sandtray. Unless the child has a problem with oppositional behavior, the therapist can spontaneously address the rules as needed. For example, she may say, "This drawer is off limits," or "Fragile objects are not for throwing," or to a child playing ball, "We both have to be careful not to hit the lights on the ceiling." Sometimes a child may not like a rule, but the therapist's holding clear boundaries contributes to trust and sets the child at ease to explore the room. There can be exceptions to rules that are intuitively based on the therapist's best clinical judgment for each child.

In addition to setting the timer, the therapist may introduce several playroom rituals that help the space feel safe for the child. One can be that the therapist always opens and closes the doors. This is helpful in that the child will not have the habit of just walking into the playroom at any time. It also provides a safety net in the event that a child wants to suddenly bolt out of the room. Children learn that, although there is ample freedom in the session, the therapist holds the authority, the boundaries, and the safety of the space. Letting the child set the timer can lead to a power struggle if he decides to give himself an extra five minutes or tries to prevent the timer from ringing at the end of the session. The response of the therapist, "That's my job," makes it very clear that she is in charge.

A common pattern of exploring the playroom begins with looking around and approaching a number of areas. Children are curious, and they may stay playing for three to five minutes or longer in each area. Eventually they select one area of the room to stay playing in for a more extended time, even up to 20 minutes. Sometimes, a child who is presently feeling trauma, anxiety, or deep sadness may skip looking around the room and go directly to expressing his experience through metaphors of play.

The initial task of the MBPFT therapist is to respond to the child in child-directed language. She uses reflective listening to keep the communication between the child and herself in the realm of imaginative play. She does not initiate random conversation but rather responds to the child's words. From the beginning, the therapist's speech educates the child about how the playroom works. The child learns that, if possible, he is expected to take the lead in initiating the play and in choosing the themes of the play. When a child is not able to play spontaneously, the therapist interacts with the child using more directive methods of play therapy while following the child's themes and direction.

It is equally valuable that the therapist be comfortable with silence.

Many children are quiet during parts of the exploring stage. The therapist's complete presence and "being with" the child are very important. This is not time to straighten shelves, text, or be mentally distracted. Electronic devices should not interfere with the flow of the session. Some children explore the room and play with the toys without involving the therapist directly; she then serves as the witness. Other children engage the therapist with ball playing or sword fighting as they explore. Both styles are appropriate. Once the therapist has demonstrated her availability, she follows the child's lead regarding whether she should simply witness the play or be involved in its themes. Most children will use both kinds of play at one time or another, although some children do have a consistent preference for just one approach. It is essential to understand the power of the symbols of the specific toys selected by the child. Whether the child plays with puppets or sand miniatures, arranges dollhouse people and furniture, creates figures out of Play-Doh or clay, or makes drawings, the therapist is aware that the child's unique choices are a reflection of his inner longings, desires, hopes, and fears. The magic of the play is that the symbols energetically hold the child's inner landscape. The selection may seem random, but it is not. It is as unique as handwriting. No two children will play the exact same themes identically.

Generally, the therapist does not emphasize the availability of new toys. It is reassuring to the child that the playroom has a reliable continuity. He does not need to think about it, and this nonthinking prepares him for deeper-awareness play.

Moving Toward Mindful Play Therapy

Play therapy can be compared to mindfulness meditation. Early on in play therapy, children want to know the boundaries and limits. In meditation, one often sets a specified time frame, which ends when a bell rings. A child in play therapy gets one block of time, also ending with a bell, and learns to expect this same amount of time each week. In the initial stages of play therapy, the child usually moves around the room and plays with various things for a few minutes until his mind settles into one area of the play-room. This is similar to the clatter of the "busy mind" that meditators often experience when they first sit down on the cushion. Gradually the child begins to play, possibly creating a pretend story or painting a picture. This puts him into a receptive mode. Once involved in the play, his mind, like the meditator's mind, is free to let go and to be.

When a child is ready for the inner freedom that comes with letting the busy mind become quiet, he will lead himself to the heart of the matter that needs reworking or healing. When children are holding trauma, this sometimes happens immediately. As witness, the therapist needs to trust the child's propensity to move toward awareness. Therapists who are new to a more quiet method of being present may find it challenging to trust in the regenerative potential of silence. The effectiveness of MBPFT is grounded in the power of simple unconditional presence.

For example, when spontaneous play involves taking roles, the therapist asks the child for cues and adds to the play according to the child's indications. She does not introduce her own themes and ideas but elicits the child's. She may whisper, "What does Alligator say to that?" rather than assuming it. She is sensitive to the child's pacing. She does not interrupt or interpret the play. Sometimes she hypnotically reflects back what the child is saying, and at other times she is comfortable connecting through silence. She may occasionally reflect a feeling in the play metaphors when it is clear from body language that this is what the child is feeling. Or she may neutrally and simply state what is happening. The reliability of these guidelines allows the child to find his way deeply into the unconscious and into a source of awareness. It is recommended for the therapist to be quiet, reading body cues while being a fully present witness (see chapter 5).

While the child is still in Macro Stages II and III of the play therapy, the therapist and family may see a decrease in the symptoms that brought the child to therapy. For example, a child having nightmares may see a decrease in frequency or cessation of the nightmares altogether. A child acting aggressively may begin to behave more appropriately, or a depressed child may seem happier. Although these are good signs and we want the families to enjoy the symptom relief, *it is very important that they understand that this is not the time to stop therapy.* During the initial sessions, the therapist, parents, siblings, and the MC child are getting to know one another, building trust, and preparing for the work that lies ahead. An issue that is very traumatic or deeply rooted does not quickly make a reliable shift. It is essential that there be a willingness to persevere until real healing occurs. Eventually, usually in Macro Stage IV, the tide will change and the roots of the issues will become evident.

As the roots of problems are being reworked, the initial symptoms often reappear with the intensity that they had when the family first entered therapy. This is the "getting worse before getting better" phase, and it can be a very challenging time for families. Parents may question the value of the therapy. The therapist must work to help the parents see that it is often in this very turmoil that healing occurs. Sometimes it is beneficial to have additional sessions for the parents, family, or the MC child during this period of upheaval.

Stage IV: Deeper Awareness

Through both the language and the silence of the play, the child is propelled into the meditative deeper awareness stage. This phase is best invited and nurtured when the therapist helps the child to stay in imaginative play, free of the concerns of life outside the playroom. By now, hopefully, a trusting relationship between therapist and child allows for being as completely in the present moment as possible. Their sympathetic attunement allows the intuition of both the child and the therapist to manifest itself. The child who comes to weekly play therapy is aware that there is a thread of continuity that supports him to gradually locate, open up, and rework and heal the places inside that need it. Research affirms that the brain regenerates gradually, through steady effort. This may help to explain why play therapy is most effective on a regular basis. As in mindfulness meditation, the actual dawning of truth may take only minutes within the child's play sessions, often after months of preparation.

Eckhart Tolle (1999) describes three themes in his work that are relevant to Stage IV: (a) the power of the Now, being as completely as possible in the present moment; (b) experiencing stillness by calming the mind; and (c) opening to sacredness. These three interconnected themes apply to MBPFT. The goal of the therapist is to nurture an environment in which the child can experience the power of the Now. The main reason for keeping playtime in the imaginary realm is that this offers the child access to a place of internal freedom where he has a chance to be fully present in the actual moment. "Real-life" thinking may be so loaded with complex relational conditions that the child is prevented from having the equanimity he would need to come to terms with these very complexities. During imaginary play, when the child learns not to chatter about the past, the present, or the future, he shifts into the right brain of imagination, which is the doorway to the meditative, deeper-awareness healing state. In *The Present Moment in Psychotherapy and Everyday Life* (2004, p. 112), Daniel Stern states, "Because the present moment is mentally grasped as it is still unfolding, knowing about it cannot be verbal, symbolic and explicit. These attributes are only attached after the moment has passed."

Tolle tells us that when we become truly present, we are able to find the sacredness everywhere, but that it is easier in certain places that we call sacred, where "there is less density in forms and there is a transparency that shines through the forms" (Tolle, 2005). It is best when the playroom reflects such transparency, generally containing nonelectronic toys that encourage imagination, allowing the child to commune with his own stillness. The space of the playroom, no matter how small or simple, needs to offer safety and sacredness. An ideal space is aesthetically pleasing with a variety and abundance of multicultural toys that allow for the unfolding of the play themes that match the expression of the child's inner pain.

This emphasis on the practice of mindfulness in the Now is a corollary to the MBFPT principle of *child-directed* or *spontaneous play*. The child's freedom to be in the present moment, as nurtured by the therapist's commitment to providing a truly open-minded presence, means that the play will be conducted by the child's implicit voice, in the most authentic form available at that moment of his therapy process. Although MBPFT is very similar to and is rooted in a child-centered play therapy approach, one may accurately say that the MBPFT philosophy is *not* "child centered" in the particular way that that play therapy method is often defined.

One difference between the two frameworks is that in MBPFT, the first stage includes a 15- to 20-minute parent–child dialogue. The problems are understood to be openly shared within the family domain, so the therapist does not emphasize a relationship of confidentiality with the child. With few exceptions, the child does not talk negatively to the therapist without the parent present. The advantage of avoiding real-life situations in the play stage of therapy is that their presence encourages left-brain, analytic, "busy-mind" thinking, whereas their absence allows the child to have fuller access to his implicit right-brain experience, as in meditation.

Another major difference is that MBPFT relies more on the attuned intuition of the therapist as silent witness to the child's words and nonverbal body language, and less on the therapist's verbal reflections, particularly during the deeper awareness stage. By avoiding being interpretive, this approach allows space for the true nature of the child to be at center. In actuality, many children using various play therapy modalities naturally create play in the imaginary realm without the intrusion of reality, especially when the therapist is a mindful witness. While client-centered, experiential, and even structured play can lead to the same quality of healing, MBPFT loads the deck by having the intention that the therapist and child's time together be dedicated to pretend play. This is similar to the freeing of the mind to be with itself that occurs during a formal meditation session with a group of mindfulness practicioners. The dedicated space trains the mind to focus and to be.

"The moment you enter the Now with your attention, the stillness arises. The essence of the present moment, no matter how mad it may appear on the surface, is always stillness. It is also sacredness" (Tolle, 2005). Most experienced play therapists know this in their hearts. Children generally want to play in "pretend," and, if given the space and time, they will eventually get to this deeper space. Play therapists can tell when the child is in the space of sacred healing. They often describe it as "awesome." Many a therapist has remarked how her sense of the significance of a play session brought tears to her eyes. When the therapist *intentionally* holds the space of the Now, children tend to go deeply into their hurt places and symbolically, through the energy of the play toys, bring their hurts with them into the realm of the sacred, for healing.

Sometimes, we think of this as the child going into the unconscious, but it is more than that. As though he were meditating, the child's thinking mind slows down. His energy sinks into the mind of the body, the body–mind. During trauma, for instance, the child's focus goes to the right brain; he loses access to the left brain. Because MBPFT is a whole-body modality, it offers the opportunity to heal the effects of trauma through the integration of the left and right brain. This brings healing deeper than the symptom relief achieved by helping the child to cognitively understand the trauma. Bonnie Badenoch notes that people living with post-trauma experiences will often perceive a threat to be greater than it actually is. This can make daily life a dysregulating experience. "Mindfully identifying the hindrances . . . often leads to an ability to do deep emotional work in a more intentional way that widens the window of tolerance and modulates the intensity of the memories" (2008, p. 193).

In his body-mind-spirit experience of play therapy, the child may move with his whole body. He may make noises, sighs, grunts, groans, and guttural sounds during the deeper awareness stage. In the play, through the process of desensitization, the child gradually has the capacity to go to the edge of his sadness, fears, anxieties, and past or recent trauma. The content of the play is not as important as the intuitive experience. There may be extended silences. Noting the child's bodily changes, the therapist remains a connected witness, holding the sacredness and safety of the space. The therapist knows when to be silent and how to stay completely present. Although she is just being a witness, or mirroring or tracking the child, her language and stance may subtly shift with the child's cues. Sometimes, the child is in a hypnotic-like state, with eyes averted. At other times, the therapist may meet the child's request for direct eye contact and, nodding affirmatively and carefully *using the child's own metaphors in his speech*, she will acknowledge that she understands just what the child wants her to understand. The child will stay with various qualities of play for as long as he needs, over the course of however many sessions he requires. When his inner state is ready, there may be a stillness, which is minutes long, in which an observant therapist can see how moments of powerful awareness crack like lightning through the psyche of the child with healing power. The child is gradually facing into and healing the trauma.

If ever there was a child who benefited from a mindful play therapy approach, it was Sandy, a client of Bruce Perry's. Sandy is poignantly introduced to us in *The Boy Who Was Raised as a Dog* (Perry & Szalavitz, 2006). Sandy witnessed her mother's brutal rape and murder, had her own throat cut, and was left for dead. She survived alone with her mother for eleven hours and, after healing at the hospital, was put into foster care with the doctor's recommendation that she receive therapy. However, the unenlightened social worker did not see the need for therapy. Sandy was in hiding and was moved from several foster care families because her life was in danger for fear she would testify against the murderer whom she knew. The foster parents did not know what had happened to her but they were concerned because she was pervasively anxious and had profound sleep problems. She had an increased startle response, and she would have angry outbursts and at other times hide in nooks in the house and cry. These concerns and a new case manager motivated the play therapy referral. What is beautiful about her play therapy is that she knew just what she needed for her healing. From the first session, Bruce Perry wisely took cues from her, and for months she started her play silently. She led her therapist to a place and position that she designated, and told him not to talk. She taught him exactly what to do and what not to do in the play reenactments that would help to heal her inner world. Perry states, "I had to do exactly what she wanted: don't talk, don't move, don't interfere, don't stop. She needed to have total control while she performed this reenactment. And that control, I began to recognize, would be critical to helping her heal" (p. 52).

Dr. Perry describes how healing trauma happens. The victim needs to be in a predictable and safe space.

> Our brains are naturally pulled to make sense of trauma in a way that allows us to become tolerant to it, to mentally shift the traumatic experience from one in which we are completely helpless to one in which we have some mastery. (2006, pp. 53–54)

Sandy controlled the play in a way that enabled her to "titrate" how much stress she could tolerate each session.

> Sandy regulated her exposure to the stress through reenactment pretend play. Her brain was pulling her to create a more tolerable pattern of stress; a more predictable experience that she could put in its place and leave behind. Her brain was trying, through reenactment, to make the trauma into something predictable, and hopefully, ultimately boring. Pattern and repetition are key to this. Patterned repetitive stimuli lead to tolerance. (2006, p. 54)

Small doses of recall allow the brain to calm the gradual breaking through of the implicit memories from their dissociated state by developing tolerance to the traumatic events. "The more intense and overwhelming the experience, however, the harder it becomes to 'desensitize' all of the trauma-related memories" (p. 54).

There are moments in a mindful approach to play therapy when the observing self is realized and the child can straightforwardly experience shifts that lead to healing. *Clarity, vividness,* and *wider perception* are terms used by Arthur Deikman in *The Observing Self: Mysticism and Psychotherapy* (1982) to describe the experience of meditation. These also apply to the experience of the child in the deeper awareness stage of Mindfulness-Based Play-Family Therapy. Deikman writes that although the state of the clarity does not last long, one can be profoundly changed by it. How do we know that this has happened to the child? Close observation shows the play starting to change. After the child has been permitted to spend as much time as he wants in playing out the themes of one who has experienced horror, the therapist notices the more light-hearted entry of normal, healthy play. The difficult patterns the child has been struggling with show increasing resolution. As his self-esteem strengthens, the child is gradually entering the next stage: integration.

Stage V: Integration

It is best to not rush the integration stage. A child's play at this time is more creative than previously, and the energy is lighter. He may make up games or create wholesome art. His play themes will include working out problems and feeling in charge. At Talk Time, prior to the play, he will often begin to discuss his problems or past traumas openly, sometimes for the first time. He will have fewer fears and less shame, he will be more at ease with himself, and he will be generally happier.

A very aggressive five-year-old boy, who had been adopted at birth and who felt quite angry about his world, began to play, for the first time, with soft animals and puppets during the integration stage. One day he picked up a mother kangaroo, hugged her, removed the baby joey from her pouch, inserted a soft baby turtle, and hugged them both. This experience was far more powerful than words for letting me know that we could head toward closure. The experience of becoming more kind also paralleled his new-found ability to express anger appropriately, another signal of integration.

As the child progresses, the therapist will observe changes in his play and a steadier sense of well-being; this may signal that the child has moved into the integration stage. The noted improvements are not mere symptom relief, such as may have been observed earlier during the exploration and limit setting stages. By now, the therapist will have seen that the child has found a way to re-create, in play themes, the issues that needed healing. Playing at these themes releases the effects of trauma that have been trapped in the body and opens the child to moments of awareness that may facilitate healing at a profound, cellular level. The suffering that all children feel at one time or another, and the trauma that occurs in the lives of many children can be soothed and healed in the present moment through the experience of silence, the empathic relationship, and the power of the chosen symbols. This is play therapy at its best.

It is recommended that a therapist pursue training that allows her to fully understand what she is witnessing. She learns to notice the energy in the room when a child has reached a significant level of awareness. If she is not catching on, the child will give her many chances. It is amazing that, if the therapist simply follows the language of child-directed play, the child tends to heal. The therapist may understand the events only later on; there is mystery in what happens that we will never understand.

Badenoch affirms the value of nondirective play for children's trauma. She states that, when the child leads and the therapist follows, stress-healing chemicals are released in the brain.

> Sometimes, under the pressure of parents' need for rapid behavioral change, we may feel strongly pulled toward "making something happen." That almost never goes well, and we soon find ourselves returning to our faith in the power of the relationship and an organic pace that can't be rushed or manipulated. (2008, p. 302)

It is important to emphasize that the healing process is dynamic, not static. Issues that are rooted in deep pain may come up again as children grow, and they may need to be readdressed every two or three years. However, when a child has had play therapy at an earlier stage, closer to the time of the trauma, there is substantially less work later on. When he returns to rework formerly addressed traumas at his new developmental stage, with newer understanding, integration suitable for the present time of his life will probably require only short-term "developmental catch-up" therapy.

Stage VI: Closure

The closure stage of the play therapy session is signaled when the timer goes off, usually indicating a five-minute warning. (It is easier for the child not to take the signal personally if it comes from an object.) This allows the child to begin to protect his inner landscape, which has opened vulnerably during his time with the therapist. The therapist may say, "It's almost time to end. You have just a few more minutes. How would you like to end your puppet show?" Most children hear the bell, use a few minutes to end their play, and ease into the transition. Some need the whole five minutes to end and may even want more time. When the child requests more time, unless there is a good reason, the therapist usually adheres to the boundary. However, there may be times when the child is doing a very deep piece of work and the therapist agrees to give a few more minutes. When the clinical benefit is clear, the therapist can intuitively adapt the structure in the moment.

Although the therapist may do all of the cleanup following trauma focused play, there are several reasons why it can be valuable for the therapist and child to clean up together when it will not interfere with healing. Putting things back helps the child feel helpful. Responsible behavior also bears the quality of personal empowerment: The child experiences some ownership of the elements of his play themes, and, by extension, of his own life. This is amplified by his alliance with the therapist. Cleanup provides a grounding activity for the child to move from imagination back to reality. During the process, the child may chatter about life; he may say that he and his dad are going to the playground on the way home, or that he has a lot of homework. Sharing the work contributes positive energy to the child-therapist relationship. The child often takes pride in cleaning off sand pieces and taking care of the space, and the cleaning process models what can happen at home.

Sometimes, a child who is being oppositional at home will say he does not want to put the toys away. On occasion, he may refuse to do so. When the negative response comes during the limit setting phase of the relationship, it gives the therapist a chance to be firm and not take the refusal personally. "I'm glad you can tell me that you don't want to put the blocks away." If he continues to refuse, she can say, "The way it works in here is that we need to put these away together, and if you don't, then I will put them away and put a little note here to remind me that you are choosing not to play with the blocks next week when you come." The therapist lets the child know that this consequence will last for just one week; after that, he can play with the toys in mention again. Although a boundary is set, it is not done punitively. Usually, the child's desire to have the toys available at the next session will motivate him to cooperate with the cleanup. Many children will refuse to clean up only once or twice; when they come back the next week, they almost always remember the consequences! Because this part of closure is reality based, the therapist may mention it casually to the parent: "Jacob didn't want to clean up the blocks today, so next time he won't be able to use the blocks. We already talked about this, and it is good that he told me directly how he really feels. I think he will clean up next time." I make it clear that the parent does not need to do anything about this, although talking to the parent provides a model of how to handle similar situations with the child at home.

As with all the basic guidelines of MBPFT, there are clinical exceptions. On days when the child is deeply engrossed in Stage IV meditative play, the therapist takes the lead in suggesting that she can clean up for him. The child is almost always very happy to receive this accommodation. It can be much better for the child not to clean up when he has been in profound play. This is especially true with sandtray therapy (see the section on sandtray therapy later in the chapter), although sometimes the child may want to wash the sand objects in water. In this case, it seems that the ritual of closure helps to ground him. When the moment to leave the playroom arrives after such deep play, the therapist can make a transition by talking about reality and by having the child stamp his feet on the ground. She accompanies the child back to his parent and lets the parent know that he may need a little extra support today. Then she goes back to the playroom to finish cleanup alone.

I notice that the issue of whether or not a child should be involved in cleanup elicits strong opinions from therapists during training sessions. I see advantages and disadvantages of both options. As with most guidelines in this book, I recommend that the therapist trust her own experience. Do what works for you in your setting; when in doubt, get supervision. It is okay to be flexible and respond to different children differently to meet individual needs.

As mentioned earlier, I recommend, for the sake of clarity and safety, that the therapist be in charge of opening the door. At the end of the session, she leads the child to the waiting room, and occasionally at this point she has a brief conversation with the parent, being careful to keep the child out of hearing range. Since the child is used to seeing his parents talk to the therapist, he will probably take this chat for granted and show no more than curiosity. The therapist will *not* talk about the actual content of the play themes, which are considered confidential. She might discretely say, however, "His play was very expressive of sadness, and he seemed to be dealing with his grief today. Jacob may benefit from extra hugs tonight." This inclusion of the parents, ever so briefly, gives a message that their importance to the child is greater than the therapist's in the long run of life. The therapist then shakes the child's hand and says good-bye while making eye contact with him.

The closure stage of MBPFT offers the child conscious awareness that the play sessions and Talk Time meetings will be coming to an end. Perhaps the child has been in therapy for a year. Many children admit that they will not miss the Talk Time but are sad to end the playtime. However, when closure follows a full segment of the integration stage, most are also happy and ready to be moving on. They realize that it is time. They have activities and friendships drawing them into the larger world.

When the therapist and parents have worked well together and the parents are doing mindful parenting work or their own therapy, the end is not a surprise. Generally, as the appropriate time for closure approaches, the therapist and the parents will notice how well the child is doing. The parents will feel much more competent in addressing the problems that come up, not only with the MC child but also with other children in the family. Through the mindful parenting meetings, they have learned much about relational issues with their child. They better understand how to work with their own reactivity, and this brings warmer feelings of connection between them and their MC child. Sometimes, they will want to have another child start therapy after they see how helpful the experience was for the initial child.

While the child will have his own thoughts and feelings about the timing of closure, it is important to let parents know that this is a clinical decision best made by the adults. They decide at parent discussion and feedback meetings without the child present. Once the therapist and the parents are in agreement, they let the child know and test his reaction. Occasionally, children ask for more time, with a firmness that convinces the adults that a little more time would be beneficial for him. In this case, closure may be postponed for the immediate future. Otherwise, the therapist and parents make it clear that coming to the play center will end in a few weeks. Generally, it is helpful for the child to have three closure sessions, and the therapist explains what will happen during those final sessions. For example, if three sessions remain, he may have two in the playroom and one as an activity session with his parents. The therapist also tells the child that on their last day, he himself may open the playroom door at the end of the session. Children seem to enjoy this transitional ritual at closure, which helps them to "get" that therapy will be ending.

The adults let the child know, when it is true, that the therapist will still be there and, in fact, that they would like to have the child visit her after about three months. The follow-up session is important for letting the child know that the therapist still exists, and that he can see her if he needs to. It is also a helpful way to make sure the child's changes are holding steady.

One favorite activity for a closure session with both of the parents and the child together is making a poster-board-size collage that can be taken home. The therapist can have available hundreds of pictures that are already cut out from magazines, magic markers for writing words or drawing designs, and some interesting crafts materials. The child is in charge of designing the collage. He selects his own pictures and decides which pictures to accept or reject from his parents' choices. He chooses where to place the items. I encourage parents to help with the glue, and the family works together while they discuss what they liked and did not like about coming. The parents can take this opportunity to acknowledge the positive gains that the child has made.

At the last session, it is repeated that if the child ever wants to return, he can tell his parents, and the therapist will be happy to see him again. It is usually the parent who is aware of the need to come back; if the child has asked to return, he is really reaching out for help, and it is best to honor his request. The reconnection is usually brief, unless the child is experiencing a new trauma, life adjustment, or wants to work on a specific issue that is coming up at home or at school.

After therapy, parents often admit that they like their child better; they may report that family members and friends see a big difference. Most report about 75% to 80% improvement overall. They are usually quite happy with this; the goal, of course, is not to have perfect kids. Parents feel notably more competent communicating and working on problems with their children and with each other. They feel better about their parenting differences even though they cannot resolve all of them. Because part of every session has been devoted to Talk Time, with parent and child together, parents are left with a lot of confidence regarding how to talk to their children when difficult issues come up. They are grateful for this skill.

Variations in MBPFT Sessions

Play therapists have asked whether having the parent–child dyad session first might raise an angry response in the child, and they question whether this might interfere with his availability to connect with the therapist in the playroom. It is important to remember that the content of Talk Time can often influence the relevance of the pretend play themes that will emerge. Usually, if the therapist models a successful shift from Talk Time to playtime, then the child will also make that shift well. Perhaps this works well most of the time because, in MBPFT, the play therapy is kept in "pretend."

If the child occasionally struggles and is unable to make the shift, the therapist can stay with the child's feeling. She can give the struggle itself space to happen. In fact, it may become the focus of therapy that day. Upon entering the playroom with a child who is resisting the play experience, the therapist may repeat the child's verbalized sentiments.

THERAPIST: You don't want to play with anything today?

CHILD: Yeah, and I don't want to play with you!

THERAPIST: Oh, you don't want to play with me either! Well I'm glad you can be honest with me about that. We just had a hard time in the other room. The way it works is, as usual, you can decide what to do in this room; you can even decide not to do anything at all.

Being with the child and accepting him without any agenda can actually be a rather significant use of time. The mindful therapist will trust the silence and wait until something changes. It is important to note that if the therapist has been multipartial with the parent and child during the Talk Time, it is unlikely that the child will refuse to play. Knowing that he can choose to do nothing in the playroom often gives him the freedom to engage. But even if the child *does* choose to have a seemingly meaningless and wasted play session, the true benefits may be priceless. The therapist holds the space of unconditional presence, understanding, and acceptance; this stance can deepen the therapist–child relationship.

It is recommended that a child not be allowed to leave the playroom even though he does not want to play. He can get the message that while all his feelings are acceptable, including being angry and not wanting to be with the therapist or in the playroom, the agreement is to be together through whatever comes up. In play, the child learns to tolerate these uncomfortable feelings. While making it clear that she accepts the child and his feelings, the therapist decides which option may be clinically more helpful to the child: simply being with him and offering unconditional presence in silence, or perhaps taking a lump of clay and beginning to make something. Or, after 10 minutes of silence, the therapist may use puppets to tell a creative story that reflects the child's feelings, providing an effective response to the child's "stuckness" (Davis, 1996).

Depending on the age of the child and clinical issues, the therapist may invite a parent to join them—provided the parent can accept that the child needs space, even to do nothing. In one of my recent sessions, the child curled up and fell asleep. The parent and I used the time to process parenting issues that did not require the child's attention, while being careful to avoid any discussion that should not be overheard by the child.

Negotiating Changes in the Session

It is generally preferable not to disrupt the continuity of the usual play process. However, it occasionally becomes clear that the entire session is required in order to attend to what has come up in Talk Time. When the therapist realizes that such a change in the agenda is necessary, she can renegotiate the time with the parent and the child, explaining that finishing with the topic under discussion is most important right now and that it may not leave enough time for the play. They process this all together until they find an agreeable solution, perhaps negotiating to have 15 minutes of play. It is very important to explain to the child why the playtime is being shortened so that he will not feel treated unfairly.

MBPFT is not meant to be rigid. Therapists are encouraged to listen to their own experiences and to adapt the framework to their unique dynamics and settings. A certain child may benefit from a reversed order: having the play session immediately after the positive check-in and leaving the hard-to-talk-about part of Talk Time until the latter part of the session. Then the child will have entered her imaginary realm, accompanied by the therapist, *before* engaging challenging issues. For example, an oppositional child struggling with disruptive attachment issues may do best to check in only on what was fun or on what the parent can offer that went well during the week. Then he is most ready to proceed into the playroom. The therapist sets the timer so as to leave 15 or 20 minutes for discussing the relational challenges. The therapist may observe for a few weeks, or even a few months, before deciding whether or not this seems to be a good clinical decision.

Challenges Connecting

Children come to play therapy with various degrees of willingness. Sometimes, an immediate connection is made. At other times, the therapist and child may not feel drawn to one another for a while. It takes time to build a trusting relationship. This is normal, and it is the therapist's job to be aware of this and to seek ways to develop trust with a reluctant child. Before entering the playroom alone with the therapist, the child has had at least one session in the playroom with his parents and siblings. He has also spent some time talking with the therapist. Yet the child may mistrust the therapist, possibly because of painful experiences from his past history. The therapist needs to be honest, direct, and trustworthy. She must not take personally any of the child's negative expressions. Even in the act of refusing to shake hands or to make eye contact, the child may be testing the therapist's acceptance—a form of connection in itself. She may say, "Maybe after I get to know you better we will be able to have a handshake. I am glad you can tell me how you really feel."

Many children realize intuitively, when they enter the playroom, that the room provides tools for their expression, and they are often readily engaged. Children who are at first uncomfortable in the playroom will usually lose self-consciousness through their curiosity. It is diagnostically important to note a child who does not know how to play. The therapist may need to teach preplay activities. The inability to play may indicate a history of deprivation or trauma, a developmental delay, or a child who is too occupied with his family's issues.

Experience has shown that a child's reluctance to play may mean that an approach other than spontaneous play therapy may be more appropriate, at least initially. In Mindfulness-Based Play-Family Therapy, since the most direct route to the child's healing is through spontaneous play therapy, we tend to use other modalities only if the child is not responding to self-initiated play. Assessment of the causes that may be inhibiting spontaneous play will dictate which alternative modality is preferable. Possible start-up options include family therapy and parent education, as well as more directive approaches to the child's play that include the involvement of a safe parent. Parents can participate in Floortime, developed by Stanley Greenspan (1992), or Theraplay, developed by Booth and Jernberg (2010). Some children do their best connecting by working for a long time in mindful art therapy activities such as water play or wet sand. Each child and family has its own best way, and it is helpful to be fluid enough to offer a variety of options. *Helping Abused and Traumatized Children: Integrating Directive and Nondirective Approaches* by Eliana Gil (2006) is a valuable book that offers a number of ideas. In all these activities, the therapist will weave his silent presence into the texture of the more verbal, often directive work.

A Word About Mindfulness-Based Sandtray Therapy

Mindfulness-Based Sandtray Therapy is a body–mind approach that integrates sandtray theory with mindfulness meditation principles. It nurtures the formation, from elements of the unconscious, of an awareness of a person's whole-life experience. Such awareness can allow one to live compassionately and exist fully in the present moment. As in any transformational psychotherapy modality, the therapist-client relationship is grounded in respect for the conscious, preconscious, and unconscious factors of each lived experience as it unfolds. Spontaneous sandtray therapy provides a simple yet profound way to be with people through the joys and pains of living. Bonnie Badenoch notes that sandplay has the "ability to awaken and then regulate right-brain limbic processes," making it "a powerful way to address painful, fearful, dissociated experiences" (2008, p. 220). Directed sandtrays can be effective for all children and families, including children who have ADD, ADHD, or developmental delays or who are on the autism spectrum. The following brief description serves merely as an introduction to this wonderful way of engaging clients of all ages in deep and meaningful experiences.

Mindfulness-Based Sandtray Therapy is rooted in the practice of meditation that I first encountered, and studied for many years, with Buddhist psychologist and prolific author John Welwood. He taught therapists how to use the principle of unconditional presence by instructing them in meditation-inspired practices, including somatic awareness, Focusing, recognition of the voice of the inner critic, and a method of case presentation using a process called "body, mind, and speech." All of these were practiced parallel to meditation practice. Mindfulness-Based Sandtray Therapy is my eclectic integration of Welwood's teachings and those of other teachers of Tibetan and Zen meditation along with traditional sand play and sand tray theory.

A sandtray area has a display of at least 300 hundred miniature figures, including representations of people, animals, nature objects, and abstract symbols. They represent a wide range of emotions, situations, personalities, and fantasies. A large collection may have thousands of miniatures. There is usually at least one moist and one dry sandtray. These may be on tables or, for some children, on the floor. In Mindfulness-Based Sandtray Therapy, it is recommended that the sandtray be an integrated part of the play therapy room so that the child has a choice of materials to work with during a single session. A child may begin playing with puppets, then go to the dry sandtray, then paint a picture, and then head to the wet sandtray. He may make a story that combines use of the dollhouse with the sandtray, or he may make a sandtray scene and then pick a large alligator puppet to disturb the peaceful picture he created. Many children will use both trays, and a third can also be brought out. In these ways, use of the sandtray is woven throughout the child's imaginative experiences in the playroom. That said, having the sandtray set up in a space separate from the playroom also seems to work for some therapists. Consider the physical layout of your office and trust your own experience.

Sandtray Therapy with Children Ages 3 to 12

When working with a single child between the ages of 3 and 12, it is important that the therapist have a solid grounding in play therapy theory. Sandtray therapy is not a separate theoretical modality, but a combined intuitive and somatic approach to exploration and expression of the inner self. It is useful in working with anxiety, depression, oppositional defiant disorder, trauma, and attachment issues and is recommended for both verbal and nonverbal children.

The same philosophy of play therapy described earlier in the chapter applies to working in the sand. It is, therefore, recommended that the therapist study the six stages of MBPFT and build her practice of sandtray therapy on that framework. For the therapist already trained in play therapy, additional sandtray training will help her use this modality with children in a more effective manner. The training enhances the therapist's skill with metaphors and tends to be an enjoyable experience.

It can be valuable to use sand miniatures to engage reality during Talk Time or family meetings. When working with a child alone, it is important to keep the experience in the pretend realm, just as in MBPFT. The child may either play and have the therapist witness, or he may engage the therapist to enact a role using the sand miniatures. In this case, as in play therapy, the therapist takes cues about her role from the child's projections. She stays with the metaphors and does not make interpretations for the child.

When a child enters the playroom for a session with the therapist, he may indicate that he would like to begin by playing with the sand materials. He and his family may have already made up a sand story during the second evaluation session, so the sandtrays may be familiar and feel like a natural choice. He may spontaneously move his fingers through the sand. If not, the therapist may suggest that he compare the wet and dry sand. When a child is playing with the sand and water without objects, she may be reconnecting with preverbal life experiences. Simply being present as a witness can be the therapist's best response.

Some children initiate working with the sandtray and therefore do not need instructions. In some cases, the therapist may ease a child's first solo sandtray experience by giving him a container and saying, "You can pick about 10 pieces and put them in the basket." This breaks the process into two steps so that, at first, the child can focus on selecting the pieces. After he has gathered his objects, the therapist directs him to place them in any way that he wants, into whichever sandtray he chooses. Once the child has had this directed experience, he learns that he can use the equipment more freely.

Many children use the sandtray to tell a story. When this happens, the therapist may write down the narrative as the child says it aloud—but this must not be done if it takes the therapist away from being connected and present.

Sandtray Therapy With Adolescents and Adults

Mindfulness-Based Sandtray Therapy makes a distinction between working with children and working with teenagers and adults. This differentiation affects theory, process, and techniques. The intrapsychic and relational sandtray styles that are most natural for adults are rooted in understanding the individual adult psyche and in relational family therapy. A sandtray room that is dedicated to teens and adults may contain additional sand miniatures that are not in a collection for children. Adults tend to do sandtrays that are more reality based, although they can be invited to create a fairy tale or an imaginative story, particularly when working with painful or traumatic content. Sandtray therapy can be very effective for individual adults or couples, as well as for addressing family-related issues. When used in individual work with adolescents and with the family, sandtray therapy often releases more profound communication than numerous sessions that rely on talk alone (see the couple sandtray example in chapter 9). It can be a sacred experience with a potential for depth so great that it surprises therapists and clients who are new to this way of working. Mindfulness-Based Sandtray Therapy with teens and adults is integrated with the somatic awareness work of Focusing (Gendlin, 1981, 1996).

Relational sandtray therapy is an adaptation rooted in the theory of family therapy. As the name implies, it is the creation of a sandtray as a means of communication between two or more people, for example, between a child and his mother or within a couple.

Recommended Reading

There are many wonderful books available that offer an in-depth exploration of sandplay and sandtray therapy training. This material is quite useful, but the reader should be aware that all resources for sand therapy recommend that the practitioner receive training and have experience in her own sand process before using this modality in therapy. Supervision is essential as the therapist begins to work with clients.

Sandplay: A Psychotherapeutic Approach to the Psyche (1980) by the originator of sandplay, Dora Kalff, is a basic book that values personal development rooted in Jungian psychology and Eastern thought as influenced by Zen Buddhist scholar Suzuki Roschi. In *The World Technique* (1979), Margaret Lowenfeld developed a way to communicate with children through sand miniatures. Rie Rogers Mitchell and Harriet Friedman offer a valuable, informative, and entertaining resource on the history of sandplay in *Sandplay: Past, Present and Future* (1994). This book provides a solid grounding in various sand modalities. Mitchell and Friedman also edited the first publication on sandplay supervision (2008).

The second edition of *Sandtray Therapy: A Practical Manual*, by Linda Homeyer and Daniel Sweeney, was published in 2011. It is an excellent first book to read about sandtray therapy and includes everything from the rationale of the work to selecting and organizing the collection to conducting and processing the sandtrays. We have used this book for years at the Family & Play Therapy Center for our sandtray training that focuses on working with children ages 3 to 12, and is greatly appreciated by our students. For adult and adolescent training, we also use *Sandtray: The Sacred Healing*, by Kate Amatruda and Phoenix Helen Simpson (1997), and *Sandplay for Diverse Populations* by B. Labovitz Boik and Anna Goodwin (2000).

In addition, I highly recommend reading chapter 16, "The Integrating Power of Sandplay," in Bonnie Badenoch's book *Being a Brain-Wise Therapist: A Practical Guide to Interpersonal Neurobiology* (2008). Badenoch's philosophy is compatible with Mindfulness-Based Sandtray Therapy, and she explains the healing events that occur in the brain during the process of sandtray therapy:

> The insula gathers all of this sensory data into an emotionally meaningful context, helping all this information converge in the middle frontal cortex, and a rich *relationship* with the sand often unfolds. People get absorbed in arranging the sand just right. This whole experience encourages vertical integration, linking body, limbic regions, and cortex in the right hemisphere. (p. 221)

5

The Language and Metaphors
of Play Therapy

ONE OF THE aspects of play therapy that is most challenging to convey, both in teaching new student therapists and in explaining to parents, is just how meaningful and valuable it can be for the inner life of the child. Many adults seem to have lost touch with the valuable experience that play provided in their own childhood. Experience shows that most children, though not all, are able to reach deep into their minds by creating their own healing stories in the play therapy room. This is most likely to happen when an empathic therapist is competent in two essential skills: using mindful language and relating to the metaphors of the child's play.

In this context, the term *language* describes the means by which the therapist communicates with the child in the pretend realm of the playroom. It includes both the spoken word and silence, as well as nonverbal messages such as tone of voice, facial expression, gestures, and demeanor. These are elements of normal human communication. The play therapist can work most effectively by becoming aware of the quality of each of these elements during interactions in the playroom. Such awareness develops through patient attention and practice.

The term *metaphors* describes the symbolic character of the play imagery that is created during the child's play. The therapist's skill lies in understanding how the metaphors may symbolize the particular child client's life history and situation, and how they offer an accessible vehicle for the child's psyche to confront and heal deep hurts that could be painful or even unapproachable in their raw state. The metaphors follow a logic that is personal to the child rather than objectively rational. Learning to appropriately interpret them may be one of the most challenging skills the play therapist needs to master. Fluency develops over time. Sometimes, the metaphors of a child's play are very obvious and easy to understand. But at other times, the meanings are hidden in the repeated themes of the play and are harder to discern, requiring observation over a period of time.

Note that, while using language and relating to metaphors are necessary skills, their main importance lies in the fact that they contribute to the quality of the connection that is established between the therapist and her child client. It is the healing relationship that is the first goal of practice.

The initial focus for the trainee is to learn about the use of language within play therapy and, as time goes on, to learn to interpret the more challenging metaphors. The therapist develops the skill of responding mindfully with words and silence to the child's play. This establishes a tone that allows the child to create the metaphors needed to develop the character of his psyche, sort out the complexities of his world, and heal his pain.

Generally, the play can proceed successfully even if the therapist only partially understands the meaning of the child's metaphors. However, a child's play does sometimes remain stuck until the therapist has a more complete understanding of the metaphors. Supervision sessions offer therapists a valuable opportunity to gain that understanding, particularly when the supervisor sees the video playback of the play therapy and reviews the themes that appear over time. Interpreting metaphors can also be studied by viewing play sessions of the supervisor or of other therapists and writing down observations about the play themes. For an expansion of the theory of metaphors, I recommend chapter 8 in *Reaching Children Through Play Therapy: An Experiential Approach* (Norton & Norton, 1997).

The final segment of this chapter will offer a concrete example of another skill that is very challenging for therapists to learn, namely, how to communicate to the parents about the child's metaphors. The therapist needs to have a sense of what may be revealed about the child's play and what needs to be left private, as well as when and how to discuss these matters with parents.

Imagination and Reality

In his classic book, *The Uses of Enchantment* (1976), Bruno Bettelheim writes about the value of fairy tales. The introduction opens with words about our hope to live consciously, in the present. It continues,

> Our greatest need and most difficult achievement is to find meaning in our lives. . . . An understanding of the meaning of one's life is not suddenly acquired at a particular age. . . . [G]aining a secure understanding of what the meaning of one's life may or ought to be—that is what constitutes having attained psychological maturity. (p. 3)

Bettelheim believes that access to the imaginary world of fairy tales helps the child to start on this life journey.

Bettelheim's writing applies with striking aptness to the stories that are often created in the playroom, where a child may use costumes and pretend to be a hero, a dragon, a sword fighter, a prince or a princess, an evil witch, an alien, a bossy child, a pony, or a loving or abandoning mama or papa bear. Or he may use miniature figures of all kinds to explore his story themes in the sandtray. He can create his own "fairy tales" to explore his inner landscape and to express the conflicts and pain that are part of childhood. In fact, reading fairy tales aloud or telling them orally can enrich a child's participation in weekly play therapy.

It is important for parents to expose their children to literature that addresses inner conflicts. This may be the value of Star Wars and Harry Potter. Fairy tales deal with all the deeper feelings that children normally have: jealousy, anger, fear of abandonment, sadness, depression, death, loss or fear of loss, and anxiety about separation from Mom or Dad or siblings or about growing up. Although adults have concerns about gender roles, class distinctions, and stereotyping in fairy tales and the perpetuation of the happily-ever-after myth, Bettelheim proposes that in rejecting them, we are throwing out the baby with the bathwater, so to speak. Fairy tales are about the struggle for meaning in life and provide a way for parents to address life's complexities with their children through the imagination. Because children have more access to their imaginative world than adults, Bettelheim notes that they will identify with the hero or heroine regardless of sex. A goal of the fairy tale is to locate the story in the pretend part of the child's brain.

Because the imaginary world of the fairy tale is such a close parallel to the imaginary world of play, Bettelheim's words are an affirmative expression of the value of play therapy. Following are a few of his thoughts about the child's experience of fairy tales, presented either as direct quotation or as paraphrasing and accompanied by comparisons with the process of play therapy.

Similarities of Fairy Tales and Play Therapy

"Fairy tales address, in a most imaginative form, essential human problems and manage to do so in an indirect way." (p. 17)

The same is true of play therapy, which allows children to address essential human problems, and one of its primary values is its indirect manner.

"Fairy tales offer new dimensions to the child's imagination which would be impossible for him to discover as truly on his own. Even more important, the form and structure of fairy tales suggest images to the child by which he can structure his daydreams and with them give better direction to his life." (p. 7)

Play therapy offers a way for the child, with a little aid from the therapist, to discover the unconscious on his own by accessing preconscious implicit memories. Play therapy also offers "new dimensions," which materialize for the child as he discovers the stories that he carries within himself. His play metaphors offer him a structure to house a sense of meaning for his life. In this way, play therapy can be beneficial for children who are not exhibiting problematic symptoms as well as for those who are.

When life is bewildering, children need even more opportunity to understand the complexities of their world in order to create order and to cope. "To be able to do so, the child must be helped to make some coherent sense out of the turmoil of his feelings." (p. 5) "Fairy tales are experienced as wondrous because the child feels understood and appreciated deep down in his feelings, hopes, anxieties, without these all having to be dragged up and investigated in the harsh light of reality that is still beyond him." (p. 19)

Sometimes a child has profoundly sad or disturbing things happen to him. We think, "This should never happen to a child"—and yet it has. In trauma play, the child's metaphors eventually go back to the harshest of experiences, and though the story is set in an imaginary format, trauma play can be upsetting for parents to watch, even if they have witnessed or participated in the play up to this time. Reliving the trauma and releasing the traumatic effects that remain in the body are important for a deep level of healing to happen. Therapists offer the child the gift of being sincerely understood by a respectful witness. When they end therapy, many children say, "Why did we come here? All I did was play!" As with the fairy tale, children do not need to cognitively understand the magic of the healing of play. They know intuitively that they feel more whole.

> "When unconscious material is to some degree permitted to come to awareness and worked through in imagination, the potential for causing harm—to ourselves or others—is much reduced; some of its forces can then be made to serve positive purposes." (p. 7)

This is how play therapy works, and this is the reason why, when the family stays the course of the treatment, children not only get symptom relief but may also achieve a healthy integration of the self—rather than, as Bettelheim says, being diverted from what troubles them the most. He tells us that "parents wish to pretend that the dark side of life does not exist" but warns that "a struggle against severe difficulty in life is unavoidable and is an intrinsic part of human existence" (p. 7). Children with nameless anxieties often have parents and even grandparents who want to expose them only to happy, positive realities, and to deny the harsher ones. For example, a parent may flush a dead goldfish down the toilet and replace it, rather than having the child experience the death with some acknowledging ritual. The death of a pet allows a child the opportunity to grieve and to have an understanding of death, which is an inescapable part of life.

> "Explaining too much to the child destroys the story's enchantment, which depends on the child's unawareness of why she is delighted by it. Intrusion risks losing the power of the tale. The value is increased when the child struggles to master it without adult interference." (p. 18)

The same is true for spontaneous play therapy, and that is precisely why it is important that therapists learn language that is not intrusive to the child. The therapist follows the child's lead in the play as the he tells her the script to follow. She needs to be able to tolerate the child's struggles, without jumping in and saving him. Play therapy pioneer Eliana Gil describes how to work with the different characteristics of dynamic and static post-traumatic play (2006, p. 160).

"It is intrusive to interpret a person's unconscious thoughts, to make conscious what he wishes to keep preconscious, and it is especially true of children." (p. 20)

In Mindfulness-Based Play-Family Therapy (MBPFT), as with many forms of play therapy, the therapist does not share interpretations with the child. She *does* discuss with the parent the significance of the play. She does not reveal the details of the actual play drama, although a parent who was present during the play will be aware of these details. The therapist also humbly acknowledges that she can never really completely know what a child is thinking.

Another eloquent expression of the value of the pretend world in play therapy is presented in *"If You Turned Into a Monster": Transformation Through Play: A Body-Centered Approach to Play Therapy* (2007) by Dennis McCarthy. The author expands on the benefits that come from children's drawing and creating monsters in play therapy as a way of dealing with their shadow. He notes that humans are positively transformed by their encounters with beasts, and by their ability to accept the beast completely. He affirms the value of accepting the monster in fairy tales: "These stories and many others like them, move us because they describe a transformation in which what is vital in the person is affirmed, freed or reborn" (p. 22). The author addresses the power of symbols that relate to the hopeful, as well as hopeless, experiences of living. "The child can say through symbols things that are unspeakable in any other form. Speaking about the unspeakable is the essence of our therapeutic work" (p. 31). McCarthy points out that the unspeakable can include "the great joy of being alive or the discovery of new parts to ourselves" (p. 31), as well as negative experiences. He states that for a child to feel affirmed, both positive and negative need to be experienced and then expressed in the play therapy process.

Speech and Silence in Play Therapy

One of the most important skills for the play therapist to learn is how to speak mindfully to the child during playtime, including knowing when to talk and when to be a quiet witness. As a default, when it matches the child's needs, the therapist is reflexive in a Rogerian way. A goal of this chapter is to demonstrate how unconditional presence, which is the goal of Carl Rogers's work, can be actualized in the child-therapist relationship through the modality of play. As adults, we often reflect by using synonyms to convey the meaning of what someone is saying. In play therapy, although the therapist may not repeat all of the words, it is usually best to use the same words that the child has used—not synonyms. This minimizes disruption of the child's flow. Remaining in the intuitive right brain can enable the child to approach the deeper awareness state.

Parents often ask what makes play therapy different from the play that children do at home. The therapist, who has established a safe environment and a trusting relationship with the child, encourages play that is often quite different from that which a child does at home with his peers. In spontaneous play therapy, the therapist's responses encourage the child into a hypnotic-like trance that enables him to address life's pain and traumas in a way that is healing. The therapist trained in MBPFT assumes leadership to keep playroom time in the pretend realm. At the same time, she does not develop her own themes but allows the child to express his own unique take on the world, uncontaminated by the therapist's agenda. When the therapist minimizes her own imaginative themes while maximizing the child's play projections, the child is offered the grounding for his authentic self to emerge.

Of course, the play that children do with their friends at home and at school is very valuable for their growth and development. In fact, there is a high correlation between learning problems and an inability to do imaginative, theme-related play that includes a beginning, middle, and end. Children having difficulty developing play themes and engaging in play with other children may benefit from a more structured developmental play therapy. Examples of both nondirected and directed play therapy are included below.

MBPFT reduces the problems children have in experiencing their world. It allows them to identify and express their feelings; develops deeper character, including more empathy for themselves and others; and helps with creative problem solving in a complex world. Play therapy can also be a constructive, preventive, short-term experience for the child who is exhibiting issues of concern, as well as for the parents.

The next section offers exercises and examples based on real metaphors that children have enacted in play. It is important to note that, depending on the stage of play therapy, the same statement by a child may elicit a different therapist response.

The Use of Language During the Exploratory Stage of MBPFT

The following examples show typical responses to a child who is able to play spontaneously during the *exploratory stage* of MBPFT. The therapist responds using the child's own words, allowing the child to know that she is present and hearing him. In this approach, the therapist whispers as she asks questions that help to create the role that the child is assigning him. The child naturally understands these communications as "stage directions." The therapist generally does not ask questions out of curiosity, but trusts that if she stays present and responds reflectively, the child will unfold his inner world according to his own timetable. During the first few sessions of the exploratory stage, phrases such as, "In here, you decide how you want to play," are stated occasionally.

GIRL, AGE 6: I am going to fill this house with furniture!

THERAPIST [matching the child's tone]: You are going to fill this house with furniture!

UNMINDFUL RESPONSE: "Here, I'll help you so we can put all the furniture in." (This shows that the therapist has an agenda and is ahead of the child.)

BOY, AGE 10 [gathering sand miniatures]: This volcano is going to blow up the world.

THERAPIST [matching the child's tone]: This volcano is going to blow up the world.

UNMINDFUL RESPONSE: "Why would it blow up the world?" (The therapist is leading, and the response is inconsistent with letting the child move into experiencing a rhythmic flow in the play. It implies that there is a reason. The child's feeling that he has to answer the therapist's need to know can bring him to his left thinking brain and intrude on the pace of his imaginary unfolding. Occasionally, the child's responses to "why" questions can be helpful when used in short-term structured play therapy. But in spontaneous play, it is better to say, "What's happening?")

BOY, AGE 8 [putting all the stuffed animals and a box of weapons in the tent]: They want to be safe.

THERAPIST: They want to be safe. (Especially during the first stages, consistent with a child-centered approach, Rogerian reflection of what the child says is often the most present response.)

UNMINDFUL RESPONSE: "How can they be safe?"

GIRL, AGE 10 [using Play-Doh]: "These bombs are explosives to plant [in the sand] where we can't see them."

THERAPIST [giving full attention and presence]: Hmmm, bombs where we can't see them. (Adults need to remember that most of the time these words, spoken in pretend, are metaphors of the child's feelings and thoughts, not actual plans. On the rare occasion when a child is really thinking about doing something dangerous, the therapist would suspect it from the whole context.)

UNMINDFUL RESPONSE: "That's scary." (The child may or may not be feeling that it is scary.)

Comment: Simply repeating aggressive content with neutral energy gives the child the message that these ideas are completely acceptable in play therapy. Children test the therapist in the exploratory stage to see whether they are permitted to explore their more scary thoughts. Given the therapist's unbiased reflection, a child will usually go deeper and say more.

BOY, AGE 7 [gathering cats, dogs, and horses]:   These two dogs don't want to get on the school bus.

THERAPIST [matching the child's tone and pointing]:   These two dogs don't want to get on the school bus. [She waits for the child to continue.]

UNMINDFUL RESPONSE: "Why not? What happens to the dogs on the school bus?" (In spontaneous methods of play therapy, if the therapist asks something like this too soon, the child may get self-conscious and stop playing. Some children will not return to that theme again for awhile.)

Comment: Simple reflecting lets the child feel safe that the therapist will wait for him to be ready. A different approach may be appropriate in directed, short-term play therapy. Sometimes a child will ask the therapist not to repeat his words. At first the therapist might say, "Well, the way it works in here is that I need to be sure I am getting just what you said." If the child is really distracted by this, the therapist may make other adaptations. She needs to find a unique attunement with each child so that communication flows unselfconsciously. If the therapist's verbal response does not adequately match the child's, then the child will often stop to make a correction. This act of correcting causes some interruption of the child's right-brain state and disconnects him from the flow of the play.

BOY, AGE 4:   [Crashes trucks and makes noises.]

THERAPIST: [Gives full presence and makes similar noises.] (Simply repeating the noises may be a more mindful response than saying, "You are crashing trucks and making noises.")

GIRL, AGE 10 [using a medical cart and handing the therapist a girl doll]: I'm the doctor and you are this sick girl.

THERAPIST [taking the doll and speaking for it, as for a puppet]:   I'm a sick girl.

ALTERNATIVE MINDFUL RESPONSE: Therapist whispers, "Can the girl have a pretend name?" (In the exploratory stage, an important goal is to help the child to learn to keep the play in pretend. Naming the doll a pretend name, not the child's sister's or friend's name, for example, keeps it in pretend. This allows the therapist to become the doll, the projection the child is addressing.)

Comment: In MBPFT, the best response is one that is most present to the moment, and that takes the cues from the child's projections. These initial responses are similar to child-centered play except that the therapist has the intention of keeping the play in pretend. In addition, there are fewer verbal responses and more non-verbal responses while the therapist encourages the child to have his own themes.

BOY, AGE 4½ [taking two puppets]:   Once upon a time, there were two dogs, a mommy dog and a baby dog. I'll be the mommy dog and, here, you be the puppy dog. [Hands therapist the smaller dog puppet.]

THERAPIST [taking the dog puppet]:   Mommy dog [pointing to child's puppet], puppy dog [pointing to puppet in hand]. [Whispering] What is puppy's name?

BOY: Bruno. The puppy did something bad and he didn't want his mommy to know.

THERAPIST [using the puppet]:   Bruno did something bad and [moving mouth on puppet] I don't want my mommy to know. (The therapist tries not to take the lead by asking what the doggy did and instead uses the exact cue that is given).

BOY [to puppy, in a bossy voice]:   Go to your room!

THERAPIST [whispering]:   Does puppy go to his room? (The therapist does not want to be creative in her responses or anticipate the child's narrative, as he might in directed play, so she will not say, "Am I also angry?" or "What did bad doggy do?" This theme may unfold more in the current session, or the child may be ready in a future session to say what bad doggy did. Accepting that the play does not have to be logical helps the child know that he is leading it.)

BOY: Yes.

THERAPIST [whispering]:   Where is his room?

BOY [whispering]:   Under the stool. (Children often take the therapist's cue and whisper too.)

THERAPIST: Bruno did something bad and is going to his room. [Moves puppet under the stool.]

BOY: Yes, and he is sad because he isn't getting any dinner and he's hungry.

THERAPIST [speaking in a sad voice and moving the puppet's mouth under the stool]:   I'm sad because I'm not getting any dinner and I'm hungry.

GIRL, AGE 3:   What do I do with this slinky?

THERAPIST: In here, it can be anything you want it to be. (This phrase is often repeated, especially during the exploratory and limit setting stages. It helps to free the child's mind so that he can create whatever props are needed, which is especially important later when he enters deeper play. For example, the slinky can be a telephone, a bridge, or anything the child imagines.)

The Use of Language During the Limit Setting Stage of MBPFT

When a child acts in such a way that the therapist needs to set a limit or explain an expectation, the pretend realm is broken—the interaction takes place in reality. Therefore, whenever possible, the therapist's statements are short and simple, and then she can direct the play back to pretend. If a child continues to demonstrate oppositional behavior, not responding to these efforts, the therapist may decide to get the parent and do more parent–child dialogue in the playroom. In his book *Play Therapy: The Art of the Relationship* (2002), Garry Landreth provides an excellent treatment of limit setting. He states that this can be a very challenging area for therapists and gives lots of concrete ideas for dealing with it.

The following section gives examples of the use of language during the *limit setting* stage of MBPFT. The therapist should not hesitate to use her "I-mean-what-I-say" voice when suitable. Frequently, the child is not pushing limits, but merely learning what to expect ("How does it work here?"). Initial sessions teach him this. The following therapist's responses are illustrative examples; many other good responses are possible for these situations.

SCENARIO 1. THE CHILD HAS DEVELOPED A THEME
PLAYING WITH ZOO ANIMALS, INCLUDING MONKEYS

CHILD: My mom just came back from her trip and she brought me a monkey. (This is a reality statement.)

In the exploratory stage, the therapist will engage this statement, more with some children than with others. On the child's first day in the playroom, she may acknowledge it briefly: "Hmm, a monkey." In the limit setting stage, however, since the goal of MBPFT is to keep the playtime in pretend, the therapist tries to give minimal responses, using brief or nonverbal answers, when a child utters random thoughts. Often the child gets right back to the play, In the present example, the child says more:

CHILD: Yeah, it has a long curly tail.

THERAPIST: Sounds like you like the long curly tail. Maybe you can tell me more about it after our play time.

That response may be sufficient. However, by the fifth day in the playroom, if a child continues to bring in reality, the therapist may say, "Telling me about the monkey sounds important. I want to hear about it at the end." By the 10th session, she may add, "Remember, in here we are pretending, and when we finish playing you can tell me more about the monkey." Then she may direct the child to the last pretend sentence of his play: "So the monkeys and lions are trapped in cages at the zoo. . . ."

At the end of the session, after the bell rings, the therapist may say, "Oh, I want to hear more about your new monkey with the long, curly tail." Most children learn quickly to keep discussion of real things in their lives for the end of playtime.

SCENARIO 2. THE THERAPIST AND THE CHILD ARE PLAYING BALL AT AN EARLY SESSION

BOY, AGE 11 [tossing a beach ball]: I miss my dad now that he lives in Washington. I don't see him as much.

Giving a response may be more tempting because of the sensitive content; however, the therapist may not want to have an extended discussion without a parent present. With such a sensitive moment, the therapist may choose to engage reality more than she usually does during play time. However the therapist may not want to have an extended discussion without a parent present.

THERAPIST: Hmmm, you miss your dad since he moved. . . . That is hard for you. . . . Maybe at the end we can talk with your mom more about this. (In this case, the child nodded and said a few sentences as we continued to throw the ball.)

One question that comes up is, does the child have the ability to tell his mother these feelings of missing Dad? If so, then the therapy can be a bridge back to the mom, generally at the end of the session. If a child feels split loyalty and is therefore unable to say these feelings to his Mom, that becomes an important topic for parent dialogue and feedback meetings (see chapter 6 on family therapy and chapter 7 on mindful parenting).

SCENARIO 3. DURING PLAY, THE CHILD HITS THE THERAPIST, WHO IS PRETENDING TO BE A WITCH

The therapist needs to set limits on behaviors that could hurt her or the child. At the same time, she wants to allow the child some way to enact his feelings. She can affirm the fact of the aggressive emotion without letting the child do actual harm. For example, she may hold up a pillow in front of herself and say, "You can hit the pillow and pretend you are hitting the witch," or, "I'm not for hitting; here, you can pretend Bobo [a punching doll] is the witch."

The child's limit testing breaks his concentration on the pretend play. The therapist intervenes because the safety of people and objects is important. She may say, "The ambulance stays in the room. We could build a pretend window with these blocks to throw it out of." This response gives the message that the feelings behind the wish to throw the ambulance out the window are acceptable, but it sets a limit on behavior that is not safe or appropriate for the child to carry out—either in the office or at home. Spontaneous child-directed play does not mean that the child is allowed to do whatever he wants.

If a child is angry and insists on doing something that is not safe, then the therapist can get the parent and discuss the problem with the parent there, since this is now reality. It may indicate that more parenting or family therapy is needed before the child is ready to be in the playroom.

The therapist watches and tries to understand the clinical implications of the situation. Her thoughts might go, "Child needs to be destructive . . . hmmm. Knocking the puppets off the shelf may take only a couple of minutes to put back. Knocking off all the animal miniatures will take half an hour to clean up." These are things to consider in deciding what to do. The therapist may be more tolerant of a child who never acts out and misbehaves, whereas she may set limits sooner with a child who has problems with limit setting or with a child who will push boundaries too far. Children use the playroom to learn to modulate their impulses and to learn a range of appropriate restraint.

Thus, depending on her sense of the situation, there are several ways the therapist might respond. She may say, "Wow," and wait to see what happens next. An alternative response may be, "All the animals, whoosh!" and, again, waiting to see what happens. A response for a child who needs inner restraint might be, "The toys are not for knocking off the shelf. You can pick out some animals and knock them off *this* shelf" (implying that the feeling of wanting to knock things is OK but that this is too big a mess to clean up).

SCENARIO 6. THE CHILD STARTS TO MIX ALL OF THE PAINTS TOGETHER BY PUTTING THE SAME PAINTBRUSH INTO EACH COLOR WITHOUT CLEANING THE BRUSH

The therapist may just watch and let this messy play happen. Finding a way to make a mess with paints, wet sand, or water seems to be an important part of a child's play. Sometimes it indicates that he is going deeper into trauma play, and it is also common for a child to mix paint or Play-Doh as part of the integration stage.

I had large jars of paint in the playroom when the above example happened. I taught the child to clean the brush. Later I realized that if I put the paint in smaller containers and had a small brush for each color, the child could keep the colors separate; or, if he mixed the colors up, it would not spoil the entire supply. This child had experienced severe trauma, and it seemed clinically important to permit him to make a really big mess.

SCENARIO 7. WHILE PLAY FIGHTING WITH THE FOAM BATS, THE CHILD ALMOST HITS THE LIGHT BULB

THERAPIST: Hmmm, danger . . . I need to keep it safe in here . . . bats lower . . .

If the action is repeated, she may say, "I need to put the bats away until next time. Safety is important."

The therapist may give advance warning about this consequence. It is important that she address safety and take responsibility for it. If a dangerous action is repeated by the child, she can set a limit on that specific play until the next session.

SCENARIO 8. A FOUR-YEAR-OLD CHILD BEGINS TO STRIP TO HIS UNDERWEAR WHILE TRYING ON A COSTUME

THERAPIST: In here, you want to put the costume on over your clothes.

One little boy really did not like to wear his shirt in warm weather. I asked the parent about this, and she gave permission. Generally, however, children need to keep their clothes on. In addition, I always ask the parent to be available in case the child needs help in the bathroom, since that falls outside the appropriate boundaries of the child-therapist relationship.

SCENARIO 9. THE CHILD IS DEEP IN THERAPY AND CUTS UP
ARMY SOLDIERS WITH THE EDGE OF A SHARK

Because this play seems very important to the child's clinical issues and because toy soldiers are so easily replaceable, the therapist may just let him cut them up, maintaining an attentive silence.

The Use of Language During the Deeper Awareness Stage of MBPFT

Silence can become sacred in the deeper awareness stage of MBPFT. The child may stay in this stage longer than in the other stages, and it is rewarding and meaningful to accompany him on his healing journey. As the nonverbal presence between therapist and child goes deeper, the therapist continues to reflect the child's words, but with less frequency. She may just nod more, say simpler and fewer phrases, and communicate more with body language. She observes when the child's silence is actively healing and holds this space quietly with the child.

On the other hand, when the child has been reworking trauma, usually for many sessions, there is a point at which the therapist may feel called on to give very direct and specific verbal reflections. These are framed in the terms of the pretend themes that reflect the child's feelings of powerlessness. She lets the child know that she understands what is happening, *but only in metaphoric form*, because she wants the child to be able to stay in the meditative, right-brain healing state. It is through the child's metaphors that the trauma is revisited, reworked, and healed. When the child stays in metaphor, it does not allow the reality of the trauma to intrude in its overwhelming actuality. The case study in chapter 9 provides an extensive example of a therapist's use of language during the Deeper Awareness Stage.

The Use of Language During the Integration Stage of MBPFT

The use of language suitable for Stage V, integration, is similar to what has been discussed. The difference lies in the more integrated themes and the relative lightness of the play. The child may become more assertive in teaching the therapist games and in taking the lead in the play. The child is more at ease once he has faced his trauma through powerful play metaphors.

Case Example: The Use of Language During Directed Play Therapy

In MBPFT, directed play is generally recommended when the child does not naturally use spontaneous play, as may be the case with children with developmental delays, ADHD, selective mutism, or obsessive thinking. In addition, certain settings may be more conducive to using a combination of spontaneous and directed play, for example, when working with children in the hospital or school, or when treatment time is limited. In these situations, the therapist may make available specific toys that tend to address the themes of the child's issues. Here I might recommend using a partial Floor-time model (see Greenspan, 1992), where the therapist makes up her side of the play to follow the child's interest.

The following is an example of *directed play therapy* with a child I will call Malik, after about four months of play therapy. Malik is a very bright six-year-old boy whose emotional and social development were delayed even before the sudden death of his father, an African American Muslim, who was hit by a car when the family of four was crossing the street together. Due to a high level of anxiety for both children and Malik's oppositional behavior, which increased after his father's death, we began the therapy working as a team. Two therapists each saw one of the two children in sessions together with their mom before starting individual play therapy. The narrative follows what happens the first time Malik allows himself to externalize thoughts and feelings about medical aspects of his father's death.

The session opens with Malik initiating a game of ball. In earlier sessions, the therapist has had longer periods of playing ball as a way of joining with Malik, particularly working on eye contact and connecting.

Impatiently, Malik says, "Come on. Let's play ball. Come on, put your tea down." The therapist responds, "How do we do that?" inviting him as usual to set some guidelines for the play. By this time, Malik is accustomed to starting the play session with a limit of just one ball game of about 10 minutes. Malik keeps score, and today he wins.

The therapist then directs Malik to drawing materials, since she has been concerned about the immaturity of his past drawings and wants to have another sample. When he is finished, the therapist asks, "What's happening?" Malik replies, "I made all boys, no girls. It's the boys in the clubhouse. No girls allowed or they would get beat up. OK. I'm done." This very bright six-year-old has drawn four people as stick figures floating randomly, with stick arms protruding from their heads, as a three-year-old might draw them.

After the drawing is finished, the therapist purposefully busies herself with writing a note in order to encourage Malik to choose an area of the room in which to play. Many children will, on their own, select an area of play. This is ideal. However, the therapist has observed that Malik tends to initiate playing with more independence and less oppositional behavior if she is a little preoccupied and gives him space in the transition. Malik's bossy, oppositional, distracted style of playing made him a challenge to engage interpersonally.

Malik says, "Are you almost finished?" He walks around impatiently. "I'm going to play!" He chooses the medical cart.

The therapist puts down her notes and joins him by taking a boy doll, a black basketball player. She has the doll speak, using a pretend voice: "Are you the doctor? Is this my skull?" She has the doll point to the X-ray machine that Malik is holding, along with the X-ray of a skull that he is inserting. (This is the therapist's way of joining with a child who has been diagnosed with ADHD and who has difficulty with the back-and-forth of symbolic play.)

Malik is engaged with the toy and doesn't respond to the therapist. She waits, quietly bringing full presence, then speaks as the doll: "Doctor, would you take care of me? I was playing basketball, and I hurt myself."

Pretending to be the doctor, Malik says, "Look at that." He shows the therapist an X-ray of a hand. Speaking as the basketball player, she says, "I see it." Malik turns the X-ray machine away from the doll and toward himself.

In all of these examples, the therapist projects the dialogue onto the black basketball doll. This allows the play to stay in pretend.

THERAPIST [speaking as the doll]:   I can't see it.

MALIK [speaking as the doctor, with a concerned voice]:   Now look at that.

THERAPIST [picking up his tone of concern]:   I'm in trouble. [She waits to give him a chance to respond.]

[Malik does not respond. The therapist decides to ask some questions. She has learned from the past that reflecting what Malik says is not effective, as it is with spontaneous play. The questions have the purpose of helping him to learn how to develop themes in symbolic play.]

THERAPIST: Did I break something?

[Still no response. Malik is playing with the X-ray machine and inserts the X-ray of the hand into the machine.]

THERAPIST [after waiting]:   Did I break my hand?

MALIK [with concern]:   Look at that. [He has put the X-ray of the ribs into the machine.]

THERAPIST: Is that my chest? Did I break a rib in my chest?

MALIK: I'm the doctor. [He finds the siren on the medical cart and puts on the stethoscope. He fidgets with things, then removes the stethoscope. He turns off the siren noise, then turns it back on. The therapist is sitting directly across from him with quiet presence. Malik makes almost no eye contact. He is self-absorbed in his own play, as a three-year-old might be, but not in a way that feels connected to the therapist. Another child doing the same action could be meaningful play, connected play. In directed play, the therapist listens to her intuition and decides when to initiate more dialogue within the themes of the child and when to be quietly present. After a few minutes, the feeling of not being connected urges the therapist to initiate more interaction.]

THERAPIST: What's happening doctor? Am I breathing, doctor? Am I okay?

[Malik ignores the basketball player's words as he moves things around randomly on the cart. The therapist waits, staying fully present.]

THERAPIST [the basketball player displays some frustration]:   You're not answering me. Am I OK? [This is very different from spontaneous play and the therapist uses it when the child struggles to create themes using symbolic play. There was a quality of Malik being stuck in his own world.]

MALIK: I'm doing my job.

THERAPIST: You're doing your job, but am I OK? That thing is all red.

[Malik asks what the IV drip is. With a child who can do spontaneous play, the therapist would say, "It can be whatever you want it to be." In this case, the therapist lowers her voice and explains that medicine can come out of it and drip into someone who is hurt or sick. Malik turns the siren back on and says, very quietly, "Emergency," as he looks down and scratches his head.]

THERAPIST [whispering]: Emergency. [She waits quietly.]

MALIK [handing the therapist a real stethoscope]: I'll be the person who is sick.

THERAPIST [taking the stethoscope]: I'll be the doctor?

MALIK: Yeah.

THERAPIST *[in doctors voice]*: Do you want to hear your heart?

MALIK: Yeah.

[The therapist turns off the siren, explaining that they can't hear his heart if it is on. She finds Malik's real heartbeat and invites him to hear it himself. Malik breathes more deeply and makes eye contact with the "doctor." A real connection is experienced.]

THERAPIST [using a doctor voice, as she searches with the stethoscope for his heartbeat]: Let's see. Do you want to hear it?

[Malik nods assent. The therapist finds his heartbeat and says, in her doctor voice, "There you go." This is a very quiet, present moment. Malik holds his hands on the ear tips of the stethoscope for a moment and listens, then removes the stethoscope as the therapist speaks.]

THERAPIST [speaking as the doctor]: Can you hear your heart, son?

[Malik nods seriously. At first, his gaze is averted; then he looks the therapist in the eye. He is quietly present—a connection, a moment of shared silence.]

THERAPIST [speaking as the doctor]: Then you must be alive. [She waits mindfully.]

[Malik sticks out his chest and breathes heavily seven times. Then he sits down.]

MALIK [in a slightly impatient and demanding voice, while moving his arms]: Do the doctor stuff.

THERAPIST [speaking as the doctor, matching Malik's tone]: Well, what shall I do now? [Trying to encourage him to develop the play themes]

[Malik hands her the X-ray machine and taps on it. Since he is developmentally not able to give the therapist verbal directives, she decides to rely more on nonverbal communication and supplies words that indicate the theme he is implying.]

THERAPIST [putting an X-ray into the machine]: I think you have—let me look at your hand—let me see. [She looks back and forth from the X-ray machine to his hand, which he holds up in the air. She puts the machine down, takes Malik's hand in hers, and presses the fingers and palm of his hand.] Oh my, let's check it out. Oh, yes, broken. [It would also have been suitable to whisper, "Is it broken or okay?" There is lots of physical touching of hands between "doctor" and "patient" as they sit face to face. The therapist takes advantage of the opportunity to connect appropriately through touch. Malik seems very attentive now. The therapist continues to feel his presence.]

THERAPIST: It's only in one place. Should we fix it?

MALIK [in a low voice]: You do that. [The "doctor" attends to Malik's hand briefly.]

THERAPIST: Now let's look at your skull. Let's put your skull into the X-ray machine. [She touches his head as she puts the skull picture into the machine.] What a nice skull you have. Perfect.

[Malik pulls out the X-ray, and the therapist takes this as a cue to look at the third X-ray.]

THERAPIST: How are your ribs? I should check them. [She shows him the rib picture. Malik nods. The therapist still feels his presence. She looks at her "patient," whose eyes are averted.] How are your ribs feeling lately?

[Malik gives a nod of his head, indicating "OK."]

THERAPIST: Guess what, they're fine. You're perfect. [She leans down to catch his eye and make a moment of eye contact.] Just that little broken piece in your hand. The rest is fine.

[Malik hands the doctor the machine and nonverbally indicates that she should remove the X-ray. The therapist removes the X-ray and attends to his hand. Malik is beginning to feel more engaged.]

THERAPIST: Now you will have to wear a bandage for a month. [She puts on a play bandage and makes another moment of eye contact.]

[Malik responds with a very present "OK" and turns his body around on the floor away from the doctor. He immediately says, "It's almost a month. The month is up." He turns toward the therapist. He picks up, then puts down the X-ray machine.]

THERAPIST: OK, a month is up.

[Malik reaches his arm out to the doctor as he continues to engage.]

THERAPIST AS DOCTOR: I'll take it off. [She reaches for his arm and a tool to remove the bandage. Then she tries to make contact with his averted eyes.] Well, how have you been? How was your month?

MALIK [nodding his head]:   Fine. [His eyes are averted, but he is present.]

THERAPIST: Fine . . . all right . . . you are better now. You're perfect.

[Malik gives a satisfied sigh and is quiet. The warning beeper goes off to end the session.]

Comment: In his pedestrian accident, Malik's father had hurt all the parts of his body: his ribs, head, and hands were hurt, and, of course, the ambulance came. As Malik and the therapist engaged more and more in the play during the session, the therapist could feel that Malik's presence was becoming clearer and stronger.

Talking to Parents About the Child's Play

In MBPFT, as in many forms of play therapy, the therapist does not share interpretations with either the child or the parents. She does discuss, with the parents, the significance of the play, although she does not reveal the details of the actual play drama. She also humbly acknowledges that she can never completely know what a child is thinking.

Generally, both therapists meet with the children's mother, Fatah, about the scenarios of Malik's and his sister's play. Malik's scenarios had been typical of his preceding four sessions, since the last parent meeting. However, in this session he had begun to let the play help him externalize, mostly nonverbally, his understanding of, and feelings toward, the past trauma. I reported that Malik's play was beginning to be a little more self-initiated, and that he was able to stay with each play theme for a longer time than previously. However, he was still prone to distraction of details, and that was slowing down the flow of the play. I admitted feeling challenged in my efforts to establish a connection, which is not uncommon with children who initially present with oppositional behavior. I let Fatah know that, during his last session, I had sensed that Malik had let down his guard to engage me more than he had done in the first few months in the playroom. I told her my perception that he is gradually using themes that address his father's medical trauma and Malik's own consequent trauma. And I let her know that he had recently begun to open, in his play, to vulnerable emotions that were difficult to for him to express in words.

Fatah's main concern about Malik, his oppositional behavior, had already been a problem before his father's death. I spent much of this parent dialogue session coaching her to listen kindly to Malik, despite his bossy, demanding style, and also to set firm limits, something she had relied on his father to do. I offered her compassion for her bereavement and understanding of how difficult was her abrupt shift into single parenting. At this meeting, Fatah was able to cry for the first time during a session, as she allowed herself to acknowledge her feelings of disorientation, sadness, and anger.

Malik was exhibiting learning and behavioral problems at school and agitated anger at home, making regressed drawings, and inhibited in creating symbolic play. Such a child may have sensory integration issues as a consequence of developmental interruptions. Sensory integration therapy can often reach these problems at their root level and thereby reduce or eliminate the need for medication. His mother had completed a simple two-page checklist that indicated that such concerns applied to Malik. I recommended that he have a sensory integration evaluation, and she agreed to consider it.

6

Family Therapy in Mindfulness-Based Play-Family Therapy

THIS CHAPTER ADDRESSES the value of family therapy for both higher- and lower-functioning families who seek help for a wide range of concerns and problems. Special attention is given to the crucial issues of loss and bereavement, as well as to cultural and ethnic diversity within families. Two theoretical family therapy frameworks are highlighted that are particularly valuable in Mindfulness-Based Play-Family Therapy (MBPFT):

- Contextual Family Therapy, developed by Ivan Boszormenyi-Nagy, a trust-based approach that is at the heart of Mindfulness-Based Play-Family Therapy.
- Structural Family Therapy, developed by Salvador Minuchin, a power-based therapy that values the hierarchical order of the family.

A primary goal of family therapy is to offer families new options for defining and achieving healthy relationships. The therapist engages, at an intimate level, the dynamics among the participating family members: couples, adolescents, children, and, when appropriate, extended family. The entire family is not required for family therapy. In fact, family therapists often utilize a dyad format, such as one parent with one child or an adult client with a sibling or parent. Each person in the family is invited to seek and express his or her authentic self while also allowing and respecting different points of view. Family members who come to therapy have chosen to discuss the difficulties of life with a trusted "outside" person; consequently, they learn to respond to one another in new ways. When they are at home between sessions, a new kind of accountability may enter their relationships.

Family therapy offers participants the chance to enhance their experience of intersubjective intimacy. Stern notes, "For the fullest connection between people, attachment and intersubjectivity are needed, plus love." However, "People can be attached without sharing intersubjective intimacy and can be intersubjectively intimate without being attached, or both, or neither" (Stern, 2004, pp. 101–102).

Resilience in Higher-Functioning and Lower-Functioning Families

The distribution of both higher-functioning (HF) and lower-functioning (LF) families extends across the entire socioeconomic spectrum. The continuum of quality relates to the degree of interpersonal trust among family members and their capacity to show care for each other. Families who come to therapy are on different points of the continuum. In *Parenting From the Inside Out: How a Deeper Self-Understanding Can Help You Raise Children Who Thrive* (2003), Daniel Siegel and Mary Hartzell describe parents' actions as "low road" and "high road." The "low road" includes reactions that lead to emotional disconnection from the child. The intensity of the reactions suggests that they are connected more to the parents' past than to what is happening in the moment with their child. Our culture does not generally help parents see this phenomenon; instead, the child is often seen as the problem. The "high road" requires a willingness by the parents to look at their own attitudes and behaviors, especially those that may be nonproductive in the parent–child relationship. By understanding something of what is happening in the brain when the child or parent "flips his lid," parents can bring a more compassionate response both to themselves and to their children.

As we will discuss later, ancestors have an impact on what is happening in the present moment; both problems and resources from the intergenerational history affect the present level of functioning. Ideally, the therapeutic process helps individuals and their whole families progress toward healthier living. "Like existence itself, therapy can be understood as part of an ongoing life process that is a mixture of burdens and resources" (Boszormenyi-Nagy & Krasner, 1986, p. 201).

In HF families, it is likely that the symptoms of a problem will be noticed before they become too "out of control." HF parents will seek help sooner rather than later. The idea of therapy may be uncomfortable, but these parents will probably consider it the best option, preferable to living too long with a problem. The parents may be thinking preventatively or may intuit that their child's symptoms are more intense, or longer lasting, than is developmentally appropriate. They may have been referred by an observant teacher, who is sometimes able to notice a problem that the parents have not seen. High-functioning families sometimes come to therapy because a series of difficult events have occurred, causing undue stress on one or more members of the family. Sometimes, they are simply seeking help in negotiating the normal issues of parenting or family life. Even happy events can raise the tension level in a household when those events contain elements of high stress. All parents, whether high or low functioning, are subject to some misattunement with their children. What marks a difference between the two is that high-functioning parents know how to repair ruptures in a timely way by addressing the child with both warmth and accountability. Relational stress is disruptive to the healthy functioning of the brain, and this kind of relational repair is healing (Badenoch, 2008, pp. 100–101).

In his introduction to *Family Therapy in Clinical Practice* (1978/2004), Murray Bowen states that his theory "developed slowly when several key ideas began to coalesce into different ways of understanding the human phenomenon. . . . Family Systems Theory contains no ideas that have not been a part of human experience through the centuries" (p. xiii). Higher-functioning families are referred to as an "open" relationship system, indicating a family system that expects reciprocity among the members: they can express authentic thoughts and feelings. Conversely, a "closed" relationship system is one that lacks transparency: differences of opinion and topics that are uncomfortable to discuss are avoided (Bowen, 1978/2004).

Daniel Hughes's formulation in *Attachment-Focused Family Therapy* (2007) integrates reliable family therapy practice with an understanding of attachment theory and intersubjectivity. Hughes writes that, for healthy attachment to occur, family members need to have attachment, security, and intersubjective connection with each other and with the family as a whole. By intersubjectivity, Hughes means shared attention that contains affective and cognitive attunement. Building on Allan Schore's work, Hughes discusses how high-functioning parents coregulate their children's affective responses from infancy on. The cocreating and coregulating of the space between the parent and child manifests both verbally and nonverbally. In the family therapy session, the therapist takes a similar lead: She facilitates the comingling of the thoughts and affective states of all family members and of herself. "Healthy function, then, is an achievement in human life rather than an automatically given privilege to be taken for granted" (Boszormenyi-Nagy & Krasner, 1986, p. 205).

Higher-functioning families can be playful and do not use sarcasm in their humor. Stuart Brown has researched the topic of creative play and has written a delightful book, *Play: How It Shapes the Brain, Opens the Imagination, and Invigorates the Soul* (2009). He reminds us that we are "built to play and built through play." He notes that we do not need to be playing all the time, but that when we engage playfully, it helps us to enjoy and be more productive in the other parts of our life. A world without play would be "a grim place to live" (pp. 5–7).

Higher-functioning families can have pillow fights and playfully wrestle. In a serious book, *The Archeology of Mind: Neuroevolutionary Origins of Human Emotions* (2012), Jaak Panksepp and Lucy Biven have provided a mind-opening chapter titled "Playful Dreamlike Circuits of the Brain: The Ancestral Sources of Social Joy and Laughter." I particularly appreciate how much they value "rough and tumble play," which meets their partial definition of play as a "spontaneous activity done for its own sake." The authors believe that it may be part of the development of the architecture of the social brain and is sequentially learned before other kinds of play. In their research, rough-and-tumble play helps animals to learn when to cooperate and when to back off, including how to prepare for the unexpected in life (2012, pp. 354–355).

Along the evolutionary path of play therapists learning to work more closely with parents is Deborah Killough McGuire and Donald McGuire's book *Linking Parents to Play Therapy: A Practical Guide With Applications, Interventions, and Case Studies*. This book emphasizes the importance of being aware of developmental issues and offers concrete examples. It also discusses meetings with parents and includes concrete homework assignments for parents.

As mentioned above, families on the lower end of the functioning continuum occur across the socioeconomic range. Sometimes individual members function at high levels in their careers while their personal relationships are quite dissatisfying. LF families usually come to therapy in a crisis that feels complicated and out of control, perhaps motivated by the unbearable emotional pain of one or more family members or by a school or court referral. Because these families tend to resist change and do not usually ask for help when it is needed, they may arrive with multiple layers of long-term problems. Their style may be mistrustful and more blaming. They may not be self-reflective or aware of intergenerational connections. In their handling of children and teens, parents in lower-functioning families may be very strict on issues where their children could benefit from more freedom. Conversely, they may be too permissive on issues where it might be more appropriate to tighten up. The process of unwinding these parenting styles can be confusing and challenging for both the family and the therapist.

LF families tend to be more isolated from the world, and members may not have nurtured close relationships with extended family and friends. These conditions may indicate embedded family dynamics that will take a lot of time to rework. There may be long-term unfairnesses, relationship cutoffs, damaging family secrets, and even the pretense of secrets that children actually know about but honor as forbidden ground. There may be poor communication skills, including name calling, mind reading, not listening to one another, and narrow thinking. In addition, family members may exhibit a range of controlling or abusive behaviors. Children are deeply affected by such dynamics. Both verbal and nonverbal experiences become internalized in the early years of life and play a part in a child's developing values and self-esteem. "If the attachment is toward an unhealthy figure, he/she learns unhealthy or negative self-esteem" (Wickes, 2000, p. 123).

In his World Health Organization report from 1951, John Bowlby lists the following as deprivations that can lead to serious problems in relationships: deprivation from severe separation or outright rejection of a child; an unconsciously rejecting attitude underlying a loving one; a parent's excessive demand for love from the child; a parent's obtaining unconscious and vicarious satisfaction from a child's behavior, while at the same time condemning it (Bowlby et al., 1951/1966). The genogram of the very low functioning family may reveal a pattern of dysfunction that spirals downward generation after generation, becoming ever more complex and hopeless.

> Partial deprivation brings in its train acute anxiety, excessive need for love, powerful feelings of revenge, and, arising from these last, guilt and depression. These emotions and drives are too great for the immature means of control and organization available to the young

child. The consequent disturbance of psychic organization then leads to a variety of responses, often repetitive and cumulative, the end products of which are symptoms of neurosis and instability of character. (p. 12)

Bowlby adds that deprivation can completely cripple the capacity to make relationships. Meeting families who are presenting with intergenerational hopelessness may feel overwhelming to the therapist, but it takes just one person on this family tree to begin a process of conscious living. Although it may be enormous work, the downward spiral can gradually be halted and turned around, if family members are motivated; the present moment has the capacity to start the healing process.

When families, whether high or low functioning, come to therapy feeling hopeless, it is important for the therapist to offer hope, if she honestly can. This is tricky, because the therapist certainly cannot guarantee a resolution of problems. However, she can point even the most desperate families in a positive direction by clarifying their problems and demystifying the therapeutic process. It helps to acknowledge how challenging the therapy will be, and to frame the problematic situation within the expanded intergenerational context. The therapist makes clear who needs to be involved in order to achieve a positive outcome. She may say to them, "I've worked with families who have come in with very stuck issues, and who felt at least as hopeless as all of you in the beginning, but to their surprise, they felt much better at the end of the therapy. We need to develop trusting relationships together and to hang in there, even when the going gets really tough."

The Brain

Understanding how the brain functions can reduce guilt and help people be more compassionate as well as accountable to themselves and other family members. Past traumas, and emotions associated with them, are stored as preconscious material inside the parent's right brain in the form of memories that are implicit—beneath the level of conscious awareness. These feelings can surface when triggered by the child's behavior. The parent may be influenced by "low road processing" to act impulsively and then regret it afterward. That is, the parent is being controlled by emotions that may cause a freeze or shutdown. The inflexibility "impairs your ability to think clearly and maintain an emotional connection to your child" (Siegel & Hartzell, 2003, p. 154). The prefrontal cortex shuts down. "You may become flooded by feelings such as fear, sadness or rage. These intense emotions can lead you to knee-jerk reactions instead of thoughtful responses" (pp. 154–155). Mindful responses become nearly impossible. Instead, the parent behaves in ways that frighten and confuse the child, who is entitled to feel safe.

In the brain plasticity literature, Norman Doidge (2007) explains that, in people whose anxiety leads them to attack a problem, they move from "feeling the mistake" (p. 169) in the orbital frontal cortex to becoming anxious. This then motivates them to fix the mistake. Once the correction has been made, "an automatic gear shift in our brain allows us to move on to the next thought or activity" (p. 169). He notes, however, that such is often not the case with obsessive-compulsive behaviors. Brain scans show that, with obsessive-compulsive disorder (OCD), all three brain areas are hyperactive as the person continues to obsess and the anxiety builds in intensity. This has a range of causes, including learned behavior, genetics, and infections that cause swelling in the brain. Understanding these factors of OCD brain function can help parents respond to their own and their child's low-functioning habits with the compassion that is necessary in healing both past and present issues. As brain research advances, more options for healing are being revealed (p. 169).

Doidge compares healing to a process that happens in mindfulness meditation: "They *observe* its effects on them and so slightly separate themselves from it" (2007, p. 171). His research found that positive results came not from staying in the anxious reaction to a stimulus, which would be a cognitive behavioral approach, but rather from learning to change the channel to lay down new circuits. This highlights two laws of neuroplasticity: "Neurons that fire together, wire together." By doing something pleasurable in place of the compulsion, patients form a new circuit that is gradually reinforced instead of the compulsion. The second law is "Neurons that fire apart, wire apart." According to Doidge, acting on the compulsion reinforces the compulsion. Exposure therapy eases anxiety in the short run but in the long run exacerbates it. The most effective and long-lasting solution is in avoiding the compulsion while replacing it with something pleasurable.

Mindful awareness of this process can help the parent to step back from the situation at hand, take a deep breath, and eventually reflect on the self-created nature of the drama of his own life. He may begin to see that the intensity that is being experienced in the present is not proportionate to the present situation, but rather is being directly influenced by the unseen force of implicit memory. A growing awareness of these factors can help bring the parent toward an increased accountability for his own emotional states and behaviors. This repaired accountability may, in turn, lead his behaviors to have a positive—instead of a negative—impact on the child's future.

This mindful awareness parallels Contextual Family Therapy, where rage is seen as a "generation up" issue. This means that even though a parent can legitimately feel angry at a child, enacted rage is not relationally fair to the child. Such actions are considered to be the parent's destructive entitlement, rooted in his history of felt unfairness in relation to his own parents. The approach for healing is not only to address this in his own adult therapy, but eventually to create a relational context for healing with his parents, whether they are alive or deceased. This root-level healing can clear out the impact of painful implicit memories and greatly benefit the next generation. Given the understanding of how change can work across the generations, parents may become positive agents for healing in their children. Badenoch states it like this: "The particularly good news of neuroplasticity gives parents hope that their family dynamics can change, if they gain the personal awareness and tools to parent differently" (2008, p. 300). Boszormenyi-Nagy and Krasner (1986) recommend that parents rework unstable relationships, when possible, for the benefit of the next generation. Whether or not this occurs, they recommend considering that the parents' needs are different from the children's needs. "Yet, by now it surely must be clear that the satisfaction of parents is inseparable from their children's welfare" (Boszormenyi-Nagy & Krasner, 1986, p. 206).

Finally, regarding children in low- versus high-functioning families, Bowlby refers to the research of Ainsworth as well as Main and Weston, noting that

> children with a secure relationship to both parents were most confident and most competent; children who had a secure relationship to neither were least so; and those with a secure relationship to one parent but not to the other came in between. (Bowlby, 1988, p. 10)

We need the secure base that an attachment figure provides, not only in childhood but throughout our entire lives (p. 62).

Loss in the Family

Addressing loss offers the family in therapy an opportunity to improve their level of functioning. It is very important that the therapist carefully track the family's history of losses and their emotional impact. How to do this sensitively will vary with each family. This information is routinely recorded as part of the family history during the fourth segment of the evaluation (see chapter 3). The therapist can slow this process down when a family has suffered a recent loss. In "Loss and Family Scripts" (Walsh & McGoldrick, 2004), John Byng-Hall builds on the wisdom of Elizabeth Kübler-Ross, addressing the topic of loss in a deeply meaningful intergenerational way. Byng-Hall describes how a therapist might help a bereaved family not only prevent long-term emotional damage but also "rewrite the family script and thus strengthen the family in other ways[.] For instance, a family can be helped to get closer than ever before in their mutual grief" (p. 85).

CASE EXAMPLE OF THE INTERGENERATIONAL IMPACT OF DEATH

Ruth came to me for therapy just after the death of her mother and three years after her husband died of leukemia. The bereavement process for her and her two children was quite "stuck" and would be considered low functioning, despite their higher level of functioning in many other areas of life. Ruth had good intentions to help her children, who were six and nine years old, but they were both becoming more fearful and anxious. After the evaluation, I saw the whole family together a number of times. Then, because of the children's anxiety, I included Ruth in the separate weekly play therapy sessions with each child. In addition, Ruth came weekly for her own therapy. The children's play sessions were sometimes directed and sometimes spontaneous. At first, neither child would do spontaneous play on a regular basis, and both seemed very worried about their mother. After six months, the younger child became comfortable enough to have play sessions without his mother, and he became able to play spontaneously. When his mother was not present, he used the sandtray to express his deeper feelings of sadness and anger. The older child needed her mother in the room for a longer time. This was partly caused by her fear that her mother could die, as had her father.

After a year and a half of weekly therapy, all three felt a greater a sense of equilibrium. There was not only symptom relief but many major changes. The son began to behave better at school, particularly after several team meetings with the teachers and his mother. He also started to sleep through the night for the first time since his father had died. Over many months, the daughter made a life book, recording happy and sad times in her life. She slowly addressed her separation anxiety in Talk Time and through spontaneous sandtrays. She began to accept her mother's occasional weekends away, and she was able to enjoy visiting friends and, eventually, to stay overnight.

One day, Ruth came in feeling sad that her father's best friend had died. This brought up the fact that Ruth's father, a retired physician, had always shown an extreme aversion to death and would not be attending the funeral of his friend. Here was an intergenerational key to this family's anxious and impeded bereavement process. When Ruth told me that her father never wanted to see a dead person and had made only a minimal appearance at her husband's funeral, I began to better understand the nature and the source of their stuckness. As their therapy went on from this point, an unusual number of deaths took place, including the parents of children at school, relatives, and acquaintances. Ruth would typically not tell the children when she first learned of a death; each time, she first had to process the loss herself. I encouraged her to work through her own feelings and find a way to be honest with the children. Among other things, I would say, "It is better that they hear the truth from you, rather than find out you didn't tell them. Hearing it from someone else can feel like a betrayal to a child."

Awareness of these factors helped focus Ruth's individual sessions. Her work included more sandtray and somatic body work as well as coaching in relating to her father and siblings. If Ruth assents, her therapy may eventually include an authentic dialogue with her siblings and her father at my office. She was also able to rework the couple relationship with her deceased husband, a process that helped her clear a path for a new relationship. This is a clear case of rewriting a family script for a brighter relational future.

Another excellent resource for understanding the often hidden reverberations that death can have on a family system is Murray Bowen's "Family Reaction to Death" in *Family Therapy in Clinical Practice* (1978/2004). It is well worth reading and also worth sharing with clients who are able to benefit from clinical reading. Bowen's first sentence goes straight to the point: "Direct thinking about death, or indirect thinking about staying alive and avoiding death, occupies more of man's time than any other subject" (p. 321). He warns that it is important for therapists not to avoid this topic in the therapy room.

> The "Emotional Shock Wave" is a network of underground "aftershocks" of serious life events that can occur anywhere in the extended family system in the months or years following serious emotional events in the family. It occurs most often after the death or threatened death of a significant family member, but it can occur following losses of other types. (p. 325)

Although shock waves are also caused by the addition of family members (e.g., through birth or marriage), the deaths of significant members usually cause more intense waves. Bowen points out that marital affairs and divorce frequently happen within a year or two after the family system has had a significant death, and that they may be partly motivated by the conscious or unconscious fear of dying. The aftershocks may appear to be unrelated to the death that preceded them. Bowen (1978/2004) states that families are more often than not in strong denial of the connection.

> The emotional dependence is denied, the serious life events appear to be unrelated, the family attempts to camouflage any connectedness between the events, and there is a vigorous emotional denial reaction when anyone attempts to relate the events to each other. (p. 325)

When families come to therapy with a child for whom they have concern, it can be very helpful to view the family with an awareness of recent and significant deaths, especially when making the genogram during the initial evaluation. When clients can acknowledge the impact of the emotional aftershocks, they may better understand what is happening in their families. This can lead to life decisions that are less reactive and more individuated.

Diversity in Families

There is no single body of therapy called McGoldrick Therapy, but in my eyes, Monica McGoldrick's important contributions hover over all the fields of family therapy. For 50 years, she has offered ways of thinking and of intervening that penetrate deeply into the therapist's human psyche. These translate into more authentic ways for the therapist to be with an individual, or a family, regardless of the particular framework being used. Many examples of "McGoldrick Therapy" are scattered throughout this book and are used in MBPFT. McGoldrick has continually kept multi-ethnic and multicultural issues at the forefront of the field. Adding to McGoldrick's creativity, her forward-thinking ideas have primarily been executed in a team approach with coauthors who share her vision.

Contextual Family Therapy: Resources in Relational Ethics

Contextual Family Therapy (CFT) is an essential basis of Mindfulness-Based Play-Family Therapy. Two original texts that offer in-depth understanding of CFT are *Invisible Loyalties: Reciprocity in Intergenerational Family Therapy* by Ivan Boszormenyi-Nagy and Geraldine Spark (1973) and *Between Give and Take: A Clinical Guide to Contextual Therapy* by Ivan Boszormenyi-Nagy and Barbara Krasner (1985).

"An important operational principle of family therapy should be remembered here: to secure alliance with healthy resources rather than with pathology in the families" (Boszormenyi-Nagy & Spark, 1973, p. 142). These "healthy resources" are the tangible and intangible realities in our life circumstances, for example, physical health, positive childhood experiences, acknowledgment of others, financial prosperity, the ability to enjoy our life work, the capacity to give to the next generation what one did not receive as a child, the capacity to trust, and the ability to be honest, joyful, and hopeful. Resources are highlighted over the dysfunctions that families also bring to therapy meetings. The degree of emphasis that Boszormenyi-Nagy gave to exploring the resources even in dysfunctional relationships was a significant departure from other contemporary theoretical frameworks. According to him, therapy could lead people to find reservoirs of trustworthiness, often at exactly those times when long periods of mistrust persist and seem to belie the worth of any new effort on the part of a family member. Contextual therapists operate out of an empirically derived conviction that there is a universally valid reality in the order of human existence. (Boszormenyi-Nagy & Krasner, 1986, pp. 12–13)

More recently, Alicia Lieberman and Patricia Van Horn put it this way: "Helping the parent and child remember and cherish positive experiences and health-affirming moments is an integral part of the treatment because these pivotal aspects of life are often overlooked in the midst of suffering" (2008, p. 25).

The Five Dimensions of CFT

Following is a brief overview of the five dimensions of CFT. The books mentioned above primarily focus on the fourth dimension, the ethics of living. The five dimensions integrate rather than oppose the spectrum of valid therapeutic approaches and methods. Neither purely an individual therapy nor exclusively a family therapy, CFT encompasses both. Even when seeing only an individual, the therapist maintains an awareness of at least a three- or four-generation context. Dr. Boszormenyi-Nagy initially called his work Relational Family Therapy. In later years, he referred to it as Contextual Therapy to emphasize that it could be used when seeing individuals as well as family groups. MBPFT is rooted in this model, which integrates both the individual child and the family system.

The First Dimension: Objective Facts
This dimension includes the circumstances and realities of each person's life, for example, disabilities, genetic and medical conditions, temperament, and the life situation into which we are born. These facts include the "*unavoidable existential conflicts* among family members" (Boszormenyi-Nagy & Krasner, 1986, p. 48). The therapist can be a compassionate witness to both the resource side and painful side of the facts in people's lives. Acknowledgment of these facts can often play an important role in allowing people to move ahead to dialogue and healing and increase the level of healing possible.

The Second Dimension: Individual Psychology

This dimension includes psychological makeup, such as personality traits and each individual's unique way of viewing life events. One family member's way of holding the resources and pain of growing up can be quite different from another family member's way. It is important that the therapist understand each individual's point of view.

Dimension II highlights the need to be aware of the personal issues that each family member, of whatever age, holds within the larger system of family problems. In *Doing Contextual Therapy: An Integrated Model for Working with Individuals, Couples, and Families* (1986), Peter Goldenthal writes that CFT is about the ordinariness of how to live wholesomely, and to freely give and take. He emphasizes that, more than a psychological theory, CFT is an ethical way to live that encourages people to care about those with whom they are closest. Goldenthal encourages giving freely in open dialogue with our family.

> Thinking of families as systems can be very useful; it is important to remember however that these systems are made up of people who have thoughts, feelings and complex inner lives. Individuals are systems too, not just cogs in a systemic wheel. (pp. 6–7)

A similar awareness of the individual and systemic issues in families is at the root of MBPFT. Play-family therapy offers a constructive and safe way for children to have their individual needs attended to while also helping the parents and ultimately the entire family. The somatic basis of play therapy allows the child to heal her existential pain, which is born of trauma and experiences in her family and society.

The Third Dimension: Systems of Transactional Patterns (Systems Therapy)

This dimension includes all of the systemic formulations of therapy that go beyond individually based therapy. The foundation of systems thinking is that a change in any part of the structure impacts the whole, and a change in the whole affects the individual parts. Systemic formulations observe family patterns and subsystems to work with systemic processes such as double-binding, triangulating, scapegoating, labeling, distorting communication, withholding, power, and competing. Various intervention styles may include reframing, sculpting, restructuring, cognitive behavioral interventions, and creating metaphors for prescribing and blocking change (Boszormenyi-Nagy & Krasner, 1986, p. 55). Structural interventions, such as realigning the power of parents and children, are often made early in therapy and help achieve symptom relief. Structural Family Therapy, founded by Salvador Minuchin, is elaborated below. It is a valuable example of what Boszormenyi-Nagy refers to as Dimension III.

The Fourth Dimension: The Ethic of Acknowledging, Earned Trust, and Fairness

Dimension IV emphasizes the therapist's attitude, which is trust based, and affirms the resources in people and relationships. It is the center point of Boszormenyi-Nagy's work and also of MBPFT. This dimension emphasizes the importance of keeping the "give-and-take" of relationship in balance. Although its therapeutic options are built on the first three dimensions, it greatly expands the potential for deeper healing and transformation. Dimension IV acknowledges that the root-level issues addressed in therapy are more deeply healed when dialogue occurs in familial relationships rather than through the relationship with the therapist alone. Dialogue is encouraged and effective whether relatives are dead or alive—they may be available, seemingly available, or truly unavailable. CFT is oriented toward clients performing constructive action within their relationships, at some point, whether early or late in the therapy. Such actions in the present can rework past hurts and offer health to future generations.

Multidirected partiality and dialogue are two jewels of the fourth dimension. Multidirected partiality is the primary intervention that allows the therapist to care for *all* family members by hearing each one's side. As a model of fair behavior, it helps families learn to accommodate differences. Dialogue is a key to optimal healing when engaged from this perspective. *Doing Contextual Therapy* is a good resource for the therapist who is beginning to study CFT. Goldenthal presents the concepts in a clear and comprehensible way. He explains that CFT can be used for shorter-term therapy, although it is often a longer-term experience because of its invitation to go beyond symptom relief into healing deeper life issues. I also recommend *Truth, Trust and Relationships: Healing Interventions in Contextual Therapy* by Barbara Krasner and Austin Joyce (1995).

The Fifth Dimension: The Ontic Level of Relating

The fifth dimension was added by Dr. Boszormenyi-Nagy very late in his career, in 1990; it concerns a relational ethics—namely, the idea that self can exist only in relation to other. Although always present in the work, it was formally introduced by Boszormenyi-Nagy in one of his last conferences and then elaborated by Catherine Ducommun-Nagy in *Ces loyautés qui nous libèrent* (2006). Contextual Therapy is rooted in Martin Buber's concepts of dialogic relating. Buber, not a psychologist but a philosopher and anthropologist, is known for "first formulating the principles of therapy on the level of caring and just interhuman relationships" (p. 28). "Genuinely trustworthy relationship requires relating partners to consider the validity of each other's interests, rights and needs as well as their own" (Boszormenyi-Nagy & Krasner, 1986, p. 28).

Buber's I-Thou dialogue is fundamental to Contextual Therapy. Terry Hargrave and Franz Pfitzer state it cearly:

> The basic idea behind Buber's work is that without another person reflecting back to me interpretations about ideas, actions, and physical being there is not an effective way for me to understand what I think, what I do, and how I look. (2003, p. 6)

The contextual family therapist relates to the client with just such honest reflecting. As Daniel Hughes describes it,

> Buber is speaking of something more than empathy and more than imagination. He is describing "a bold swinging" into the intersubjective experience of other, so that it is now an aspect of one's own subjective experience as well, enabling one to understand the other "from the inside out." (2007, p. 10)

This also resonates with Allan Schore's writing about the right-brain-to-right-brain connection. As Schore (2009) explains, the brain develops based on the energy connection between the mother's and infant's right brains. There is a similar connection in the therapy relationship, where there is an empathic secure holding of the client.

How Does the Contextual Therapist Intervene to Promote Healing?

People often say, "Why bother? Do all this work? Stir up the past?" One reason is that the ghosts from the past *do* come out and haunt us. Our society is not set up to see how the present is connected to the unworked problems of the past. Similarly, we may not be taught to appreciate the positive benefit that accrues to future generations when we put out the effort to repair old grievances in the present. Many therapies do not emphasize the challenges of honest dialogue, but CFT invites all family members to grapple with topics that may challenge everyone, while offering the possibility of deeper intimacy. Engagement is difficult when strong differences arise; when hurts, disappointments, jealousy, anger, revenge, fears, and apathy keep loving people from showing their care. In therapy, all family members can earn merit through listening to and acknowledging others and speaking truths that may be hard to say. This can be the basis for nurturing the trust resources in the family, which are requisite for healthy relationships but may be dormant.

Contextual theory is supported by neurological studies, which find, as Bonnie Badenoch writes, that "the way we embody warmth and awareness helps children integrate their brain circuitry—literally. . . . If we can get parents fully on board, even more change is possible" (2008, p. 302). In MBPFT, the child responds to the therapist's unconditional presence, which is, ideally, a bridge to the growth of the parent's compassionate unconditional presence with his child. A major goal of CFT is for the parent–child relationship to become a source of warmth and love. "Acknowledging the truth of the genuinely positive core of a child may extinguish his need for symptomatic behavior. Addressing deeper truths fosters hope, trust and resource-oriented relational patterns. Conversely, manipulating a child's feelings of trust is in itself untrustworthy" (p. 60).

Weaving CFT With Mindfulness-Based Play-Family Therapy

This section is intended not to simplify CFT, but to introduce it, while highlighting those aspects that tend to be most used when working with families in MBPFT. Many families arrive with worries about one of their children more than the others. Rather than the traditional term "identified patient" (IP), we refer to this child as the "MC," that is, the child for whom the family has the most concern. Ironically, this child often is, indeed, the "master of ceremonies" whose behavior has been unconsciously working to bring attention to overt or hidden family problems.

While MBPFT avoids scapegoating one child, the therapist cares about the MC child and is willing to see her in individual play therapy. At the same time, the therapist is equally interested in broadening the view from just one member's problems to the whole family situation. It is helpful to highlight how family members have handled the difficult situations that have come their way. It is important to ask about the strengths and the problems of the other children and adolescents in the family. This communicates that the therapist wants to understand the whole family context. He attempts this with an attitude of humility and respect.

A primary technique for the contextual family therapist is to ask questions nonjudgmentally. This provides a secure base of trust. He acknowledges resources and strengths and brings attention to issues of fairness. The environment created by this approach allows participants to feel how the giving, taking, and receiving can be played out in relationships. Acknowledgment is a crucial experience, somewhat akin to compassion. The MBPFT therapist also works this way. In sessions with parents and children, he invites each parent to make eye contact with each child individually and to say what they like about each child. What are her strengths? It is also important that the therapist acknowledge the adults, and that the adults acknowledge one another, even, when possible, amid painful and confusing situations. Badenoch reminds us that when therapists are as nonjudgmental as possible to parents, they also can heal the neural circuits that support self-regulation. This then enables the parents to develop new and durable ways of parenting (2008, p. 307).

Root Causes

Contextual Family Therapy aims to address not only the symptoms and behaviors that are bringing pain, but also their root causes. These roots comprise the residue of past experiences stored in the implicit memories of the current family members, and also those passed on from previous generations. They can remain invisible if one does not ask the questions that bring them up. To avoid recognizing these roots, one must maintain some mental anesthesia against them, which is costly because it also inhibits intersubjective intimacy. Consequently, the possibility for I-Thou relating is severely handicapped. Daniel Stern's definition of "implicit knowledge" conveys a sense that it is accessible: "The term 'unconscious' should be reserved for repressed material where there is a defensive barrier to entering consciousness. More precisely, implicit knowing is nonconsciousness. It is not repressed. . . . Accordingly, the implicit is simply nonconscious whereas repressed material is unconscious" (2004, p. 116). It is as if the light has simply not shone on the material until now. When family members engage the CFT process, they are embarking on a journey of willingness to shine a light directly onto the truth of the past that they already know implicitly.

The goal of this inquiry into the past is to not indulge in regret and blame. Rather, it is to let grievances come to the light of compassion, acknowledgment, and resolution. Ideally, each family member can gain a new, less victimized, and more hopeful view of himself as well as of other family members, living or deceased. Parent and child can become closer; couples can become more appreciative of one another. Boszormenyi-Nagy admits that the contextual therapist must be brave, for he must be willing to raise sensitive family issues and be able to discuss even those things that elicit the most resistance. The therapist needs courage to be willing to address challenging topics such as physical, emotional, and sexual abuse; despair; suicide; family cutoffs; and criminal actions. The ability to eventually give voice to "forbidden" topics is a quality of true intersubjective relating.

Mutuality, Dialogue, and Intersubjective Relating

Daniel Stern describes intersubjective consciousness as being similar to Buber's I-Thou, which is at the root of Contextual Therapy. He describes intersubjective consciousness as

> a form of reflectivity arising when we become conscious of our contents of mind by virtue of their being simultaneously reflected back to us from the mind of another. . . . What is shared in a moment of meeting is an emotional lived story. It is physically, emotionally, and implicitly shared not just explicated. (2004, pp. xvi–xvii)

In MBPFT Talk Time, the therapist creates the ground, week after week, for intersubjective dialogue with one parent and one child. This serves to encourage emotional closeness as well as healthy attachment. MBPFT shares Contextual Therapy's concern not only for the people who are in the room for the ongoing therapy, but also for those family members who are not able to be part of the weekly meetings. The therapist raises awareness of the conflicting interests of various family members, including anyone who could be impacted by the outcome of the therapy.

A fundamental intervention of MBPFT is in the dialogue among family members concerning the misunderstandings, pains, and seemingly insurmountable differences that deserve healing. Healing the past in the present offers grace not only to the present participants but also to future generations. Sometimes, the awareness of this benefit to the next generation is the primary motivator for moving toward healthier family dynamics. For example, when a parent is cut off from his parent, the child may fear that there will, in turn, be an inevitable rift between herself and her own parent. Because a child may not have words to express her fears, it is easy for the parent to dismiss this invisible effect of his estrangement from his parent. In fact, the child's withdrawal or destructive behavior may be the unconscious expression of her fears. As the play therapy proceeds, these hidden themes may be contained within patterns of her play metaphors. In *Family Therapy as an Alternative to Medication*, the contributors, who have years of combined experience, offer theory and case studies to encourage increased use of family therapy and decreased use of unneeded medications. The editors, Phoebe Prosky and David Keith, state, "Our book acknowledges the usefulness of medication, but expresses skepticisim about the way the medication model has been embraced by practioners and patients" (2003, p. xii).

Past pains that interfere with present relationships are worth revisiting, since a process of dialogue may allow genuine love to flow from parent to child. For example, a client once told me that she realized explicitly for the first time that the rage she was feeling all weekend at her son was the rage she still felt toward her father. "The only other person who can make me feel like this is my father." The honest examination that followed allowed her to differentiate her relationship with her son from her relationship with her dad. Action such as this not only helps the individual, but can also bring great healing to the MC child and to the entire family.

Like many symptoms, parental resentment can have a healthy source. It may expose a power imbalance that can be corrected by the parent's exercise of more effective limit setting for the child. Or it may indicate that something else is out of balance in the parent–child relationship. A mindful parenting response is to realize that, if resentment seeps in, the parents need to change something in themselves, not just blame the child. Sometimes the resentment may be rooted in a parent's relationship with his own parents or siblings, either in the present or the past. Locating the roots of the resentment can be the first step in a sequence of healing actions. Drawing inspiration from the Contextual Therapy framework, MBPFT offers a rich array of options for parental discussion, insight, and change. At Talk Time and at monthly mindful parenting meetings, parents are encouraged to observe when their "buttons" are pushed by their children and to seek the causes. This knowledge points the way toward deep and lasting change.

Structural Family Therapy: A Systems Approach

Salvador Minuchin's landmark book, *Families and Family Therapy* (1974), describes Structural Family Therapy (SFT). This theory's focus on the family as a system has become standard practice for family therapists. An understanding of hierarchical relationships, emphasized in SFT, is essential for Mindfulness-Based Play-Family Therapy. Following is a brief highlight of some of Minuchin's most important concepts and their application to play-family therapy.

In systems thinking, one must consider that an event that affects one family member impacts the whole family. Minuchin challenges the labeling of the "identified patient" when meeting with several family members; he does not assume that the person presented by the family as "the problem" is the only one who needs help. He envisions the therapist as seeing the family through a magnifying glass, able to see it as a whole and also to focus on its individual members (1974, p. 7). The structural therapist focuses more on present issues than on the past. He becomes part of the family system in order to help induce change. Minuchin's framework helps therapists to place families on a continuum between "disengagement" at one extreme and "enmeshed" boundaries at the other. A goal is to help families achieve a balance of healthy boundaries: not too enmeshed and not too disengaged, having connection without intrusion.

The therapist's attention to hierarchical family structure is a major contribution of Minuchin's work. Structural Family Therapy describes subsets of the family system. The parental subset is in charge of the family; aiding parents to work as a team is pivotal to addressing the goal of healthy relating. Various subsets may be defined, for example, combinations of spouses, parents, children, grandparents, or older siblings who play an executive role, depending on circumstances. There is an emphasis on the boundaries of the subsystems, that is, the rules of who participates and how. According to Minuchin's theory, boundaries function "to protect the differentiation of the system" (1974, p. 53). For example, the spousal subset needs boundaries that do not allow excessive intrusion from the children or the in-laws.

Minuchin instructs therapists to notice how family members enter the session and where they sit, which may be metaphoric of "alliances and coalitions, centrality and isolation" (1974, p. 143). The therapist can also serve as a director who choreographs the family seating in order to restructure a particular subset or induce a healthy hierarchical structure. The therapist's role is to be the leader and to "resist being sucked into the family system" (p. 139).

It should be noted that Structural Family Therapy as it was originally practiced did not include play therapy. The following sections provide concrete examples of circumstances in which Structural Family Therapy has proven to be an invaluable component of MBPFT meetings. This approach can be applicable during Talk Time, in coaching parents during mindful parenting meetings, and in the whole-family therapy sessions that are scheduled for each family as needed. Later in his career, Minuchin began to appreciate the power of addressing the family history as part of therapy.

Realigning Power

When first meeting a family for therapy in MBPFT, the therapist assesses the power differential. After examining the history of the problem, the developmental history of the child for whom the family has the most concern, and a three-generational family history, he can often see where misalignment has occurred. This misalignment is especially notable when a family presents with a child who holds inappropriate power. A child who has either too much or too little power in the family structure is suffering some disruption to her healthy development.

Minuchin is clear about the role that parents need to take. They may have fears or confused thoughts that perpetuate the hierarchical misalignment. It is the therapist's job to understand their misconceptions and challenge the family dynamics that allow the child to have inappropriate power. As Minuchin explains,

> Parents cannot protect and guide without at the same time being controlling and restricting . . . parenting always requires the use of authority. Parents cannot carry out their executive functions unless they have the power to do so. Effective functioning requires that parents and children accept the fact that the differentiated use of authority is a necessary ingredient for the parental subsystem. (1974, p. 58)

It is essential to balance autonomy and interdependence (Minuchin, 1974, p. 139). In a healthy hierarchical family system, parents share authority so that children gain autonomy gradually. This is particularly important for parents who have been trying to run the family as a democracy. Virginia Satir, a well-known family therapist, has written that, in healthy families, parents see themselves as "leaders, not bosses" (1972, p. 16). In MBPFT, it is recommended that, in order to avoid overly harsh parenting, the parents first compassionately hear and reflect on the child's authentic feelings. After the parent has established this attunement with the child, she then sets the limit. There are exceptions, of course, such as with issues of danger and safety.

Assigning Tasks

In MBPFT, Talk Time with the child and parent before the play session provides an opportunity to coach them in new ways of relating. Exercise tasks may be suggested by the therapist during this family session.

Example 1: Enacting tasks in the session. For a parent who is frustrated by a child's constant interruption of conversation, the therapist may suggest that the parent and therapist role play a conversation and discuss what the child can do if she wants to interrupt. One suggestion is to have the child place her hand on the parent's elbow. (Many families find that having a tactile way to connect allows the child to be more patient and to feel successful.) The parent is instructed to continue to converse for an amount of time that is reasonable, given the child's age and capacity to wait. She can then turn to the child, acknowledge her waiting, and respond to her question.

The family can practice at home. It helps to suggest tasks with a light touch, unless they relate to realigning the hierarchy. Whether or not the family adopts the suggestion, it is valuable to discuss, at the next session, what the family did with it during the week. If the parent forgot to practice the task or needs more instruction, then the therapist can patiently help the parent and child try it again.

Example 2: Assigning chores to do at home. The therapist may ask about a child's participation in the family. Can Amir begin to help with the dishes or the trash? How did it go with the chores this week? How does it feel when Amir resists doing work that encourages responsibility? Amir, what would you rather be doing than chores? Does it feel good to make a contribution to the family work, or do you resent it?

Enacting Transactional Patterns

It is effective to use what actually happens during Talk Time or family sessions to engage a family in addressing problems. For example, when there is a need for limit setting, the child will invariably provide opportunities for practice when the therapist is present. The therapist may first watch to see how the parent handles the problem. He may then assist by pointing out patterns of communication, by coaching the parent to reclaim authority, or by advocating for the child if a parent's response is too severe. The parent should not threaten to punish the child later. Whenever possible, it is best to resolve the situation within the session. Negative behaviors can be expected, as the child understands that therapy is a place to get some help.

When conflicts arise between parent and child, the most constructive approach may be to work with the parent–child dyad. The conflicts thus stay within the parent–child relationship, and, over time, the parent can become very competent in addressing them. The child, too, becomes more comfortable addressing conflicts openly with the parent. The result is often a more trusting connection.

Conflict during therapy sessions may take the form of objectionable behaviors, such as a child hitting her parent or using abusive language. This acting out indicates that the hierarchy is misaligned. It may be coming from a child longing for a deeper connection than the family system has been able to provide. Because trust in the parent–child relationship is damaged if a parent allows these behaviors, it is essential to attend to changing them early on in the therapy, prior to resolving the underlying problems. The parent's task is to address the child directly with kind yet firm limits, modeling how he would like the child to be. This can be balanced with "time-ins," one-on-one time between parent and child to build the close attachment that augments the process of realigning appropriate power. When a child's behavior is oppositional, a combination of time-outs and time-ins helps to establish that the parent is the leader. The parent needs to stay in control of her own triggers, use her "I mean what I say voice," and offer calm amid the storm.

Boundaries and Relating: Using Good Communication Skills

It is important for family members in therapy to listen well to one another and to use good communication skills. Structural Family Therapy encourages family members to address one another directly during the session. At clinically appropriate times, the therapist can ask one person to turn to another family member and say directly what he is thinking.

A helpful structural guideline is that the person who is asked a question should be the one to respond. Often in enmeshed families, a more verbal spouse or sibling repeatedly responds to questions, even when the questions are not directed to him. Bringing awareness to this communication dynamic will help the family, not only in the family sessions but also at home and beyond.

To promote individuation, the therapist needs to ask questions that differentiate the children from the adults, and the siblings from one another. Are defined family boundaries too rigid or too diffuse? Do children of different ages have different bedtimes? Do children have assigned chores? Do they receive an allowance? What happens in their daily life with regard to eating, sleeping, and using the bathroom? Is there enough privacy? Who picks out what the children wear? Who decides where the family goes for vacation? What about summer camp? What is the teen's curfew? How does the family prepare for a member's entering or leaving the nuclear home? These questions can stimulate a discussion about the similarities and differences among the experiences of individual family members and their perceptions of fairness and unfairness. A healthy family system can accommodate differences in a way that offers a degree of autonomy appropriate for the age and character of each member. In family therapy meetings, the therapist can be sensitive to how a child or teen's issues impact not only that child but also the siblings and parents.

Twelve Core Concepts of Contextual Family Therapy and Their Application to MBPFT

Following is a treatment of 12 concepts that are essential to both Contextual Family Therapy and Mindfulness-Based Play-Family Therapy. These are basic tools for treating children in families, with the goals of encouraging mindful parenting and seeking the root level issues that underlie symptoms. The discussion will use clinical examples to show the application of CFT concepts to MBPFT practice. This treatment is necessarily brief, and I recommend further reading and training for therapists working with all ages. It is important to keep in mind that other modalities are integrated into this eclectic approach.

1. Multidirected Partiality

Multidirected partiality, also called multilaterality, is the primary intervention a contextual therapist uses to show care for every person in the family—whether present at the session or not. It is "the most important guiding principle for the contextual approach to therapy with individuals, couples or families" (Goldenthal, 1996, p. 4).

The multipartial therapist serves not as a judge but as a person with enough empathy to connect to each family member. He also maintains sufficient separateness such that he does not become unwittingly embroiled in family dynamics. He recognizes everyone's strengths and allows each person's side to be raised. A person's "side" is how she thinks and feels about life, about the topic at hand, or about what is important to her to communicate at the time. Family members are encouraged to have their own ideas and to express them, rather than to say, "I think the same thing." If this is said, the therapist may reply, "Tell me in your own words. How would you answer the same question?" He may repeat the question. The therapist places more emphasis on the responses of the family members than on his own. At the same time, the therapist brings authentic, present-moment responses to the dialogue. The therapist is real, rather than playing a role.

The therapist does lend therapeutic leverage as needed by emphasizing, highlighting, and rephrasing the dialogic moments of the therapy. His speech demonstrates transparency. The intent of the contextual therapist is *not* to be neutral, but rather to encourage healthy, honest responses by family members to one another.

> We have a global or strategic orientation to move a person, a couple, or a family away from a situation of despair, suffering, having symptoms, or dysfunctional behavior. We want to help them change toward suffering less and getting along better in life and in their relationships by using the powerful resources of love and trust. (Hargrave & Pfitzer, 2003, p. 50)

Looking through the multilateral lens, the therapist may perceive that a particular party has an acute need for focused attention. Throughout their book, Lieberman and Van Horn are consistently sensitive to both parent and child in their approach with young children.

> When the parents are so depressed, angry or self-absorbed that they cannot respond to their child's needs, the therapist may need to focus first on decreasing the intensity of the parents' emotional states and on helping them to notice the impact that they are having on the child. (2008, p. 2)

They recommend that the parents have individual therapy as well as guidance based on child development to sort out which issues are the parents' and which are the child's.

Multidirected partiality offers a way for the therapist to be fair and empathic to all family members over time. In working with couples, Badenoch recommends having a "flexible, curious, wise, warm openness with the ability to cultivate *equal empathy for both partners.* This capacity is at the heart of successful work with couples, and it rests on our ability to compassionately hold each partner's history" (Badenoch, 2008, p. 274; italics in the original).

2. Questions and Dialogue: Secrecy vs. Privacy

There are different ways to accomplish multidirected partiality. In one method, the therapist addresses each family member with questions about the matter at hand. Everyone responds directly to the therapist while the other family members listen. Especially when family members have strong differences, this approach often allows them to listen to one another without interrupting and without being distracted by planning a response. Many questions are based in the ethics of contextual thinking. Thus, the therapist considers all family members when formulating and asking his questions. His inquiry invites them to reflect on life and its fairness or lack of fairness. He asks about the giving, taking, and receiving in family life. Of concern is how family members treat one another "for better or for worse." The therapist's questions may compare current family issues to similar ones from the past. Family members may also find themselves starting to ask questions that connect the present with the past. Family crises are often connected to losses that are part of the family history, whether recent or more distant. "Crisis is a terrible thing to waste" is a good Contextual Therapy attitude.

Dialogue is the honest back-and-forth created in the space between and among the individuals. Its most intimate form occurs between two people: "I" and "Thou." In a family session, all members are part of the dialogue. "Contextual Therapy is not simply another theory on how to help individuals. It posits that relationships have their own identities and deserve due consideration, just as much as do the individuals who participate in the relationships" (Hargrave & Pfizer, 2003, p. 73). The dialogue respects and nurtures the family as a relational body that is more than the sum of its parts.

By its nature, dialogue is meant to be truthful. Although consideration is given to people's feelings, telling the truth usually outweighs worrying that someone might feel hurt. Rather, emphasis is placed on how the truth is delivered, with care and consideration and without accusation and meanness—although that too may occur when family members are suffering. Harsh words are understood to be reflective of the depth of inner pain. Those in pain must have their feelings acknowledged, but they are also encouraged to find ways to communicate that are less judgmental so as to better deserve the attention of the listeners.

While family members are not expected to share everything, trust and intimacy can be sabotaged by omitting the truth from communication. It is important to know the difference between privacy, which concerns matters that can be kept confidential without compromising relationships, and secrecy, which is a destructive withholding. Secrecy in parent–child relationships can cause unseen havoc in children. Adult secrets should be discussed with the therapist. Consideration of the child's age and stage of development is a primary guideline for sorting out how to approach secrets that may be causing unconscious harm. Children do well in being told about difficult family matters when the information is delivered with age-appropriate content and in small doses. They should not be asked to keep secrets between their parents. They should not be expected to pretend they do not know a secret when they actually do. Mindful parenting meetings can be used to sort out serious concerns in this area. The parents and the therapist can develop a plan for gradual disclosure of difficult content that is in the child's best interest to know.

Even if the party addressed cannot respond in an intersubjective way, healing can come to the initiator of dialogue as a consequence of his honest efforts. His constructive action can reconcile his own inner conflicts with regard to the other. The parent, sibling, or teenage child addressed may be too emotionally inaccessible to engage in an authentic give-and-take, or the therapy client may have chosen to break connection with family members as the only response he could manage in the past. Such a strategy cannot resolve the inner conflict that is being ignored. The bias in Contextual Therapy is to bridge cutoffs by addressing relationships as constructively as possible, even though primary relationships may be extremely uncomfortable. It can take a long time to know how to safely mend them. Sometimes truly satisfying relationships cannot be achieved. In this case, the most constructive option may lie in grieving the loss of compatibility while finding at least a thread of connection in the basic fact of the ancestral bond.

3. Trust, Love, and Care

When therapy is sought, there has often been some breakdown of trust in family relationships. It is important that there be an acknowledgment of this situation, and a process of rebuilding. The therapist may begin by acknowledging the resources of trust that are still evident, but perhaps unnoticed, within the current family system. There is a foundation of trust in the parents' providing shelter and the needs of survival, rearing children from infancy without the expectation that they will ever be repaid, and carrying out actions in daily life that are caring and empathic. Children need to be able to trust their parents to be fair and honest role models for them in the world.

Children need and deserve acknowledgment, fair consideration, and discipline that is neither too loose nor too tight. Ideally, they receive *unconditional love* from their parents. This is not to be confused with loving all of their behaviors; many behaviors of children are in fact quite unlovable. Parents do well to find a way to make children feel deep inside that they are loved, no matter what they do. After parent and child have been angry with one another, making up includes the parent's message that "No matter how angry I get, I love you." With this comes its complement: The child learns she can be very angry at her parent and still love him. When families arrive with a child presenting with a problem, the unquestioned status of unconditional love may be insecure.

Care is learning about the giving and receiving inherent in significant relationships. Care begins with honest speech and continues into actions of giving. In the therapy session, it can manifest as words and actions among family members and the therapist that show their concern for others. Care is developed when parents take charge of the adult problems of life. It is also built when parents invite children to participate by generous actions that help, in age-appropriate ways, with the needs of the family or of the wider social community. Parents can encourage and expect altruistic behavior. All family members benefit from being comfortable enough to give and take what is fair and to receive from each other.

4. Fairness in Relationships: Giving, Taking, and Receiving

Issues of long- and short-term fairness are fundamental concerns to the contextual family therapist. Fairness in the family is best estimated through an examination of a three-generational history of giving, taking, and receiving. Family relationships are kept fair through a balance between the actions of giving and taking. Boszormenyi-Nagy encouraged families to have a commitment to fairness. "Perhaps nothing is as significant in determining the relationship between parent and child as the degree of fairness of expected filial gratitude" (1973, p. 54). He taught the therapist to remain aware of the clients' perceptions of fairness and unfairness, and to invite the family to process these issues as they come up. Long-term fairness should be a regular part of healthy living. While short-term unfairness may need to be endured as part of life's conditions, it is important that the therapist and other family members acknowledge when life is unfair. When unfairnesses occur, repair work is essential both in couple relationships and in good-enough parenting.

During a therapy session, issues of fairness are heard multipartially. During family sessions, the therapist elicits each person's side, including his or her thoughts, feelings, and perceptions of past or present hurts or injustices within the the family system. He may help the younger or more vulnerable members have a voice. In addition to negotiating fairness, the therapist models fairness by his attention to each person and to the family as a whole. The therapist's own engagement in the present moment gives authenticity to his interpersonal connections.

By hearing and amplifying *each* person's true voice, the therapist helps family members balance perceived unfairness, even in the face of fundamental differences between parties. The intention behind this compassionate approach is to promote trust in family relationships. However, while the therapist avoids "ganging up" on any particular family member, he may occasionally give more weight to one person's side in order to facilitate her being heard. On another occasion, he may emphasize the value of yet a different family member's point of view. The therapist may share an opinion on an issue, based on relevant psychological literature or on an example from his own life experience.

Many Talk Time and family therapy sessions are spent discussing fairness in families. Parents, as leaders in the family, may make decisions that feel unfair to the children, especially in the moment. Parents should try to make decisions that will be fair in the long run, but acknowledge that children have differences in perception.

Children need to be givers in their families. Even babies give indirectly to their parents—in the case of those who have welcomed parenthood—through the joy of their presence and by providing the experience of accomplishment. However, children receive from parents without being able to reciprocate equally. "Society does not expect the child to repay the parent in equivalent benefits" (Boszormenyi-Nagy & Spark, 1973, p. 55). Nevertheless, as children grow, each developmental stage offers opportunities for them to give according to their capacity. The entire family is benefited when parents encourage and expect altruistic behavior. They do need to be aware of what kinds of giving are age appropriate, in order to avoid conveying destructive parentification or destructive entitlement to their child. When a child has been scapegoated as the family problem, the therapist may look for signs of such issues early in the treatment process. Healthy repayment of the filial debt is fulfilled when the grown child gives to the next generation, or to society.

Sometimes a child brought to therapy is living in a family where parents are experiencing long-term issues of unfairness with each other. During the fourth evaluation segment, the therapist listens to both parents for factors of inequity both within their families of origin and within their couple relationship. At subsequent parenting meetings, he may ask questions that have to do with the present unfairness in the nuclear family, and then shift back to the family of origin. For example, he may say, "You have tried so hard to be fair to your children. You are telling me that they seem spoiled, expecting everything, not giving, exhibiting hostile sibling rivalry. Tell me more about any unfairness to you and your siblings when you were raised in your families." Exploring these intergenerational issues may help parents unravel problematic family dynamics that have become tangled into the fabric of present relationships.

Many psychotherapists have been taught to disallow blame in therapy, because it can enable the client to avoid taking responsibility for his present behaviors. However, it can actually have short-term benefit: in Contextual Therapy, a time-limited discussion of blame may be seen as the best way for the client to formulate an understanding of the unfair aspects of his life, past and present, and rightfully attribute the unfairness to those who have hurt him. The therapist is compassionate about the outpouring of pain that comes in the form of blame. The client's expression of blame can lead to his holding accountable those who have done the hurt, whether they are dead or alive. The invitation to accept accountability may or may not be received by the one who has done the harm. The victim's action of "extending the olive branch" can be quite healing, regardless of the willingness or ability of the perpetrator to honor the story and apologize. When that does happen, it is quite wonderful. It often does not. Contextual Therapy teachings recognize it as a life truth that a person's relational action of speaking honestly brings its own reward, even if the party addressed does not reciprocate. Furthermore, the healing helps to prevent the suffering of future generations.

B. Janet Hibbs provides a very helpful questionnaire in *Try to See It My Way: Being Fair in Love and Marriage* (2009). The questionnaire has 69 questions divided into four categories: "General Fairness Questions," "Fairness With Your Partner," "Fairness With Your Parents," and "Fairness With Your Children." She notes that the questionnaire highlights two major mistakes in relationships: overgiving and taking too much. The book, filled with the wisdom of Contextual Therapy, provides insightful, concrete advice and recommends that, by looking at imbalances, we take "a step toward a more satisfying life" (pp. 45–51).

5. Acknowledgment

Children require acknowledgment in order to flourish. They deserve to be acknowledged by their parents for the contributions they make to their parents' lives, to their siblings and friends, and to society at large. This plants a seed for healthy relating and promotes appropriate individuation of the child from the parent. A parent's acknowledgment of the child is an essential experience in the child's growing up. This concept is an important component of the therapist's basic point of view.

A parent who is depriving her child of acknowledgment may be continuing a blueprint of injustice that was perpetrated on her as a child. During an interview on the radio show *Voices in the Family* with Dan Gottleib, CFT pioneer Margaret Cotroneo emphasized the importance of acknowledgment. She said that if you want to keep your children bound to you forever, never acknowledge their efforts and contributions. Parents tend either to imitate their own parents or to swing to an opposite pattern of parenting behaviors. Either tendency may be problematic. One may feel, "My parents never acknowledged me for anything, and I'm okay, so why should I acknowledge my kids?" Or it may be the opposite: a parent may offer flattery at all the wrong times, leading the child to feel misunderstood, self-conscious, and actually treated unfairly. In such a case, the child may eventually reject the parent's attempts at acknowledgment.

Acknowledgment During the Initial Evaluation

In the second segment of the initial evaluation, when the whole family comes together, as described in chapter 3, the therapist invites the parents to acknowledge the children. She asks what they love about each child and what they see as each one's strengths. Most parents are able to respond with what they like and love about each of their children, who are often moved when they hear this overt affirmation. If a parent is so frustrated with a child as to be unable to respond to the resource side of the child's giving, then the therapist needs to note this and intervene early in the therapy to shift this dynamic. If the therapist senses that this might happen, she may warn the parents at their first meeting that she will be asking questions about the positive side of their relationship with the child so that they will have time to think about it. However, spontaneous responses are generally preferable.

A parent sometimes has difficulty identifying positive qualities, especially with children who have been oppositional for a long time. He may be able to respond by describing activities that they enjoy doing together, or by remembering better times. The therapist may ask, "At what age *did* you enjoy your child?" One mother, who was struggling to acknowledge her son, was able to respond by saying that he was very much wanted and that she was happy to be his mom despite the present problems. Of course, this is not always the case; in such a situation, it is helpful for the parents to discuss negative feelings with the therapist alone at a parent meeting. The therapist can acknowledge the immense giving required of parents who are dealing with an oppositional child, and the tendency to have thoughts of giving up. Feelings of discouragement are common, and the parents need compassion about these feelings, not judgment. Through ongoing understanding and acknowledgment of the parents, the therapist models a healthy way for family members to credit one another, paving the way for them to eventually acknowledge their child.

Acknowledgment During Weekly Sessions

During Talk Time each week, the therapist asks the child what she enjoyed about her week. "What did you do this weekend? Did the family do something together? Did you like something about school today? Did you visit with friends?" Such questions can bring affirming attention to the child's resources. They engage the child in a back-and-forth dialogue with the therapist about positive topics. For most children, this dialogue cultivates a positive self-reflection and becomes an important part of therapy. The child has the opportunity to formulate thoughts and feelings, and then to express them to the therapist and parent. Repetition of this experience helps the child become more proficient with intimate dialogue concerning her life.

Children should be acknowledged when they are able to respond to questions that may be uncomfortable—for example, "Tell me what happened when you got into trouble at school today." After the parent, the child, and the therapist discuss the problem and perhaps do some role playing to figure out new behaviors, the therapist acknowledges the child's efforts: "You were really able to tell me a lot about that! I know it was uncomfortable for you. I hear that you really feel that the other child was unfair." If the child says she does not want to talk about the matter at hand, the therapist can still provide acknowledgment: "I know your mom wants to discuss the argument you two had just before coming here today. I appreciate that you are telling me that you really don't want to talk about it. One reason people come to me is to do just that: to talk about things that are hard to talk about. So, since your mom and dad want us to do that, even though it is hard, it is important to talk about that fight you two had on the way here." He may encourage the parent to join in and affirm to the child that it is okay to include the therapist in this matter. For example, the parent may say to the child: "Your mom and I are trusting our therapist to help our family with some of the problems that have been very hard for us. It is okay to talk here about things that are hard to talk about."

However, the child is permitted to remain silent during Talk Time, if that is her need. It is not beneficial to force her to talk, but she may not stop her parents and therapist from discussing the issues that concern them. So, the therapist may acknowledge that the child is saying she does not want to talk about the topic at hand. Then he may start discussing with the parent—the more willing participant—the recent dispute that occurred between the parent and child. The child will often join the discussion in order to correct a detail or express a disagreement.

Toward the cultivation of mindful parenting, the therapist encourages the parent to consider what might have been done differently. This question also points out that the issue with the child is a shared relational problem. Children are often quite attentive when the therapist suggests that parents examine how they may not feel good about their own actions with their child. "I was very unfair today when I gave a large punishment for a minor infraction." The parent may apologize and make an adjustment. The parent then models how to handle unfairness. This repair work keeps trust in the relationship.

A child can usually tolerate discussing just one issue at each Talk Time, for about 15 or 20 minutes. Gradually, she learns that the talking therapy, moderated by the presence of a trusted participant from outside the family, is a place for discussion, acknowledgment, and accountability, not only for her but also for her parents. Parents report that, over time, the therapist-as-witness becomes a part of family dynamics. Recalling the discussions of Talk Time motivates children to make positive changes at home, such as acquiring the habit of mutual acknowledgment.

Acknowledgment During Mindful Parenting Meetings
At mindful parenting meetings, usually held approximately monthly with the parents alone, the therapist should credit the contributions that each parent is making to the family. He can acknowledge the ways in which family members are doing well. It is rewarding when each parent takes this opportunity to acknowledge the positive contributions of the other.

6. Parentification

Parentification can be positive or negative. Positive parentification can be the needed help that a child gives to a parent, often on a temporary basis. It may even be above what is normally asked of a child, as long as this does not overburden the child. In such a case, relationships benefit when the action of parentification is clearly defined by the parent as being above normal expectations. It is especially important that the boundaries of the extra giving be clear, including an estimate of how long a time the extra need is expected to last. The parent must also take into account the child's needs based on her level of growth and development.

An example of healthy parentification occurs when an older teenage sibling takes care of his younger sibling for a few hours while the parent goes shopping. The elder child learns responsible behaviors and gains useful experience. He also earns acknowledgment for giving beyond normal family expectations. Before the parent leaves, she provides child care instructions and explains the boundaries of limit setting and nurturing. When she returns, she makes it clear to both children that the designated roles are no longer operating. Thus, the elder sibling does not continue to act in a parental role toward the younger. In some cultures or families, this substitute parenting may be part of normal expectations and not be seen as extra giving.

Negative parentification, as Boszormenyi-Nagy calls it, crosses the child's deserved boundaries, leaving him burdened with responsibilities that are not rightfully his to bear. This would occur if the teen sibling were required to watch the younger sibling frequently and without clear parameters of role or time. The teen may be unable to participate in activities that are important for a person his age. For example, when the parent's assignment to take care of siblings regularly prevents him from joining his peers in a desired sport, dance, or activity, the price is too high.

Negative parentification is most serious when the child feels responsible for the well-being of his parents and siblings. An example of this occurs when the parent confides in her child her adult personal problems and sometimes even negative thoughts about the other parent. In the chapter "Black Genealogy Revisited: Restoring an African American Family" (McGoldrick & Hardy, 2008), Elaine Pinderhughes offers a poignant, sometimes sad, and ultimately hopeful account of how she decided to research the roots of her parents' families. She was well into middle age when her father died at the age of 88. Her mother had died when she was 16 years old—the same age that her mother had been when her own mother had died. Referring to herself as a "parentified child," Pinderhughes states, "I had known that my mother, despite her unusual beauty, was often sad and depressed. I knew this well, for she was my first client, as she shared much of her sadness and depression with me" (p. 127).

Negative parentification is born when a child becomes overly responsible. She grows up without having life experiences that teach her that this kind of relating can be damaging. A parent may realize that she is repeating a harmful pattern, but have conscious or unconscious loyalty which motivates her to unwittingly replicate it. Rather than confronting the unfairnesses of her own childhood experience, the parent may attempt to seek retribution through her children or spouse. This is one of the ways that the "revolving slate" continues in families for generations. As we will discuss later, the parent may not feel guilt for this destructively entitled action. This lack of accountability contributes to the difficulty of changing the behavior. "Many abusive parents hate themselves for the terrible things they do to their children, yet still feel justified in trying to get their needs met" (Hargrave & Pfitzer, 2003, p. 79). It is the play-family therapist's job to identify hidden injustices when the family is unaware or in denial of them, and to help family members face them. An understanding of negative parentification can provide parents the leverage to break the cycle of neglect and denial. If the parentification pattern is egosyntonic for the parent, it can be quite challenging to shift to more positive relational structures.

Another kind of negative parentification occurs within the marriage relationship, when one spouse assumes the role of "parent" to the other. Each partner may be trying to get too many of their unfulfilled emotional needs met by each other. These may be needs that were, sadly, not met in their respective families of origin, where they were appropriate for a growing child to have. The parentification may manifest as repeated incompetent performance by one partner of tasks that, in fairness, should be shared. The spouse who is playing into this parentified role, whether resentfully or willingly, may take on more and more responsibility. She begins to feel like the parent rather than the lover. This may in some way answer unfinished issues from her family of origin as well.

When marital parentification presents during a family session, the therapist may choose to address the parents privately about the issue and educate them about its ramifications in an objective, left-brain way. Later, as trust builds, parents may be ready to visit the parentification in a right-brain way, by accessing implicit memories that can gradually lead to change. Couples therapy can help to interrupt the destructive patterns and facilitate healing by reworking each partner's legacy issues at the root level. Even though the benefits brought by repair work may grow into the future, insight does not yield immediate change in behaviors. Indeed, it is the therapist's job to know that a long process is required for unhealthy habits that have long been embraced to shift into healthy ways of living.

Note: You may want to read the segment of the case study concerning couple therapy, which is found on p. 295.

7. Loyalty and Split Loyalty

Loyalty is a key concept in CFT, to the extent that the title of Ivan Boszormenyi-Nagy and Geraldine Spark's book on Contextual Therapy is *Invisible Loyalties*. Boszormenyi-Nagy notes the etymology of *loyalty* in the French word *loi* (law), "implying law-abiding attitudes" (1973, p. 42).

> Families have their own laws in the form of unwritten shared expectations. Each family member is constantly subject to varying patterns of expectations to which he does or does not comply. Young children's compliance is enforced by outside disciplinary measures. Older children and adults may comply out of internalized loyalty commitments. (p. 42)

At a past American Association for Marriage and Family Therapy conference, while being interviewed by William Doherty for the Masters Series of family therapy pioneers, Boszormenyi-Nagy said that his father and grandfather were judges in Hungary (Boszormenyi-Nagy, 1992). It was expected that he and his brother would follow the same path. With humor, he let us know that becoming a psychiatrist was a departure that led him to be viewed by his family as a bit of a rebel. We might conjecture that, though he "rebelled" this way, Nagy maintained his loyalty to his family by developing a relational ethics rooted in fairness.

Who Owes Loyalty to Whom?

Committed spouses need to shift their loyalty from their families of origin to each other. If they become parents, they simultaneously reinforce their loyalty to their line of ancestry. Parents owe loyalty and affection to their children. Although the nature of parenting can require postponing adult needs to benefit children, parents can find ways to be loyal to and maintain the larger family system while still attending to their own individual needs. If they succeed in this, they avoid long-term resentment. Husbands and wives owe loyalty to their aging and incapacitated parents, balancing their parents' needs with their own needs, their spouse's needs, and the needs of their children.

Children owe appropriate loyalty to the parents who raise them. Siblings owe loyalty to one another. Children and their grandparents owe loyalty to one another. All family members owe loyalty to preserving the whole family system. To allow separation and individuation to unfold, they need to adapt to the changes that come with the developmental growth of each member, including accepting new members through birth and marriage and welcoming friends and affiliates. A family cut-off is a breakdown in positive loyalty. It does harm within the contemporary family context and also to future generations. A contextual therapist seeks to understand possibilities for healing a cut-off, or for finding the most humane way to deal with one that is beyond the client's control. (This section, "Who Owes Loyalty to Whom?," was adapted from Boszormenyi-Nagy & Spark, 1973, p. 51.)

Split Loyalty

Split loyalty classically occurs when children feel forced to choose allegiance to one parent over the other. Such a dilemma can develop when the parents have a competitive or adversarial couple relationship, whether living together or apart. All children deserve to love both of their parents. When one parent criticizes and belittles the other, whether overtly or by intimation, a child is burdened with the feeling that she must take sides. It is important that this be addressed first in a meeting without the child present. The therapist needs to articulate some of the painful ways that couples are critical of each other. Often, indeed, their criticisms inform the therapist about the parents' honest frustrations and injuries. When the couple live in the same household, an important intervention at mindful parenting meetings is to coach each parent to talk directly to the therapist about his or her frustrations about the other's parenting style, while the partner witnesses. This may allow their strong feelings to be heard and defused enough so that they can then have an open dialogue. If they are unable to understand each other in the parent meeting, individual or couples therapy can be suggested. Parents are warned how damaging it is when children witness a parent's chronic, direct or indirect denigration of the other.

A similar occurance of split loyalty happens when a child is cast as referee to her parents' disputes. A notorious example is the custody case in which a child is asked to decide where she wants to live. It is acceptable to let a child know that her feelings matter, but according to CFT wisdom, she should be asked her viewpoint, then instructed that the adults will decide. It is negatively parentifying for children to believe that they make this decision.

Split loyalty damages the child's trust. It is natural for her to identify with both parents; therefore, she takes the antagonism personally. She cannot trust the criticizing parent who is violating the spousal contract of respect and care, and she cannot respect the parent who is being diminished. It is such a serious problem that Boszormenyi-Nagy used to say that split loyalty is at the root of all suicide. It is often the cause of self-harming behaviors such as eating disorders, cutting, use of drugs and alcohol, and reckless sexual behavior. When working with suicidal feelings, the therapist tracks the split loyalties, which are often multilayered.

Children in stepfamilies can be subject to intense split loyalty. When a parent brings a new partner into the family, a child may worry, "Will Mom be hurt if I like Dad's new partner?" or, "Will Dad be mad if I like my new stepfather?" It helps when the child receives her other parent's permission to bond with the newcomer. Children benefit greatly when their parents have accomplished closure on their former marital relationship. Even so, the children's needs are best met if a lot of time passes before they are asked to incorporate a new parent figure into their lives. However, this is not always what happens. The needs felt by the parent may be in conflict with the needs of the children. If the parent makes life changes without regard for the children's needs, there will be unfairness toward the children. At the very least, the parent owes acknowledgment of the differences and some efforts at healing.

Split loyalty is one of the most challenging areas of therapy work, and one of the most common. It is useful for parents to know the degree of harm that can be caused by split loyalty—that it is at the root of self-destructive behavior. Constant exposure to split loyalty is one reason that a child's behaviors can become very intense and uncontrolled. When parents continue a pattern that is hurting their children, I recommend a mediator. I am particularly concerned when I see self-harming actions, either intermittent or acute, by children or teens. A child may end up in a psychiatric hospital due to intense split loyalty, and even then, parents may be unable to see the connections between their child's despair and the split loyalty they are causing her to feel. "Uncoupling" sessions are always beneficial for separating partners, and they are essential when parents allow their negativity to flow over to the children.

Loyalty to the Therapist

Loyalty within the therapy relationship is a delicate issue, whether with children, teens, or adults. The therapist's intention is to honor the fact that, for the child's emotional well-being, it is important that she be more loyal to her parents than to the therapist. There can be a warm attachment to the therapist without its competing with the filial relationship. With emotionally healthy parents, this happens naturally in MBPFT when the therapist is sensitive to the parent as the primary attachment figure.

However, it is tricky when the parent's apparent deficits or physical absence complicate the feelings of attachment. Therapists who work in shelters with families, especially those who provide long-term treatment, report that is is helpful for the child to have individual play therapy and to bond with the therapist before a parent enters the playroom. This is particularly necessary when there is an attachment problem, when the parent's behavior in the playroom is initially toxic for the child. While the parent is in parallel therapy, exploring her own implicit memories from childhood, her child may be bonding to the therapist, who is available for the more intimate relationship. This needs to be done with the therapist's full respect for the parent, whose own pain may be inhibiting her availability to her child. The therapist needs to always keep in mind that his ultimate goal is for the child and parent to bond more closely. As the parent becomes more accessible for connecting, the therapist can invite her to participate more directly in the child's healing process. Children can learn to hold several loving, caring people in their hearts simultaneously without competition. This is similar to what occurs with adoption, foster care, stepparents, grandparents, aunts and uncles, and good friends.

8. Destructive and Constructive Entitlement

Destructive Entitlement

Destructive entitlement is a concept that is very useful for working with families that are suffering victimization from the behaviors or the repetitious rage of a family member. Destructive entitlement happens when a person feels he has been unfairly treated and is, consequently, owed. In his state of grievance, he assumes "permission" to behave in ways that are hurtful and unfair to others. He feels justified in acting in ways that would ordinarily lead him to feel remorse. This is a complex phenomenon, because we often associate lack of guilt with a person who has a personality disturbance, but according to Boszormenyi-Nagy, this is not necessarily the case—especially in regard to actions motivated by destructive entitlement. The more a person has been harmed at an early age, and the longer the harm has gone untreated, the less reversible are the consequences, and the more likely that the person accumulates destructive entitlement (Boszormenyi-Nagy, classroom teaching, 1981). "The destructively entitled person characteristically overlooks the fact that he is not entitled to take out his basically justifiable grudge on innocent others. . . . [I]t is a derivative of unacknowledged and unrequited justice" (Boszormenyi-Nagy & Krasner, 1986, p. 110). A "valid factor" and an "invalid factor" operate simultaneously. The grudge is valid because of past unfairness, but the vengeful expression of the grudge, which affects innocent others, is not justifiable.

When a child has accrued destructive entitlement, the parents and the other children may bear the brunt of the desperate child's history. The therapist needs to uncover the early history of the child. He can begin treatment by validating the past harm suffered by this destructively entitled youngster, then proceed to helping the concerned parties face the truth and invite repairing actions into their relationships. Any of the various members within the family can be subject to destructive entitlement. A parent may be retaliating for childhood injustices by acting unfairly toward her children. Marital problems may have similar motivating factors. As described above, acknowledgment of the old hurt, and truthful assignment of the original injustice, are part of healing.

For example, 12-year-old Taneisha was acting out by cutting herself. When she was only five years old, she had been the caregiver for her younger sibling. In the evening when her father was working late, her mother would often pass out from alcohol and prescription drugs. Taneisha would change her sister's diaper and put her to bed, and then take care of herself. The mother blamed the father for working late hours and felt abandoned with young children. The father blamed his wife and said that she was alcoholic and that he did not want to go home.

When Taneisha came to therapy, her mother had been a member of Al-

coholics Anonymous for four years. Both parents were successfully participating in their own therapy, and family life was much better. At the age of
12, why was Taneisha behaving self-destructively? Since the couple was
doing much better, they could not understand their daughter's behaviors.
Eventually, her destructive behaviors were reduced as the parents painstak-
ingly addressed their own guilt. At a family meeting, both parents were
willing to apologize for past harm to all of the children and to particularly
acknowledge Taneisha's caring "big-sister" actions that were too much for
a five-year-old little girl. The parents worked with the therapist to create a
trauma reality sandtray with their daughter. All of the children attended.
The truth invited accountability and forgiveness and a new level of healing.

If the abuse enacted by the destructive person poses a safety issue, then
protecting everyone must be addressed first. The impulses operating in
destructive entitlement can be harmful to the person's well-being and to
others in his life. It is the therapist's task to work with this turmoil by asking the destructive person to put a halt to his harmful behavior, even if he
does not view the behavior as destructive. The therapist asks the difficult
questions that raise implicit memories from past injustices. In time, if
possible, clients are encouraged to go to the source of the abuse, often
their own parents, to attempt to rework the injustices through honest dialogue.

> Contextual therapy tries to help people discover and construct mul-
> tilaterally responsible solutions in the very situations in which their
> impulses drive them in the opposite direction. Akin to classical
> Greek drama, a victory based on disregard for significant people in
> the individual's life weaves tragic consequences into the fabric of the
> future. (Boszormenyi-Nagy & Krasner, 1986, p. 19)

On the other hand, regard for others, along with concern for one's own
needs, benefits everyone. Once the destructively entitled behavior is defused and is being reworked through acknowledging root causes, the current systemic issues can be identified more accurately and addressed more
effectively. In the example of 12-year-old Taneisha, who was cutting herself,
the parents were coached to be both compassionate and quite firm with her.
Role playing was used to give them a variety of parenting techniques that
would regain hierarchical balance.

Destructive Entitlement and the Brain

What might be happening in the brain when there is repeated destructive entitlement from unresolved trauma? In the chapter on trauma in *The Mindful Therapist: A Clinician's Guide to Mindsight and Neural Integration* (2010a), Daniel Siegel gives a couple of very clear, simple examples of his own reactions to trauma and explains what is happening in the left brain (explicit memory) and the right brain (implicit memory). As Siegel writes, "Trauma impairs integration. Unresolved trauma results in persistent chaos and rigidity. . . . This chaos and rigidity reveal a brain with impaired integration—and a mind with unresolved trauma" (p. 189). It is helpful to realize that the disruptive behaviors of a destructively entitled individual are rooted in implicit memories that may have been formed any time during the person's life span, even before birth. This does not make the outbursts any more pleasant, but it may help the parent to be more compassionate. Therapy encourages clients to make these connections so that, as Siegel says, children and adults can become "flexible, adaptive, coherent, energized and stable (FACES)" (p. 184).

Constructive Entitlement

Constructive entitlement is earned by giving. One way of earning entitlement is through efforts to engage with another party in honest dialogue about past hurts and injustices. A positive response by the recipient can be very rewarding to both the victim and the perpetrator. When dialogue of reparation is achieved between family members, it can bring a halt to harmful behaviors and result in the capacity for healthy giving. This is considered root-level healing and is an ultimate goal of MBPFT.

If the former perpetrator admits past injustice and asks for forgiveness, it can be very healing. Frequently, however, the abuser is unable to acknowledge the injustice of past actions. In this case, the therapist helps the client see that the simple act of seeking accountability still builds her power to decrease her own destructive entitlement. Equanimity is not dependent on the response of the other. When an adult child seeks a healing dialogue, a stonewalled response by a parent may at the very least expose the truth of the impasse. The effort to confront difficult matters is witnessed and acknowledged by the therapist, and the effort itself earns constructive entitlement. A person who has earned constructive entitlement has more power to stop her own unhealthy behaviors and acknowledge the injustice and harm done, and she is less likely to engage in destructive behaviors to a partner or the next generation. She also sets up the atmosphere for forgiveness or exoneration.

9. Scapegoated Family Members and Family Monsters

When the child is labeled the primary cause of the family's problems, this is called "scapegoating." The parents may be coming to therapy after years of frustration and anger. They certainly need a lot of empathy for enduring the problems of a child who has a challenging personality or a chronic physical or emotional illness. It is particularly important that the therapist give them this empathy at the first evaluation session with the parents alone. However, the parents may have little awareness of the connection between the child's behaviors and larger family problems. Or, they may see that the child is not the primary cause of difficulties, yet be unwilling to examine the emotional legacy passed on from their family of origin and admit its potential connection to the chronic problems their child is having. These parents may say that if this child would just "obey," then they would have a happy family.

The four-segment evaluation is a natural way to broaden the view and reduce the scapegoating of a single child. The therapist can note what is happening in the family life cycle, in the three- or four-generation genograms, and in the couple relationship, in order to expand understanding of the family's pain. At the same time, in addition to the family therapy, he can recommend individual play therapy, which allows the child to begin to express her feelings and to release her painful energies. These interventions often give initial symptom relief to both the MC child and her family.

Sometimes families report that there is a "monster" or two in the family history. It is important that the therapy attend to a hated family member, sooner or later. Despite the real offenses that may have brought it about, the institutionalized exclusion of a relative can have a toxic effect on the meaning of membership in the family, and may plant seeds for one of the children to become the next "monster." At the same time, it is very important to have some caution in approaching a person who may carry truly toxic elements. The therapist can give balanced guidance, attending in particular to the safety of those harmed or who could be potentially harmed.

In approaching the topic of the family monster, the therapist listens to the reasons for the hatred. How did this person become such a monster? Usually there are compelling explanations for the strong feelings. At other times, family members may not even be clear about what happened originally to warrant the designation of monster. Although it may take a while to happen authentically, in due time family members can be asked to consider that this person was once an innocent infant, too. The therapist can express that he is curious to learn how circumstances may have hurt and changed this person. Every victimizer was once a victim. His inquiry can allow the family members to be willing to find out more information about the "monster's" life, although it may take some time before they are able to talk about this person. This, too, is understandable.

This listening stage of therapy may last for a while before the "dialogue of the between" occurs, if it does indeed occur; the client, of course, makes this decision. Dialogue with a family member who has done harm can provide an opportunity for those who have been hurt to voice their viewpoint, their needs, and their entitlement to give and receive fairness. Sometimes a letter is a constructive way to start the dialogue. The truthful expression of very difficult thoughts and feelings may be more easily accomplished in writing. This is often useful for addressing a parent who tends to have toxic, repelling responses. When a parent is deceased, writing is a primary way to communicate. As the process advances, the possibility of exoneration or forgiveness can be introduced in a manner that respects the emotional needs and level of willingness of the hurt family members.

10. Exoneration and Forgiveness

Contextual Therapy accepts the premise that human beings hurt one another as an inevitable part of living. In the process of exoneration, the harmed person is honest in looking at the injustice of the harm he has received and the consequences it has had on his life. Exoneration takes time and does not bypass a deeply felt grieving process for the loss that has been suffered. The sensorial body release arrives with the opening up of connection between right and left brain, implicit and explicit memory. At the same time, the individual can try to understand the difficult life circumstances of a parent, grandparent, or any person who may have inflicted harm. He may additionally credit any positive giving by the perpetrator. The contextual therapist compassionately hears and offers witness to the person's story. It may take a very long time for this process to replicate authentic exoneration.

A client may come to therapy with an intellectual willingness to forgive those who have caused harm. Sometimes she may have a cathartic experience and feel willing to "wipe the slate clean." This kind of forgiveness may be unilateral. The client may be expressing the courage and generosity that she can find within herself. These are personal attributes of the person willing to forgive without a dialogue with the other.

A person on the journey of exoneration is able to look at the life of the perpetrator. Realizing that every infant is born innocent into the world, she may ask, "What happened in this person's history that led him to become inconsiderate, selfish, or malicious? Were his life circumstances harsh, callous, or even cruel?" Eventually, the victim may be able to see the context of the perpetrator's life and realize that he, too, was once a victim. The pathway of exoneration is both intrapsychic and dialogic. Through it, the harmed person may even be able to acknowledge that, despite the damage inflicted, the perpetrator has also made positive contributions. Contextual thinking "does not require that all of a person's actions be forgiven. Indeed, there are actions that may simply be unforgivable" (Goldenthal, 1996, pp. 76–77). When a person chooses to forgive, she may be responding to appropriate steps of accountability taken by the one who has inflicted the pain. Authentic forgiveness can arise after a process of exoneration and may come from the open heart of the one harmed; it is not assumed that the victimizer *deserves* forgiveness, although this may or may not be deemed true. The process of exoneration releases the victim from unconsciously acting in a destructively entitled way against someone unrelated to the offense. It ends the revolving slate on which former victims becomes victimizers. Perhaps it is a fifth-dimension action to exonerate and then forgive even when the perpetrator has not sought forgiveness.

Contextual Therapy is at its best when family members listen, join in dialogue, and express sincere regret. In this way, the stage may be set for reparation and forgiveness. Such right-brain-to-right-brain connection may occur first between client and therapist, and then, with time, between the client and those who are responsible for his childhood pain. In *Forgive Your Parents, Heal Yourself: How Understanding Your Painful Legacy Can Transform Your Life* (1999), Barry Grosskopf has an uncanny ability to express the inner process of forgiveness and the transformation that can come from a committment to mindful living.

An application of exoneration to a family therapy situation may occur when a therapist encourages parents struggling with their children to keep in mind the different context in which their own parents were functioning. For example, the therapist may say, "Self-help information and therapy were not as available to your parents as they are now. If they had understood the value of acknowledgment, maybe they would have been able to do better with it." Such considerations can help avoid loyalty conflicts for the parents in therapy. This does not mean that one should not hold one's parents accountable for injustices. It means, however, allowing a compassionate view of their life circumstances. Contextual Therapy theory warns against setting the parent up to be "better" than his own parent. Such competition can intensify a loyalty conflict. But because it *is* a goal of therapy to avoid repeating the mistakes of the past, parents may, in fact, be accomplishing healthier parenting then did their own parents.

11. The Revolving Slate and Concerns About Future Generations

The concept of the "revolving slate" is quite helpful when a family's problems have continued over generations. Boszormenyi-Nagy and Spark (1973) describe it as the unsettled account that stands between a person and the original "culprit" can revolve and get between him and any third person. An innocent third person may be used—scapegoated—as a means for balancing the account. The revolving slate is "a relational consequence in which a person's substitutive revenge against one person eventually creates a new victim" (Boszormenyi-Nagy & Krasner, 1986, p. 420). This problem is very confusing, because the innocent victim is treated as though he were the original perpetrator.

The revolving slate becomes apparent when we look at the difference between anger and rage, and at the manner in which rage crosses generations. In working with a child or teenager who is rageful, the therapist should track each parent's anger history. A parent's anger toward his child's misbehavior can be a very normal reaction, but if he becomes rageful, this indicates a source located back a generation or two. In contemporary expression, where nature and nurture convene, the revolving slate would be considered epigenetic. The revolving slate bears the pattern of the rageful parent's unfinished business with his own parents, or with other significant people who either raised him or abandoned him, or with his siblings. Then, through life habits, this is passed on to the next generation.

When the rage is directed, as anger, to the original source and reworked there, the revolving slate mechanism is interrupted. Then the parent can stop scapegoating his child and can be merely angry at the child's misbehaviors. This intervention, which can take some time to accomplish, is a most powerful help for the scapegoated child, who may have borne the brunt of one or both parents' rage for many years. As the child or teen experiences the healing of the parent's rage, she sees a model of how healing can be brought to her own rage. This is one of the most effective ways to help a child with her problem: allowing her to witness her parent's growth. A clear and easy-to-read book I find most helpful when family members are trying to identify their style of anger is *When Anger Hurts Your Kids: A Parent's Guide* (McKay, Fanning, Paleg, & Landis, 1996).

An example of a horizontal revolving slate occurs within the couple relationship when spouses, who have unworked past issues with their own parents, blame one another for the current manifestations of those old issues. Hibbs recommends that couples sort out the unfinished business of "yours, mine and ours."

> It's often easier to pin the blame for relationship problems on a partner, rather than claiming your own baggage. Your baggage consists of experiences that have shaped your expectations, affected your level of trust, and recharged hot buttons from childhood. . . . In order to avoid changing partners, but dancing the same dance, you need to unpack your baggage, stop repeating unhealthy patterns, and strengthen your marriage. (2009, pp. 107–108)

For example, a person's unworked issues with a parent, whether alive or deceased, can impact how he treats his spouse. Blaming the spouse in the present preserves one's loyal illusion of the blamelessness of his family of origin. If the play-family therapist becomes aware of these issues because they are also spilling over into the next generation, he should recommend couples therapy and let the couple know how it will help the whole family. Parents often find it hard to see the connections between their own and their children's problems. Children deserve to have their parents make as much constructive effort as they are able.

12. *The Self of the Therapist*

Both Ivan Boszormenyi-Nagy and Murray Bowen encouraged therapists to revisit their own family emotional systems and to struggle directly with the unresolved issues they discover. This willingness to do personal healing permits a therapist to maintain a "differentiation of self," and a healthy distinction between the client's and his own family emotional systems. After describing some serious efforts at individuating within his own family of origin, Murray Bowen refers to his enacting "the role of the differentiating one." He writes,

> The one who achieves some success at differentiation has a kind of appeal for the entire family. It is as if any member of the family can approach this one and have the advantage of an emotionally detached viewpoint which in turn helps him or her develop a different perspective. (Bowen, 2004, p. 516)

When a therapist reworks his own issues directly with his family of origin, he achieves levels of self-awareness and individuation that allow him to be comfortable with the intimacy that comes with working so closely with families. He can be committed to confronting "the emotional shock waves" (Bowen, 2004, p. 326) that follow months or years after major loss. He will encounter fewer transference problems with his clients. As he discovers and acknowledges the connections between the events in his life, whether they are joyful, sad, or unremarkable, he gains greater leverage to invite clients to take a similar journey.

7

Parent Education and Mindful Parenting

Mindful parenting meetings provide an opportunity for the therapist to meet with the parents alone. Discussion of problems and of the progress of the child and the family creates the environment for parent education that is specific to the needs of the individual family. Parents are encouraged to reflect on their parenting skills and to seek deeper insight concerning the relationship issues among the family members. They are also invited to cultivate their awareness, particularly of their own behaviors and of the root-level causes of the family issues. In a parallel fashion, it is very helpful for the therapist to be involved in her own deeper journey, facing and healing her own life pain, so that she is not merely living vicariously through her clients.

The Frequency and Structure of Meetings

The most usual pattern is to have a meeting with both parents following every four sessions of Mindfulness-Based Play-Family Therapy (MBPFT). In some cases, the therapist may decide to have the first parent dialogue meeting after only two or three sessions. An initial pattern of two or three play-family therapy sessions followed by a parent meeting may be recommended in cases such as the following:

- When seeing a very young child
- When the parents have many questions or a high level of anxiety
- When the issues presented need more immediate attention from the adults

The therapist uses the four-segment evaluation to determine which pattern of sessions is most likely to meet the initial needs of all the family members. The default monthly parent meetings often suffice because the weekly Talk Time provides a regular opportunity to address issues as they arise. Occasionally, additional appointments are needed at the beginning of the course of play therapy, or during the deeper work when the "worse-before-better" part of therapy becomes particularly challenging for the parents.

Family therapy sessions for all members, including intergenerational meetings, can be scheduled as needed at any time during the treatment, as requested by the parents or recommended by the therapist. Occasionally, a child will request a family meeting, and it can be affirming to the child when his suggestion is taken seriously by the adults. However, if the therapist agrees with this request, it must be based on sound clinical reasoning, not simply allowing a child to control the agenda.

For a family in crisis, the therapist may request weekly parent meetings throughout the crisis stage of the work in addition to seeing the child for play therapy. The more concerned the therapist is about what is happening in the family, the more meetings she will deem necessary to gain some initial symptom relief. The parents will appreciate the coaching that the therapist gives them to help reduce the child's symptoms. In the case of a child who has been thrown out of school, or who is being very oppositional or having self-harming feelings, the parents may need to be involved intensely until there is some symptom relief.

The success of the work depends on parental involvement and availability to attend the meetings. When parents are living in the same household, the monthly parent meetings are scheduled so that both are able to attend together. Most parents will honor at least a minimal commitment to parent feedback sessions once every fourth week, particularly if the therapist communicates this expectation clearly at the outset. Parents come to appreciate these meetings, even if some initially try to place the burden of attendance on the other parent. The therapist is aware that the larger family problems may relate to a perceived or actual imbalance between the levels of responsibility carried by the two parents. By requiring both parents to attend dialogue meetings, she avoids colluding with an unfair family dynamic. It is crucial to everyone's healing that the issue of fairness be raised and discussed.

The parents normally appreciate taking time for parent meetings and often arrive with topics they wish to discuss. The dialogue offers an opportunity to talk about parenting topics with someone who cares very much about their child. As is the practice in family therapy, the therapist directs her questions to both parents. If one of the parents seems to have the role of designated spokesperson for the couple, it is wise for the therapist to request that each parent respond separately. She may also invite the quieter parent to expand on the ideas that have been given by the more verbally responsive parent.

Single parents may appreciate the acknowledgment of how intense the parent–child relationship can be. They often enjoy feeling a coparenting support from the therapist during parent feedback and dialogue meetings.

The Agenda and Forms

At the beginning of the session, the therapist and parents together create an itemized agenda of topics to be discussed during the one-hour meeting. This process invites the parents to verbalize their concerns. However, the meeting may start with the therapist asking the parents to describe what is going well in the family. This enables them to acknowledge one another, themselves, and their children. If the list of problems is long, it may need to be prioritized, since there may not be enough time to discuss everything.

The therapist takes time to prepare in advance for the parent meeting, using these two tools, which can be found in Appendix A:

1. *The Monthly Talk Time Notes form.* This form summarizes relevant information from the past month of play-family therapy. It includes issues that were talked about during Talk Time; highlights of the dynamics of the child's play themes, which may be shared with the parents; and issues that address mindful parenting behaviors.
2. *The Parent Dialogue Meeting Agenda form.* This form summarizes what is going well; the parents' agenda at the beginning of the meeting; relevant child development and family history information; and a check-in on the MC child concerning life at home, at school, and with friends.

The therapist can review these forms before each parent feedback meeting and may make a list of her thoughts relevant to the upcoming meeting. For example, if a child's unhealthy eating habits have been discussed at Talk

Time, she can write on the agenda, "Discuss the family's eating habits." Or, if a grandparent's ailing health was mentioned initially as a concern but has not recently come up, the therapist may want to check in later about any changes in that situation. The agenda can also include asking parents if they have any complaints or concerns about the therapy or the therapist. Addressing the parent-therapist relationship can clarify misunderstandings and help the parents to understand the process.

There is no set order for the dialogue meeting. Sometimes the therapist starts by briefly sharing with the parents her observations of the significance of the child's play in the playroom, and what she is learning from it. Parents are curious about this. The therapist gives the parents feedback about how the child's play is progressing, including discussion of the themes that are emerging as relevant during the child's playtime. The therapist does not share the actual content of the child's play, but rather the meaning of the patterns of the play as it is revealed through metaphors.

Normal Child Development Issues

Most first-time parents have had little or no experience with infants, babies, and young children. Experience with the children of relatives or friends, although helpful, does not usually bring up the same issues as raising one's own child.

It is the therapist's responsibility to be aware of the normal development of babies, children, and teens, both in the culture of residence and in the cultures of the families of origin. During parent meetings, the therapist gives advice on normal development. At the same time, she is learning about the family's values; she needs to understand and respect family standards.

The therapist bases her advice on what is appropriate to the age and developmental stage of the particular child. Her opinion is based on her years of experience and the experience of her supervisor as well as graduate and postgraduate training in child development, and it is worth sharing with the family. The parent dialogues are not intended to be controlling. The therapist does not dictate what parents should do but rather offers suggestions with a back-and-forth discussion until her advice matches the parents' style. Generally, when there is a disagreement in dialogue with the parents, the therapist listens to their thoughts about how to implement parenting ideas in their unique household, and she adapts her suggestions so that they take a form that makes sense to the parents. They try out what was discussed, and learn to trust their own observations and intuitions.

Of course, the therapist is aware of and upholds standards for parental behavior that are dictated by law. In addition, she can share her own values, which are based on principles of child development. For example, if a child is watching too many hours of TV or spending excessive time using electronic games, or if it seems to her that a child's developmental needs for individuation are not being honored, then she expresses her concern. She may offer supporting evidence from research and from her experience in working with similar issues. For example, Brown (2009) mentions the "dark side of play," which he does not define as play per se. He is concerned about the amount of screen time children are getting with videos and particularly with addictions that are developing in all ages. He is concerned about the deep psychogical needs. "Many of those who are addicted to computer gaming are those who don't feel comfortable meeting life's varied and ambiguous challenges" (p. 187). If children are sitting this much Brown notes, they do not even feel the tug of gravity in the body. What are the long-term consequences of this?

After she has offered this information, her responsibility regarding the problem under discussion ends for the moment—provided that the actions of the parents do not constitute abuse. If the parents' own approach continues to be unhelpful, they will often acknowledge it later on, and they may then be more open to the suggestions of the therapist, who can patiently repeat her recommendations. On the other hand, through the dialogue, the therapist may learn that the cultural heritage of the family collides with some aspect of her advice. In this case, together they can define healthy parenting behaviors that are compatible with the parents' mores. Acceptance of disagreement, which may occasionally happen, is an important quality of parent dialogue meetings. It serves as a model of healthy relating when there are couple differences. For more information on this topic, see chapter 8.

Awareness of Cultural Diversity

The therapist needs to be aware of cultural differences in child rearing practices. Before beginning to work with a family from an ethnic group unfamiliar to her, it is helpful if she informs herself about their practices. One way she can do so is by reading the corresponding chapter in the book *Ethnicity and Family Therapy* (McGoldrick, Giordano, & Garcia-Preto, 2005). Using such a reference may prompt the therapist to address a situation in a way that is completely different from what she is accustomed to doing. If the family is adjusting from their original culture to a new one, she can help the parents move toward a balanced integration. This is best accomplished when the dialogic nature of the meetings is respected; the therapist is listening and learning as well as responding and informing.

When the children in therapy are first-generation immigrants or have been adopted from another country, they may or may not have parents who enrich their lives by nurturing a sense of their heritage. During the therapy, it is beneficial for families to share photographs, objects, and stories from their country of origin. *Cultural Issues in Play Therapy* (Gil & Drewes, 2005) is a valuable resource for enriching the therapist's competence to practice play therapy in a variety of cultures.

In many neighborhoods, children are growing up appreciating various household constellations. They experience families with two moms, two dads, or a mom and a dad. Others have a single-parent mom or dad or grandparents. Some children enter families through birth and adoption. For others, their conception and birth may have involved medical interventions and known or unknown donor parents. The Internet is allowing birth siblings who may never have met to communicate with each other. The therapist can keep books in the waiting room that describe a range of family constellations and convey an appreciation of similarities and differences.

Recommending Books to Parents: Bibliotherapy

Books About Communication and Discipline

The therapist can recommend books to assist the parents. Supplementary reading provides matter for discussion at the parent meetings and, during the first few months of therapy, can be particularly helpful for getting symptom relief for family problems.

Three books have proven especially useful in the areas of communication and discipline. The first is *How To Talk So Kids Will Listen & Listen So Kids Will Talk,* by Adele Faber and Elaine Mazlish (1999). If a parent tells me that she is willing to read only one book, this is the one that I recommend. It describes skills in listening, development of empathy, and reflecting that are excellent for people of all ages. Many people say that this book helped them so much that they went out and bought copies for all of their friends. Many adults tend to become locked into unskillful ways of talking to children unless they have been taught otherwise. Learning and practicing the specific way of talking to children that is described in this book requires a degree of motivation. As with any new skill, it may seem artificial at first, but the rewards are great for those who persevere. Although the Faber and Mazlish book is helpful for any parent–child relationship, it is particularly helpful with children who tend to have oppositional behaviors, children who nag and whine, and with children who, for any number of reasons, have learned not to share much of themselves with their parents. Parents learn to be compassionate, nonintrusive listeners—important skills for mindful parenting.

The second book is *1-2-3 Magic,* by Thomas Phelan (1996). This book provides an excellent framework for helping children with expectations and limit setting, offering simple, concrete, and easy-to-follow advice. Limit setting is a part of everyday life in the parent–child relationship, and it is generally felt to be among the most challenging aspects of parenting.

After reading both books mentioned above, parents have sometimes been confused, thinking that the two books seem to have opposite viewpoints. One is about tuning into a child's feelings, and the other is about limit setting. The truth is that using the ideas from *both* books tends to offer balance in two areas of the parent–child relationship that are challenging parts of everyday parenting: compassion and discipline. An appropriate blend of these two forces allows parents to offer the best environment for the unique temperament and personality of the child to unfold.

The third book that I recommend is *Attachment-Focused Parenting: Effective Strategies to Care for Children,* by Daniel Hughes (2009). Hughes describes a relational style of parenting that separates the child's core sense of self from his problematic behaviors. He uses the acronym "PACE with love" to stand for *playfulness, acceptance, curiosity,* and *empathy* held in the safety of unconditional love (or "PLACE," with the "L" standing for *love*). Multiple examples include intersubjective vignettes and actual dialogue that are well articulated for parents. He describes how such communication allows for cocreating affect and meaning, and, in turn, models these skills so parents can learn to engage their children similarly.

Books About Mindful Parenting

At this point, I would like to mention two books about conscious, mindful parenting: *Parenting From the Inside Out: How a Deeper Self-Understanding Can Help You Raise Children Who Thrive,* by Daniel Siegel and Mary Hartzell (2003) and *Everyday Blessings: The Inner Work of Mindful Parenting,* by Myla and Jon Kabat-Zinn (1997).

In 1983, I completed my master's thesis, titled *The Impact of the Birth of the First Child on the Family Dynamics* (Higgins-Klein, 1983). It is about the unsuspected growth and changes that happen in a couple as they become parents. Welcoming a wanted child into the world is often an essentially joyful experience. However, the event also frequently causes the new parents' unexamined personal issues to come to the surface. These issues derive from emotional formations in the couple's families of origin, in which the family dynamics were, in turn, formed by previous generations, going four or five generations back. Thirty years ago there were few resources that addressed what I call the secret of parenthood, the fact that both the parenting experience and our children themselves have the capacity to "push every button," especially buttons we did not know we had. This new experience confronts us with previously unrecognized anomalies in our own personalities. "Know thyself." We cannot be perfect parents, but, if we follow this ancient maxim, we can learn enough to do the least amount of harm and the greatest amount of good.

When my children were two and four years old, there were many times when I felt overwhelmed. It was then that I decided that my life would have new meaning if I dedicated myself to being the best parent I could be, and to love myself, including what I saw as my failures. Many years later, when both of the books mentioned above became available, I found they resonated deeply with me. While they are more poetic and readable than my thesis, they closely echo the tone of parenting that I have long sought for myself and the families with whom I work. Both books offer the powerful gift of leading parents into their own inner landscapes in order to reflect rather than react. The authors highlight awareness, appreciation of silence, being present in the moment, and seeing our children's oppositional behaviors as teachers when they do push our buttons. I lightheartedly caution parents that, if they read these two books, they will never be the same afterward! Parenting becomes a journey, not a destination.

In *Parenting From the Inside Out* (2003), Siegel and Hartzell remind us that children need us to be fully present in our connecting relations. "Being mindful as a parent means having intention in your actions. With intention you purposefully choose your behavior with your child's emotional well-being in mind" (p. 7). The authors cite brain research as they address the issue of nature and nurture, maintaining that they mutually affect one another. "Experience is biology. How we treat our children changes who they are and how they will develop. Their brains need parental involvement. Nature needs nurture" (p. 34). We are reminded that children learn more from watching how their parents live than from what their parents say. And for children who have had traumatic, stressful experiences, the authors explain that memory can be affected with an impact on areas of emotional relating, social life, attunement, and attachment behaviors.

Siegel and Hartzell's research also affirms the value of play in the development of the brain. They explain how children use pretend play to comprehend and define themselves and the world. "By creating scenarios of imagined and lived experiences, they are able to practice new skills and assimilate the complex emotional understandings of the social worlds in which they live. Creating stories through play, and presumably through our dreams, may be ways in which the mind attempts to 'make sense' of our experiences and consolidates this understanding into a picture of ourselves in the world" (p. 36).

Critical to the mindful parenting process and to the play-family therapy experience is that parents commit to looking at their own side of the equation in relational interactions; this helps to avoid scapegoating a child. The process of self-reflection ideally leads the parent to remember how he was parented, to gain insight from the past about what is happening in the present. "How you make sense of your childhood experiences has a profound effect on how you parent your own children. . . . Understanding more about yourself in a deeper way can help you build a more effective and enjoyable relationship with your children" (p. 1). The authors warn parents of the consequences of truncating their own development by being unwilling to examine their own hidden problems. "People who remain in the dark about the origins of their behaviors and intense emotional responses are unaware of their unresolved issues and the parental ambivalence they create" (p. 28).

In *Everyday Blessings* (1997), Myla and Jon Kabat-Zinn write about striving to keep the heart more open and the mind more clear. These efforts enable us to see our children more authentically and to accept who they are. When difficult moments arise and we are not happy with our own mindless or sometimes destructive responses to our children, we do not give up. We are committed to parenting, including the "imminent uncertainty" that is part of living with "the full catastrophe" (p. 90). Referring to our children as "live-in" teachers, the authors remind us that there are "endless moments of wonder and bliss and opportunities for the deepest feelings of connectedness and love" (p. 23). They also highlight the challenging side, where parents find themselves to be so vulnerable. "They will also, in all likelihood, push all our buttons, evoke all our insecurities, test all our limits and boundaries, and touch all the places in us where we fear to tread and feel inadequate or worse" (p. 23). In the process, if we are willing to attend carefully to the full spectrum of what we are experiencing, they will remind us over and over again of what is most important in life, including its mystery.

The Kabat-Zinns' counsel is to live attuned to our children, in moment-to-moment, nonjudgmental awareness. They share beautiful stories and many concrete examples. Chapter 10, "The River of Buried Grief," is especially moving. But this is not a how-to book, for the authors are humble enough to know that readers have their own life experiences from which to draw wisdom. They remind us that it is never too late to heal. Start now.

It is valuable for the therapist to glean the wisdom of these books and to incorporate it into the dialogue with parents.

The Dialogue: Relational Dynamics

During the monthly parent meeting, the therapist reviews with the parents relational dynamics and problems that have come up during past Talk Time sessions. The parent and the therapist may expand on concerns that would not have been appropriate to discuss in front of the child. The therapist's discretion offers families a model for appropriate ways to maintain good boundaries with their children about certain topics. For example, a therapist may find herself working with a child who is getting in trouble, at home or at school, for lying. The therapist may have observed in the family meetings that the parents avoid or hide inconvenient facts, or that they tell little, seemingly justifiable lies. The parent feedback meeting is an appropriate time for her to share these observations. Children often complain about such behavior and are confused by it. Parents may not be aware of the extent to which they make things up, but, when they look back at their families of origin, they may be able to see the roots of this behavior. With regularly scheduled sessions, parents are engaged and informed and fewer families end treatment prematurely.

Attentive parents usually bring to the parent feedback sessions specific questions about the child's progress at home or at school. It can be helpful to ask the parents for concrete examples of recent, relevant incidents *between* the parents and their children. How did they handle the situations? What did they like about how they responded? What do they wish they had done differently? The therapist focuses on the quality of the transactions, using concrete examples that happen in everyday life. Her intention is to provide a structure for addressing problems so that when the therapy ends, the parents are confident about their communication and problem solving skills. If they are not already approaching the challenging task of child rearing from a basis of compassion and awareness, do they now want to accept the invitation to practice mindful parenting? Are they willing to get to the root causes and understand their part of the family relational dynamics, which may go back to their own childhood pain? Can they try to understand their child's point of view even when it seems crazy and irrational? Can they explore alternatives and make compromises for relational fairness? Parents may be unconsciously projecting onto their children the same emotional burdens that their parents unconsciously displaced onto them. "Many parents show distortions in their ability to cope with stress as the result of their own traumatic experiences" (Lieberman & Van Horn, 2008, p. 22). It is important to take time to slow down the process so that the parents can be in touch with their own experiences of these issues. The therapist's sensitive, mindful presence is helpful in this.

Mindful Parenting and How the Brain Works

The parent dialogue meeting is about steadily engaging the parents' experiences of, and attitudes toward, the very personal and intimate journey of raising healthy children. An important component of mindful parenting meetings is offering a research-based understanding of how the brain functions in relation to the experience of therapy. Parents benefit from understanding that deep healing depends on neural change, and that such change happens over time, in small increments. It is also useful that they see that negative behavior is not completely voluntary, but is strongly influenced by traumatic damage to neural networks. The constructive response is not in blaming either child or parent, but rather in patient attention. Abuse and neglect cause improper brain development, make attachment difficult, and give rise to behavioral problems. Parents should not take personally the resulting relational problems with their child.

In *Being a Brain-Wise Therapist: A Practical Guide to Interpersonal Neurobiology* (2008), Bonnie Badenoch offers us a major resource for finding simple language for describing to parents the neural healing that is possible. Badenoch notes that when clients feel heard, neural integration occurs by supporting "linkages between the middle prefrontal and limbic circuits in the right hemisphere" (p. 117). The verbal exchange paves the way for deeper connection to the family. Badenoch states that empathic discussion about the brain can actually begin to bring neural integration.

Spontaneous play therapy offers the potential for deep healing of past trauma. Play therapy and sandplay by nature offer the optimal grounding for attunement between child and therapist. In micro-moments, the relational experience balances the right and left brain, and it is helpful for therapists to find ways to communicate this to parents. In the process whereby a child or adult connects to early trauma in play, Badenoch states, "there may be a sense of delicate tenderness, often feeling almost sacred, that can only be honored by quiet joining" (2008, p. 224). In the mystery of play though, this can contrast with "a robust story . . . around armed clashes or dinosaur wars. Always following our patients lead, we can become collaborators in the unfolding process" (p. 224). Badenoch notes that children use sandplay with less defensiveness and self-consciousness than do adults, and that it helps them to benefit in "self-regulation and emotional release" (p. 226). "Sandplay demonstrates a remarkable ability to pull the brain together" (p. 233). As parents understand how this process works, and as they see changes in their children when the family engages the whole experience of therapy, it reduces their "magic mystery" misunderstanding of play therapy and helps families to stay committed.

Therapy for Parents

Mindful parenting meetings have the capacity to foster significant change. This is especially true when the child experiences the team efforts of his parents and his therapist. For example, the frequent complaints of one rather oppositional child about coming to therapy may have related to the parents' ambivalence. Once they examined their own resistance and became clearly committed to the therapy process, their son's therapy deepened and there was a notable shift into more meaningful play.

Parents can have very concrete problems that continually present obstacles to healthy parenting. For example, they may find themselves reverting to techniques their parents used, which they may see are ineffective but feel powerless to change. Or a parent may defend his own parents, insisting that certain techniques were effective. This parent may say, "My parents did it this way and it worked for me," while the spouse disagrees, holding that they are not beneficial transactions with the children. Parents may not be able to give reflexive responses to their children, even after repeated intersubjective coaching from the therapist. Mindful parenting meetings are an essential means to understand these deeper family dynamics and to foster change.

When parents' relationship patterns with their children remain stuck after working in this model for a while, it is important to understand the causes and to assess repeated blocks in the parents' own behaviors. Sometimes, unresolved issues that are impacting current family problems can span back generations. If parent education and an understanding of relational dynamics are not giving the family the skills and competence they need, the therapist may recommend either couples therapy, intergenerational therapy, or individual (systems, psychodynamic) therapy for one or both parents. Therapy penetrates far more intimately than does mindful parent education, so it is important that a decision about adult therapy be a conscious choice for the parents rather than an unconsidered reflex. Such decisions respectfully place the responsibility for the child's progress into the hands of the parents.

Family Secrets

Sometimes the couple cannot succeed in their parenting because their marriage relationship is in too much pain. This may manifest as overtly hostile behavior or as denial or avoidance of issues that are critical within the couple relationship. These emotional situations may be grounded in unexamined or unrecognized family secrets that the parents have not shared with the children, or perhaps even with each other. The children may actually have some degree of awareness of these issues. Although there can be some private matters that should not be shared with children, at least not until they have reached a suitable age, many family secrets cause shame that can begin to heal by their being brought out in the open. A main point for the therapist to make here is that such a secret can indeed be connected to a chronic, seemingly unresolvable problem with a child or teen.

There is a wide range of family secrets that can cause confusion for children. Examples are chronic or acute depression, anxiety, or mental illness in one of the parents; the truth of parental paternity; a parent's struggle with an addiction; physical or sexual abuse; a criminal history; or behaviors or events in the family history that members hold as shameful. When it is appropriate to share some of the content of these secrets with children or teens, this honesty can have a positive impact on the parent–child relationship. Despite such honesty, addressing these sorts of issues with the children may not be very effective if the parents continue to feel burdened by their own emotions without getting help for themselves. Offering individual therapy to one or both parents can ultimately have a positive outcome for all of the children as well as the adults.

Disclosure of secrets should not be attempted lightly, and there should be good clinical reason for doing so. Preparation to uncover some family secrets may take months of therapy work, as well as weeks of discussion about the best way to tell children or teens the information. Often parents will say, "How can something the child doesn't know be part of his repeated negative behavior?" This is a good question, and it is not so easy to answer. It has to do with the power a secret has when it is embedded over time in relationships. The case material at the end of this chapter presents a powerful illustration of the impact of a secret on several generations.

Sometimes the secret is not a secret. A child may have discovered it from a relative, or overheard it in the heat of a parent argument, or seen it in a legal document or a news article. A child may have inadvertently become aware of a parental affair, and he may be afraid to tell his parents that he knows the truth. The consequences of the child's guarding the secret, or of simply carrying the myths surrounding a secret, can include the growth of mistrust, which the child may manifest in many emotional and behavioral ways. At other times, a secret may remain in the child's preconscious mind: He suspects something and may even guess it, or when told, he will say that he is not surprised. A critical point here is that the secret can indeed be connected to a chronic, seemingly unresolvable problem with a child or teen, and it deserves attention.

There is often shame attached to a secret, especially when it remains unacknowledged. Shame itself has energy, which has impact on all the relationships it touches. However, before counseling parents to reveal secrets, the therapist is advised to consult a supervisor when there is a question of discerning the difference between privacy, which can remain confidential, and secrecy, which may be shared. When revealing information of this nature with children, the parent remains in control of which material gets disclosed. The therapist can help guide the process to suit what is developmentally appropriate for the child. The parent may choose to say only a sentence or two now and postpone further disclosure until the child is older. A parent can certainly share selectively with a little child and say more to a teenager. It is often better to reveal information of this nature in small doses, like an inoculation. Telling the truth of secrets gradually as children grow up, and completing the information while children are still living at home, avoids the jarring experience of their moving out of the house and then finding out something that would have been better assimilated with the daily availability of the parents. There is much more to be said about secrets, and I recommend two books on the subject: *Family Secrets: The Path to Self-Acceptance and Reunion* by John Bradshaw (1995) and *Family Matters: Healing in the Heart of the Family* by Daniel Gottlieb and Edward Claflin (1991).

A CASE STUDY*

As part of our mentoring program at the Family & Play Therapy Center, I supervised a therapist who was working with a couple with two children. The MC child was the younger of their two daughters, Effie, an eight-year-old third grader. The parents said that she had been very challenging at home since the age of two. During second grade the previous year, her school had reported concern about her oppositional behaviors. She was perceived as arrogant and uncooperative with the teachers, and although she did have two friends in her class, Effie was occasionally being scapegoated by her peers. The father, Nikos, was a second-generation Greek American. The mother,

---

*This case study combines two family stories of secrets held about adoption.

Anna, had been adopted as a baby into a first-generation Italian American family. Anna was her parents' only child. They withheld from her the fact that she was adopted. In fact, even when she was 18, her parents denied it, despite the fact that Anna had been told the truth by a great aunt who was dying. The young parents now seeking therapy had met in their late 20s while traveling in Europe. They chose to live in Philadelphia because they were both able to find employment in their respective professions. They were very distressed by their daughter's behaviors and felt powerless to correct them. Both parents seemed to have a strong need that the girl be identified as the problem child.

Effie responded well to play therapy. She especially enjoyed creating elaborate sandtray stories. The parents took turns bringing her to weekly sessions, and each attended diligently to the school complaints as well as to Effie's problems at home with her parents and sibling. She would have periods of equilibrium followed by mischievous behavior that would cause her parents to feel quite disturbed. The parents decided to stop therapy because, after a year of weekly sessions and monthly parent meetings, there was a reduction in Effie's symptoms, improvement of her behavior, and better communication between her and her parents. However, the parents still had minimal insight into either how their personal backgrounds influenced their reactions to their daughter or how intergenerational histories laid the ground for her emotional situation.

The parents called again in six months requesting to continue the therapy, and a similar pattern was repeated. Although the therapist again suggested that they have their own therapy, they resisted. A second year went by, and once again, when they felt enough equilibrium, they chose to stop therapy. Root-level issues were still not addressed.

By the time Effie was in fifth grade, the parents finally agreed to engage in couples therapy with me, while Effie resumed her play-family therapy with my postgraduate supervisee. In the couple sessions, I invited exploration of Anna's disconnection from her roots and her feelings of split loyalty. She wanted to know the truth about her own adoption, but felt it would be disloyal to confront her alcoholic parents, who continued to deny the truth. Anna had a memory of sneaking into the attic when she was a teen and of finding her adoption papers. She was scared and never told her parents. Because her parents told her that she was not indeed adopted, part of Anna still doubted the veracity of her experience. We discussed that Anna did not owe loyalty to her parents on this issue as what they are asking (overtly or covertly) harmed her own growth and development. Anna began to have insight that her own emotional impasse could cause her to project her anger onto her daughter. It could also be the source of the imbalance that led to her daughter's inappropriate emotional power in the family. Nikos was very supportive of the possibility that Anna would talk to her parents. He himself began to explore issues in his own family of origin.

However, after six months of therapy, Anna did not want to invite her parents in for a meeting, nor was she ready to broach the subject with her parents outside of our sessions. Therapists need to respect the client's timing. To both the supervisee and me, it seemed that this big intergenerational secret kept the family stuck.

My supervisee reported that Effie, now 11, was doing quite well expressing herself during both the Talk Time and the individual play therapy sessions. During this time, Effie provoked a fight on the school bus, got into big trouble at school, and was suspended. The parents were frustrated, yet admitted that they were having difficulty changing some of their own destructive behaviors that they were addressing in couples therapy, such as calling the children names and belittling both of them when they were angry.

Often children who are acting out like this at school will also be oppositional during play-family therapy. However, Effie seemed to cooperate. She expressed herself particularly well in sand stories and during family sessions. In many ways, she was also developing quite positively: She was doing well at school academically, feeling comfortable with a small group of girlfriends, and competent in her gymnastics class.

During this time, Anna suddenly received a surprise phone call from her unknown birth brother. She learned that her birth mother had been trying to find her for many years. Anna was shocked by this call and still felt confusion and uncertainty. She used her therapy sessions to address her guilt and to help her figure out how to approach her depressed parents and tell them what had happened. They begrudgingly admitted the truth, at last. Anna felt elated and was finally able to reveal to her children her long held secret. Eventually the nuclear family of Anna, Nikos, and the two children met Anna's birth family, and there was real rejoicing. It took another year for Anna's adoptive parents to be willing to discuss the truth at more length with her. In her therapy, Anna worked on her feelings of split loyalty.

Together with celebratory feelings, this explosion of the secret initially brought temporary disequilibrium to the nuclear family. The status quo was shaken, and, with it, the emotional blockages it had contained were dislodged. The revelations caused related issues that had been previously buried to become apparent. As usually happens when such issues get addressed, the constraints they had engendered eventually become lighter. Relations between Anna and Effie greatly improved. Effie expressed overt excitement about the discovery of her mother's birth mother, and she asked many questions about the process Anna was going through. Nikos was impressed with the positive impact that these events were having on everyone. He chose to come for additional individual sessions in order to work on some early loss trauma in his own family of origin. He invited his mother in for a few family sessions. The couple reported feeling closer together than they had in a long time. After some sessions integrating the truth, Effie no longer needed therapy.

Throughout all of this, a parallel personal process was going on in the play therapist. She herself had been adopted as the youngest child in a large, multiracial family. Supervision included recommendations that she consider exploring her own birth family history. However, for years, she had hesitated to seek out her birth family, even though her adoptive parents were willing to support her doing so. Effie's family provided an inspiration for her. As she watched both the confusion and the joy of this family, she decided to begin her own journey as she began exploring her roots, tracked down her birth parents, and then met both of them. Eventually she met many members of her birth family, just before having a child of her own. Today, her two children have a very large extended family.

It is recommended by all prevalent contemporary therapies, and has long been a basic part of Contextual Therapy, that therapists need to go through their own therapy if they are to relate authentically to the therapy processes of their clients. In this case, the coincidence between the therapist's and the client's histories moved the therapist to address her own unfinished business and to explore unknown parts of her background. This is an example of the healthy reverberation that occurs when we explore our own personal truths. Author and psychiatrist A. C. Robin Skynner addresses this from his own personal viewpoint:

> Certainly I was attracted to the study of psychiatry by a need to find
> a way of dealing with my own problems. And my present interest in
> training mental-health professionals leads me to believe that this is
> not only the usual motivation for taking up such work, consciously or
> unconsciously, but also the best one, provided it leads the professional

to a real, direct, and systematic study of himself rather than a vicarious one through the study of his patients. (Welwood, 1983, p. 19)

In coaching parents in mindful parenting, we are inviting them to become aware of their experiences, their histories, and the inner motivations that are impacting their parenting and, consequently, directly affecting their children. It is essential that the therapist be firmly committed to an awareness of her own personal journey.

8

Weaving It All Together

*Child Development, Mindfulness-Based
Play-Family Therapy, and Parenting*

> In the first three years of life every human being undergoes yet a second birth,
> in which he is born as a psychological being possessing self-hood and separate
> identity. The quality of self an infant achieves in those crucial three years will
> profoundly affect all of his subsequent existence.
>
> —Margaret Mahler et al. (1978, p. 15)

ROOTED IN MARGARET Mahler's theory of separation and individuation, this chapter demonstrates the integration of multiple levels of theory in the practice of Mindfulness-Based Play-Family Therapy (MBPFT). A child's emotional state emerges through the process of his early development, and this process occurs within the environment of the nuclear family and its intergenerational history. Margaret Mahler's work provides a valuable basis for understanding *normal* emotional growth and development; the stages of separation and individuation can serve as a guideline for identifying problems. Understanding the stages can also help families navigate the course of their child's development. Following the sections that present the Mahler stages, the final section addresses attachment issues rooted in the first three years of life.

Within the treatment framework offered by MBPFT, a therapist balances an awareness of multiple levels of emotional elements in the child, his parents, siblings, and the intergenerational family. The sections in this chapter demonstrate how optimal early development may have been lacking for a child who is now coming to therapy at a later age. There is a parallel understanding of the parents' own unworked issues. When the adults use mindful parenting meetings or their own therapy to heal their unresolved problems, children benefit directly. Conversely, when parents are unwilling or unable to confront the difficulties in their own lives that are relevant to their child's issues, it is more likely that the child will develop chronic problems. The therapist can help parents to see how the family lineage is connected to present issues and to encourage choices for optimal growth and development for the whole family.

Mindfulness-Based Play-Family Therapy According to Mahler's Stages of Separation and Individuation

MBPFT for Children With Issues Originating During Awakening and Symbiosis (Birth to Six Months)

Developmental history: Symptoms may have included extended eating or sleeping problems, colic followed by an uneasy baby-mother relationship, or some failure in the baby's learning of eye contact. Situations may have included postpartum depression or unavailability of the parent; prolonged separation during the first six months; or lack of enough tummy time, which can slow down physical development and impact social development during the next stages.

Current symptoms: A child between three and six years of age may come into therapy exhibiting separation or attachment problems. This may be reflected in the child's current passivity or depression. This child may have difficulty finding his voice. He may ask his parent to speak for him and may have difficulty expressing feelings appropriately.

Family therapy/Parent–child dyad: During Talk Time, the child's nonverbal behavior is accepted, although he is gradually encouraged to find his true voice. If the child continues to be mute when the therapist engages him, the parent can gently help by answering for him with her best guess as to what he would want to say. However, the therapist makes eye contact with the child in responding to the parent's words: "Your mom thinks that you really liked having your cousin visit over the weekend. She thinks that was fun for you."

Using a puppet to talk to a shy or self-conscious child during Talk Time is one creative option. Can the child begin to feel comfortable enough to respond with her own puppet?

Play therapy: During the exploring stage of play therapy, this child may use a lot of nonverbal play, including being tactile with the sand in the tray, often without any objects or with just a few. He may explore the texture of the sand for repeated sessions or do a lot of quiet work with paints or clay.

"Being with" this child and offering unconditional presence is recommended. Developing trust between this child and the therapist takes longer than it does for children whose early development was more optimal. Including a trusted parent in the playroom may be helpful. Incorporating eye contact into the play can be a good step toward communication. The child may naturally do this, or the therapist can initiate games that encourage eye contact.

Parent education: The therapist can gently educate the parents about the reverberations of past or present depression within the family. She can seek an understanding, by the parents, of their own separation issues—for example, their fears and anxieties.

A goal is for the parents to acquire optimal attachment styles, together with an appropriate ability to separate. Parents can be coached to help their child develop a "feelings vocabulary" using simple feeling words such as *happy, sad, mad, disappointed,* and *afraid*. Parents can model using feeling words by telling simple stories from their own lives.

Adult therapy: Have the parents worked on their own depression from their past? How does the mother respond to knowing that her postpartum depression may have impacted her child? Can she be compassionate with herself? How has the depression impacted the father? Facing these issues may allow the mother to give to her child in ways that compensate for difficult past circumstances.

How does each parent's experience of separation from his or her own mother compare to what is happening in their relationship to their child? Are the parents able to express feelings well?

MBPFT for Children With Issues Originating During Development of Early Trust (Birth to Six Months)

Developmental history: The baby may have been hard to soothe. The baby's experiences may have included early medical interventions, a difficult delivery, a particularly prolonged hospital stay, or multiple early caregivers. These issues can be part of the history of a child who, on entering therapy at a later age, has current symptoms such as those listed below.

Current symptoms: If the child had early medical interventions, she may present with anxiety, fears, nightmares, frequent somatizing, or difficulty with affect regulation. Where trust has been thwarted, additional symptoms can include unprovoked aggressive behaviors, withdrawal, and difficulty making friends.

Family therapy/Parent–child dyad: At a family play therapy meeting, parents can use sandtray miniatures to tell about the facts and feelings of the child's early trauma. This session is often done with all of the siblings present. Siblings who have witnessed the difficult times of one child benefit from the healing process themselves. Generally, this kind of exercise, called a Trauma Reality Sandtray, happens after a lot of trust has been established and after the parents have begun expressing their feelings in parent meetings.

Play therapy: The child often engages in nonverbal, frequently spontaneous play. She may caress the sand but use few or no objects, or she may fill the sandtray with many pieces in a disorganized manner.

The child may use the medical kit together with repeated verbal and nonverbal themes. She may use play to reenact nightmares and release energies that are trapped in her body. She can release anger energy using the foam bats.

Parent education: Parents benefit from addressing their own feelings regarding their child's medical trauma. Did they work well as a team? Does either parent blame the other for any unfinished business stemming from that time? The therapist and parents can discuss how to model acknowledgment and expression of feelings for the children in the family. The therapist can also help to prepare the parents in advance for the Trauma Reality Sandtray, which invites them to process their own feelings

Adult therapy: After discussing feelings at the parent dialogue meeting, the parents may feel they would benefit from deeper work on the unexpressed fears they carry regarding their child having been so vulnerable as a baby. How did they feel when their baby was difficult to soothe? How may this be impacting their present relationship with the child and with each other? While sharing these feelings in mindful parenting meetings can be healing, deeper attention in couples therapy may benefit all family members. How do the issues arising for each parent relate to how they themselves were parented?

MBPFT for Children With Issues Originating During the Early Practicing Stage (7 to 10 Months)

Developmental history: When the baby was beginning to crawl, his parent may have been overprotective, restraining healthy movement, or underprotective. An overly protective parent worries too much about the baby moving into the crawling stage of development. This parent keeps putting the baby back on her lap and does not encourage pre-crawling behaviors, perhaps because she is not ready to let go. An underprotective parent may not monitor the safety of the newly crawling baby or may not stay sufficiently connected to her. Babies at this stage begin "refueling" by maintaining eye contact as they move away and come back for frequent hugs. These babies begin to learn how to interpret nonverbal body language, especially when the parent stays attentive and responds nonverbally. Mahler noted that when a baby begins to crawl at six months he is not quite ready emotionally, although he may become more so just a month later. It is recommended to hold and cuddle him a bit more, while at the same time appreciating his new movements.

Current symptoms: The overprotected child may develop anxieties or sensory integration issues. If a child feels held back, he may have difficulty trusting new experiences—especially new physical experiences. He may be afraid or awkward at making new friends. The underprotected child may not respect boundaries or may take inappropriate risks. He may develop regulation, attention, or social difficulties. For example, a four-year-old may want to make friends but may be too bossy or too physically "in the face" of other children. The child may be unaware of intruding on other children's boundaries or may not be able to pick up social cues from other children.

Family therapy/Parent–child dyad: During Talk Time, the therapist, parent, and child may discuss one issue that made the child anxious that week and then role play how to handle it in a new way. They may each take turns in different roles. If the child is hesitant, the therapist can role play with the parent alone. After observing, the child will often join in. Role playing is a very effective modality. It offers concrete ways to change behavior. It is practiced during Talk Time so that the child can experience the change.

Play therapy: The child may express themes in dollhouse play, with puppets or "pretend" stories. A child with anxiety frequently responds well to wet sand, which can be calming. However, some anxious children do not like the feeling of wet sand.

A child who felt restrained may have difficulty being spontaneous in the playroom. His play themes, which may be limited, may include scenarios of being forced to comply to uncomfortable or surprising demands.

Many children who need more than the usual limits may create enclosed spaces in their play themes, using objects like tents or blocks to develop boundaries.

Parent education: The therapist helps the parents to respond to their child's risk taking in a way that balances her need for safety with freedom that is developmentally appropriate. It is important that the parents accept their child's anxieties in a loving way, and, at the same time, encourage him to confront mild anxieties by trying new experiences.

It is helpful for the child's brain development that he be engaged in regular physical activity, such as martial arts, gymnastics, trampoline jumping, or team sports. In some cases, it may be best to refer the child for sensory integration (a field of occupational therapy) to address bodily issues of regulation and attention.

Adult therapy: When a child presents with anxieties, it is very likely that one or both parents are suffering from their own chronic anxieties. In order for the child to get the best help, it is necessary for the anxious parent to do root-level work, particularly by exploring what happened in her own parent–child experience when she was the same age as the child is now. Parents often have difficulty making these connections or choosing to work on them. However, when parents rework their own issues of anxiety, there is immediate benefit, and it helps to reduce the child's anxiety throughout his lifetime.

MBPFT for Children With Issues Originating During Development of Object Constancy and Early Practicing (7 to 10 Months)

Developmental history: At approximately eight months, the baby begins to know that the parent exists when she is not right there with him. At this point, he may express his complaint by bursting into tears even when he is left with a familiar caregiver or when he awakens at night and thinks, "Come here, I now know you exist." Although there is short-term inconvenience when the baby cries, the eight-month-old has the capacity, given proper compassionate support, to tolerate this moderate frustration. The experience facilitates the development of trust, and helps prevent future separation problems. It is important that the parent not slip out unseen in order to avoid the discomfort of this experience. It is equally important that the child's crying, which results from his parent's direct goodbye, be kindly and patiently accepted by the caregiver. In the long run, the development of trust outweighs the short-term relief gained by distracting the child as the parent sneaks out.

Perhaps when the child began to crawl away from a parent or primary caregiver, she was unwittingly shamed by these adults. Perhaps they continually ignored her, or overreacted negatively to the overtures she extended when she returned to their lap for reassurance and praise. Maybe the parent returned to work abruptly, leaving the child in a strange environment with an unfamiliar caregiver. At the object constancy stage, it is ideal for the baby to experience the gradual increase of the parent's absence rather than abrupt, long absences. This stage can be particularly challenging for a baby who has joined the family through adoption or foster care.

Current symptoms: The presenting child may have acute or chronic difficulty separating from his parent. A six-year-old child may suddenly have begun to show resentment when a parent, who has traveled regularly, is packing her bags. A seven-year-old may be having problems making friends; fear of separation from his parent is interfering with his social development. A nine-year-old may worry that a parent will disappear, or that he himself will be kidnapped. An eleven-year-old girl may begin to feel shame about her body developing earlier than her friends' bodies. Other themes of shame or abandonment may be present in the child's daytime worries or dreams. Whatever the age, earlier issues may be triggered, even though the associated body memories from the first three years of life, may not be consciously remembered.

Family therapy/Parent–child dyad: The therapist may bring play materials, such as dollhouse people and props, into Talk Time. The parent can watch or take a role in the child's play as the therapist coaches the parent. For example, the child can be guided to enact his fear of riding the school bus. The therapist helps the child use the props to gradually show his own perceptions of the scary situation. As the child reveals this fear, the adults let him know that they really understand the fear, even though they themselves are not afraid of riding a bus. It is important for the child to hear that aspects of his fears have a sound basis in reality. The school bus ride can be scary for a child. Checking the reality of what is actually happening on the bus is important.

The therapist can introduce a game that indicates how much of the child's separation anxiety may be parent driven. In one such game, he uses a big cube, its opening covered with blankets. The parent sits inside while singing a lullaby and rocking the child—even an older child if he is willing. The therapist watches to see what happens after the singing and holding are done. Often the child will leave the tent and play happily without attending to the mother, who has stayed in the tent. After the child has played for a while, the therapist may ask, "Do you think your mom disappeared?" A child who is carrying anxiety may not be sure and go back to the tent to check. Sometimes the child will engage the playroom only after the mother has left the tent with him. This game is a good tool for diagnosing and re-working problems that occurred when the child was nine months old, at the beginning of the object constancy phase.

A child with shame (for instance, a seven-year-old child who consistently has soiling stains on her underwear) can benefit from knowing that the therapist knows of his problems and understands his difficulty, and also that his parents have discussed the problem with the therapist. It can be helpful to allow the child to hear the parent and therapist discuss the issue briefly, but at first he should not be required to participate. As the child becomes less self-critical and more trusting, he ideally learns that it can be helpful to discuss such problems, despite some discomfort.

Play therapy: When there is difficulty separating from the parent, the parent is initially included in the playroom. Filial therapy or Greenspan's Floortime can be helpful in incorporating the parent in the play. Once a child is secure enough to separate from the parent during playtime, the therapist gradually implements a desensitization process until the parent can stay in the waiting room. This may take weeks or months.

Usually, the earlier the problem developed, the longer it takes to heal. Frequent hide-and-seek or burying and unburying games may be played. Children often find creative ways to play hide-and-seek by themselves or with the therapist, sometimes using objects. Frequent repetition of these games answers an earlier developmental need to understand that things seem to disappear but then return.

Blowing bubbles is a soothing game for children who suffer from separation issues. The child can control the popping of the bubbles and make them disappear. Then he can create new bubbles.

The child's anxieties may play out in themes of feeding and nurturing, or of rejecting dolls or stuffed animals. Dollhouse play may be used to express these themes. The child who has entered a family at an older age may have a special need to play out themes of feeling "stolen"—his way of expressing the confusion of moving, often abruptly, from one environment to another.

Children may use animals or puppets to express present issues of shame, projecting these feelings through their metaphoric stories.

Parent education: Through dialogue at mindful parenting meetings, parents can learn to appreciate the importance of separation and individuation. They can learn how, if the child continues to live with too much fear, he will suffer a depletion of emotional energy that will impede normal development, including a disruption of his social life. Work on parental boundaries includes learning to accept that the child may have opinions that differ from those of his parents, and even to welcome those opinions.

Children need parents who help them to tolerate the pains and frustrations of life by offering comfort during difficult times, rather than by always trying to make everything okay. Parents need to accept that their job is not to prevent normal hurts and challenges from happening. Of course, it is important for parents to do their best not to expose children to situations that are intrinsically harmful. For instance, children may ask to see movies or TV shows, electronic games, or books that will scare them or cause disturbances. Parents need to take charge of these decisions and protect children from situations that are not appropriate for their level of development.

The therapist may recommend regular one-to-one play dates with compatible children, ideally in alternating homes. Arranging for children to play with friends outside of school time can be challenging for busy families, but it is a valuable means of supporting the child's ability to make friends and to trust the outside world. When the child resists visiting friends' homes, parents can introduce this slowly by accompanying the child and staying for the first hour, gradually reducing the parent's transition time.

Adult therapy: If the child's temperament is the opposite of the parent's and this is causing conflict, individual therapy for the parent can help him or her to differentiate from the child. Sometimes the child resembles the parent's own sibling or parent. This perceived similarity may be at the root of the client child's separation and individuation problems. Having parents do their own personal work can help ease the parent–child relationship through the middle and teen years as well as the early years.

Therapy may include compassionately addressing the myth that the parent should be able to shield the child from painful experiences. When parents try too hard to do this, it can be suffocating for the child. If the parent continues to be fearful and gives conscious or unconscious messages of fear to the child, then it is recommended that she initiate individual therapy to investigate her own anxiety. Adult therapy can also include addressing how the same dynamic that is manifesting in the child (e.g., separation anxiety, shame) may have operated in the parents' own childhood experiences, as well as how the couple is handling their differences in the present time.

MBPFT for Children With Issues Originating During the Later Practicing Stage (10 to 18 Months)

Developmental history: As a toddler, the child may not have learned sufficient frustration tolerance in matters of safety and danger. He may have had too much power. He may have tried overly dangerous feats, perhaps in part because he did not receive adequate parental limits. On the other hand, the parent may have restrained the child from learning physically challenging tasks because of her own fears. The child may have been confused if his parents disagreed with each other about safety and danger issues.

For example, by 11 to 16 months, a toddler can usually be taught to climb backward down steps as the caregiver spots him. Gates are helpful for safety. Neglecting to install a gate, with the risk that the child might fall down the steps, may mean that the parent is "too loose" in addressing safety boundaries. By contrast, always using a gate and being afraid to guide a child down the steps may indicate that the parent is "too tight." When the parent is not skillful enough in matching assurance of safety with the child's immense need to explore her environment, the consequences for the child may include sensory integration problems.

Future problems can also arise from this stage when a parent has been either extremely unavailable, inconsistently available, or overly protective. Significant life experiences occur during this stage as the baby learns to regulate his affective responses to parents and caregivers. Parental responses have a direct impact on the development of the toddler's attachment and personality. A baby who is too subdued may not be having enough experience with affect regulation, whereas a baby who is habitually stressed may be unable to regulate his responses. To minimize development of unhealthy narcissism in later life, he needs to learn that the world is "not just my oyster." The continuing development of healthy affect regulation is an important part of the parent–child relationship. In a reliable environment, a child normally surpasses the previous stage in his independence from the parent. As he advances through new territory, he checks back through eye contact. The best development of affect regulation occurs when parents are consistently available for this dance of separation and reunion. The propensity for shame carries over from earlier practicing to this later practicing stage.

Current symptoms: The child coming to therapy may present with "spoiled child" behaviors. He may be whiny and exhibit anxious attachment or he may exhibit difficulty modulating sadness and disappointment. He may act bossy with peers; he may hit his parents; he may need a lot of help with boundaries and limit setting, or he may continually try overly dangerous feats despite established limits.

On the other hand, the child may be overly responsible and relate better to adults and older or younger children than to her peers. Sometimes, even though the child's energy is being drained by adult concerns or worries, he may appear to like this role, and the family may not be aware of what it is costing him in normal growth and development. They may notice that the child just does not seem happy or that he is exhibiting "high-maintenance" behaviors.

A child who is unduly fearful of challenges that are actually age appropriate may have had problems during a previous stage. A parent's mixed message may take on an enmeshed quality by unwittingly encouraging even dangerous behaviors that are not age appropriate. It can lead the child to suffer from low self-esteem and sometimes social, emotional, and cognitive delays. Many children who developed problems during the early stages of physical exploring may come to exhibit difficulties with sensory integration when they reach 5 or even 10 years of age. Among other signs, the child may exhibit tactile defensiveness, clumsiness in large and small motor control, or body image issues. A child's lack of sensory integration can contribute to the development of social problems.

Family therapy/Parent–child dyad: Talk Time sessions can focus on one area that has been a problem during the preceding week. The process slows down and attention is given to understanding the child's viewpoint. Efforts may be made at seeing the wisdom inherent in the problem—how it functions to help the child or the family. The therapist may empathize with the child's viewpoint before supporting the parents' larger responsibility to watch over the safety and normal growth and development of the child. She can assist the parents in helping the child tolerate the normal frustrations of life. She can also support the parents in gradually taking back appropriate parental authority when a child has been too bossy or has been allowed to make decisions that the adults should be making (e.g., when a young child has been allowed to choose his own bedtime in a way that creates havoc for him and for the rest of the family).

Recommended techniques include using behavior charts and role playing specific boundaries. The therapist may help the child and parents change their behaviors when there are expectations that the child be responsible in ways that are more appropriate for an older child. This can reduce the energies a child is using nonproductively and allow him freedom for more spontaneous playing.

Play therapy: The child may push physical limits in the playroom, for example, by throwing objects toward lights or windows. He may try gymnastics that could hurt him. The therapist must set clear limits for safety. The child may safely choose to play with the "danger" toys (knives, swords, guns, monsters), creating high-risk scenarios that will help him express confused feelings. He may create games relating to fires, safety, or heroes saving victims. He may create elaborate sand stories. One technique the therapist can use is to playfully mirror the child's bossiness.

All play sessions are concerned with the optimal development of the child's self-esteem. The child's play may be very distracted and unfocused. He may move from one area of the room to the next and have difficulty settling into one form of play to work more deeply. The more anxious or self-conscious he is, the less coherent his play themes or sand pictures may be. He may be unable to tell a cohesive story. He may benefit from having the play session divided into halves, one using spontaneous play and the other using a directed play therapy approach that concentrates on helping him develop play themes with a beginning, middle, and end. Puppets can be helpful; puppet play may give a voice to the "stuckness" that the child is expressing in his play. Since spontaneous play is often the most direct way to heal trauma, the directed approach may be best practiced after the child has faced the powerlessness associated with the trauma.

A child who is more shy and self-conscious, or who is physically awkward, may need help taking risks in the playroom during the exploratory stage. At the same time, it can be beneficial for the therapist to be patient with a more withholding child, and to wait for him to find his own ways to make choices. For a child with either a bossy or a withdrawn stance in the world, one goal of play therapy is to build self-esteem and confidence so that he is grounded in experiencing himself as an authentic person. A child will often create spontaneous stories in pretend that are about his sadness or disappointment. This play helps him to externalize these feelings and heal.

Parent education: Parent education works toward the goal of unconditional acceptance of the core of the child. At the same time, it helps parents realize that they can love their child while setting limits on his negative behaviors.

While acknowledging the value of the child's willingness to take responsibility, the therapist can coach the parents when their limit setting does not match the child's stage of development. She may encourage parents to give clear messages regarding hitting, poking, throwing things, or other socially obnoxious behaviors. Tolerating such behaviors continues to give the child inappropriate power. The therapist can discuss with the parents how the display of such behaviors with peers can damage the child's friendships.

When the child is exhibiting additional issues—for example, those related to ADHD or Asperger's—parents may need further supportive coaching during parent feedback meetings. It is recommended that the parents be given a checklist to identify whether the child should be referred for a sensory integration evaluation. They can fill out the questionnaire at home. If there are patterns of sensory integration problems, then the child can be referred to an SI therapist once there is a sufficient reduction of his pressing emotional and behavioral symptoms.

Adult therapy: Sometimes couples need more than parent education to explore repeated differences in their parenting habits. They may have been raised with very different parenting styles. Helping parents to "get on the same page" in regard to setting limits for their children is very important. Within the format of couple or individual therapy, parents can explore how their life issues are rooted in how each was parented. This crucial work is often the missing element when parents find themselves unable to sustain the positive changes they want to make in how they respond to their children.

Sharing with each other the pains and traumas of their own early lives can open parents up to ways they may be projecting their own experiences in a harmful way onto their children. Exploring root-level issues can greatly enhance their self-esteem and their competence as parents. They may benefit from describing to one another how issues of safety and danger were handled in their respective families of origin. Did they feel ignored or attended to? Reworking these experiences as a couple can have great benefit for their primary adult relationship, and this in turn will have a positive effect on their children.

MBPFT for Children With Issues Originating During Rapprochement (18 to 36 Months)

Developmental history: Affect regulation problems in the client child at an older age may relate back to traumatic events that happened to the child or in the family during his rapprochement stage; for example, a near drowning, medical trauma, the death or loss of a significant caregiver, having multiple caregivers, witnessing violence, or divorce.

Besides being competent and delightful, children from the age of 18 months to three years usually have occasional—or even regular—temper tantrums. Tantrums enable the child to understand and hold the knowledge that the parent who loves him is also the parent who gets angry with him. Likewise, the child begins to understand, "The parent I'm so angry with, I also love." This is an essential emotional developmental task for the toddler to achieve, and it is in this arena that the child learns affect regulation.

Parents may distract or give in to a frustrated child so much that the child skips over the stage of having normal, healthy tantrums. If a child has bypassed this stage at age two, his tantrums as a three-year-old are usually longer and more intense. If he comes to therapy, he will need help with affect regulation. On the other hand, the parent may have isolated the two-and-a-half-year-old during tantrums, perhaps making it more difficult for the child to feel warm attachment. In this case, he may not trust that his parent accepts both his unpleasant behavior and his loving behavior. Sometimes parents fail to be both firm and kind when setting needed limits, and this can lead to manipulative behaviors on the part of the child.

Clinical experience suggests that many families who come to therapy because of the oppositional behavior of a child 4 to 10 years old, or even older, may find that the child did not adequately negotiate the rapprochement stage of development. Understanding the significance of this bypass is crucial to helping such a family. If earlier stages were not optimally experienced, then this stage will be that much more challenging. The issues from the earlier "missed" development will need to be addressed as well.

Many fears develop during this phase, and in a "good-enough" environment the parent helps the child through his fears. However, if life circumstances are traumatic, or if parents are too enmeshed with or too disengaged from the child, prolonged fears may be generated. They can resurface when the child is older. Anxiety at this age may be associated with difficulty in distinguishing fantasy from reality. This is a good time to begin to teach children a simple "feelings vocabulary." The words are best taught when the child is experiencing the feeling: *happy, sad, disappointed, mad, scared, frustrated.*

Current symptoms: The child may have limited ability to tolerate frustration and thus have many tantrums at ages three to six or even older. Exhibiting oppositional behavior may be a sign that he did not resolve the "love-hate" crisis of rapprochement. This child may anxiously ask the parent, "Do you love me?" especially if he has been engaged in some problematic behavior.

Anger and rage may be out of control at home or at school. The child may be aggressive toward parents, siblings, or peers. He may be very oppositional or uncooperative, exhibiting passive-aggressive or manipulative behaviors, especially with parents. These are problems in affect modulation.

When an older child, or even a teen, carries rage that is too intense, it may indicate that he needs to rework very strong negative feelings toward his parent and to believe that his parent will still love him. Also, he needs to hold deeply that his parents can be very angry with him and still love him.

Family therapy/Parent–child dyad: Parents bring to Talk Time examples of events that occur around the temper tantrums. One goal is to help the child develop a tolerance for frustration. In giving an example, the parent slows down and attends to various aspects of what happens: Does the parent get enraged as the child's tantrum builds? Is the child fearful of the parent's anger? It is very helpful when the parent can be honest in reporting not only when she has handled the child's tantrum optimally but also when her response was less than ideal.

The therapist coaches the parent to stay with the child during the meltdown, keeping the child, the parent, and the space safe. "I love you even when you get very mad at me. I still love you. I don't like the behavior. I will help you to stop it, and I do love you."

If the child has a tantrum in the office, this can be an opportunity for the therapist to coach the parent—while refraining from being reactive herself—and attend to a fundamental reworking of development that was missed during the child's rapprochement stage.

One favorite family therapy intervention is to gather together all the family members who live in the same household and to have everyone describe their own style of anger. Then each can characterize how anger is acted out between himself or herself and each of the others. From this exercise, the therapist gains a baseline understanding of everyone's anger style, and the presenting problem is expanded beyond the symptoms of the child of most concern (MC). Also, the family members become more conscious of their multiple dyadic anger responses. Material is provided for many more sessions to come.

In addition to addressing the child's current fears, Talk Time provides an opportunity for the parent to let the child know about and discuss early events in the child's life that may have become an embedded source of fear. For example, a six-year-old boy in therapy had nearly drowned when he fell out of a canoe at the age of two. Even though he did not remember almost drowning, he subsequently developed a fear of the water and had always refused to learn to swim. Using a sandtray technique rooted in the framework of Family Play Therapy, his parents explained to him in detail what had happened. He became engaged in the story in a sensorial way, and this was the beginning of his willingness to move slowly toward learning to swim.

Play therapy: Through the metaphors that the child creates in spontaneous play, he can safely recreate the conditions needed to confront and resolve the splits he feels: "The parent who loves me is also the parent who can get angry with me; the parent I am so angry with, I also love." She may use role playing, sandplay, puppets, or dollhouse play. For example, one child made a "bad" boy out of clay using a cookie-cutter mold. His play made it clear that he was identifying with the bad boy. As the split healed, the clay boy could be both loving and naughty in the child's play.

In play therapy, a child who feels these conflicts may test the therapist by pushing limits more often than other children do. Can the therapist give unconditional acceptance to the child while firmly setting limits on her behaviors? Can the therapist tolerate both the child's and his own anger?

When a child's repeated pushing of limits is preventing him from getting into spontaneous play, the therapist may invite the parent into the playroom to discuss the oppositional behavior. She may find directed play therapy to be more effective, whether or not the parent is in the room. She may engage the parents and possibly the siblings in family play therapy with the goal of addressing the split feelings more deeply.

Play therapy is ideal for reworking affect modulation issues because they are lodged energetically in the body, and play therapy heals through the body. Cognitive behavioral techniques are valuable for regulating behavior and adjusting cognitive distortions. The combination of spontaneous play and constructive parent–child interactions provide healing for root-level problems.

Parent education: Mindful parenting helps parents track their own angry responses to the child. A child's meltdown indicates loss of ego control, and the child needs the parent to provide her with an in-control, firm, but kind presence. This may mean quietly comforting a sobbing child, because a caring response to his meltdown may take precedence over the issue at hand. It may mean containing the child in a space where he is safe, the parent is safe, and things are safe. Unless there is an issue of danger, the parent needs to temporarily drop the issue that brought on the tantrum. It is very important to return to it later on so as to process what happened and hold the limit that the child was pushing. Discussing such strategies is a significant part of parent meetings.

If the parent is concerned that her own anger will get out of control, it is important to get distance for cooling off: "Put a door between you and the child." However, the child benefits from having his parent stay there—in control, compassionate, and firm through this very difficult set of feelings that he is experiencing.

Manipulative tantrums can be handled by ignoring them, if that works, or by setting a limit on the manipulation. Parents also need to notice whether they are modeling manipulation by bribing children, or by telling lies that they do not consider harmful but are in fact duplicitous and therefore confusing to the child.

At parent meetings, the therapist can review the importance of empathically reflecting a child's feelings and understanding a child's perceptions even when they defy adult logic. The child will then be better able to hear the parents' more reality-based responses.

Adult therapy: More often than not, when a child is having difficulty with anger, he is not alone in this struggle. One or both parents may also have anger that gets out of control too frequently. Or perhaps a parent has repressed and avoided getting angry so much that the child is being explosive for his parent. Anger problems are often broadly intergenerational. Did the grandparents have anger issues?

Progress with the child is much slower when the parents are not attending in parallel to the anger dysfunctions on their own part. If the symptom of the child's rage do not abate in a reasonable amount of time, and if parents repeatedly struggle with their own 'anger issues, then therapy for the adults is highly recommended in order to heal the whole family. Many parents are grateful when the therapist makes this recommendation.

It is helpful for the parents to explore their own histories of development around the issue of anger, as well as their trauma and attachment histories. Are they parenting similarly to or differently from how they were parented? Did they too often witness their own parents' anger? What was this like for them? Or perhaps their parents rarely showed emotion, keeping it pent up inside. How can such facts help inform how they want to be with their own child? Is there unfinished business around anger issues that they need to address with their own parents or siblings? Couples may benefit from describing to each other how issues of anger were handled in their respective families of origin. This can help them to be compassionate with each other, and also to begin to clear out harmful personality assignments that they may be projecting onto their children.

Another indication for recommending therapy for the parents is when one or both of them are unable to listen empathically to their child's viewpoint. This may indicate a blockage rooted in their early years.

Play therapy is a wonderful way to help a child cope, but if the root-level issues are not addressed within the family, then the child goes home to the same difficult environment that formed his problems. Frequently, parents who were reluctant to enter their own therapy will find that the unfolding of their personal issues relates organically to the problems that are being discussed in the mindful parenting meetings. Eventually, it is satisfying for them to see themselves becoming more fulfilled as a couple and more effective as parents, and to see their child responding in healthier ways.

Integration of Attachment Theory With Mindfulness-Based Play-Family Therapy

Infants, babies, and young children who have been neglected, deprived, or physically or emotionally abused suffer serious challenges as they grow up.

Attachment problems often develop when, for whatever reason, there has been parental unavailability without appropriate substitute care, particularly in the early years of life. Unavailability may be due to situations such as the mother's postpartum depression, the child's receiving early care in an orphanage with multiple or negative caregivers, prolonged medical care in the early years, parental medical illness that compromises infant care, or the death of a parent. Anxious attachment can develop when the parent, who may be taking relatively good physical care of a baby, carries a high level of anxiety. The intensity of these problems often correlates with the degree to which a healthy, reliable alternative caregiver may or may not have been available in the early years. When the history includes physical or sexual abuse or being raised in a drug-addicted household, extensive healing experiences are needed to ensure the child's healthy emotional growth and development.

The loss of significant attachment figures causes unresolved grief and mourning . This can result in developmental delays, emotional detachment, difficulty loving and trusting, and depression. Children may have problems in an adoptive or foster care family as well as in a birth home. What is perhaps most disturbing to parents and caregivers is that very challenging symptoms continue to occur even when abuse or neglect has been halted. The repercussions come back to haunt the older child whose needs went unmet as a baby. The sometimes sudden appearance of difficult problems relates back to this earlier time, confusing the parents, since the child, who is now living in a loving environment, may have had a period without showing symptoms of concern.

The impact of attachment issues falls on a continuum, and of course a child's temperament and personality are important to consider. Some children present with tenaciously held symptoms that seriously challenge their relationships with those who want to love them. Deep down, these children want to be loved, difficult behaviors and all. Healing work in such a situation is arduous, and parenting strategies that work for children who were not neglected and abused will often be ineffective. This can become quite complicated when there are siblings in the home who need a different style of parenting.

When a child has a history of deprivation, neglect, or abuse, it is best to start therapy as soon as possible rather than waiting for symptoms to appear. The younger the child, the less time he will have had to build up defenses. The current literature clearly indicates that both parents and children benefit immensely when parents are willing to practice mindful parenting and to uncover their own attachment issues. For both therapist and parent, I recommend Beverly James's account of how to understand and work with trauma and attachment issues in *Handbook for Treatment of Attachment-Trauma Problems in Children* (1994).

Current symptoms: The client child may come to therapy unable to engage in healthy giving and receiving. Key to this problem is an inability to trust and to be trustworthy. The children often need extensive help to tolerate frustration and to regulate affect. This includes being able to identify and express feelings. Their self-aversion can be so strong that it can take a great deal of time and energy on the part of the child's caregivers to persuade him to let love in. Some children will attempt to attach immediately without getting to know people. In this case, the development of love benefits from the caregivers' making sure to allow the attachment to grow gradually.

A child will often present with an inappropriate amount of power, and the child's experience of self-hate can manifest to others as being defiant, controlling, and manipulative. Symptoms can include aggression; intense anger and rage; self-destructive behaviors; lack of impulse control or of affect regulation; stealing; lying; destroying property; cruelty to animals; hoarding; eating or sleeping disturbances; enuresis or encopresis; inappropriate sexual conduct or attitudes; defiance of rules; preoccupation with fire, gore, or evil; poor hygiene; difficulty with transitions; grandiosity or perception of oneself as a victim; lack of cause-and-effect thinking; learning and language disorders; tactile defensiveness; accident proneness; superficially engaging and charming mannerisms; difficulty with sincere, close friendships; or development of a false self (Levy & Orlans, 1998). In many cultures, difficulty making or sustaining eye contact can be a symptom.

Children who may have been neglected in orphanages but were adopted early may thrive, but many issues lie on the lower end of the continuum. Often the problems go underground immediately after the adoption and surface up to a few years later. Other children may initially cry much of the day. It is essential that parents understand that part of the process forward will include regression. Children may do basically quite well for days, weeks, and even months, and then have behavior that is completely out of control.

The parents of a child with attachment issues often arrive in therapy feeling very frustrated and confused. Discipline styles that worked for another child may be ineffective. Parents feel incompetent and are not aware of the inevitability of the difficulties they are experiencing as a result of the child's early history.

Family therapy/Parent–child dyad: Each weekly Talk Time session begins by addressing the positive experiences the child and the family have had over the past week. When establishing trust is a significant goal, this practice is very important as an ongoing frame of reference that is uplifting and self-esteem building. Connecting to the child around positive experiences allows the therapist some leverage for talking about the challenges of life.

Next, the therapist takes one symptom or concern that the family mentioned during the initial intake evaluation, especially one that has come up during the past week. For example, they may want to discuss the child's lying, waking up with nightmares, or arguing about taking a bath. Role playing can be a very effective method for working on these problems.

When issues are "stuck," the therapist may suggest that the family keep a communication log in which the adults describe the content and manifestation of major problems as they arise during the week. The log tells what happened, why it happened, and how it was resolved. This can also be done by creating a cartoon drawing with bubbles that provide the words. Was there a parental correction appropriate to the unacceptable behavior? Was the correction carried out? In what ways did the parents feel good about their actions? Was there anything to learn about handling the situation better in the future? It is immensely helpful if families are willing to take time to write down a problem at least once a week. Recording the details in writing and/or with a cartoon provides more objectivity and also establishes a healthier sense of accountability on everyone's part. For example, a child may sign an agreement based on issues that arise. This experience helps the child to develop well-needed problem-solving skills, and the record of the exchange can offer a frame of reference when the same issues come up again. During discussion of issues from the communication log at Talk Time, the therapist needs to be firm but patient. She needs to be partial to hearing both the child's side of a problem and the parent's side. Parents deserve a lot of empathy when they are dealing with an oppositional child at home; the goal is clearly to reduce the oppositional behavior. The child also deserves to have the therapist really understand his side, even when she may not be able to condone his behavior. Underneath a child's controlling behavior are vulnerability, hurt, and confusion.

The communication log can also be the basis for discussing issues at scheduled family therapy meetings with the whole family present.

Issues of fairness or perceived unfairness are addressed during Talk Time. It is very beneficial when parents learn to admit their own difficulties during conflicts with the child. For example, a parent may have said hurtful words, and acknowledging this mistake models for the child that it is okay to be vulnerable. This needs to be balanced with holding the child suitably accountable for his own actions so that he does not feel parentified. Sometimes, the therapist may think that the consequence was too harsh or too lenient. She may discuss this during Talk Time, or she may decide to wait and bring it up with the parents alone at the next parent feedback meeting.

When parents set limits on a child for an inappropriate or destructive behavior, the child often tries to usurp power by stating that nothing bothers him; he doesn't care about the punishment. In this case, it is important for the parent to firmly carry out the disciplinary action, and to tell the child that it doesn't matter that he doesn't mind; he still must abide by the parent's ruling. If parents believe that the child will learn only from the harshness or uncomfortableness of the punishment, then they can feel inhibited from taking action, and this gives the child more inappropriate control. Parents need to know that the enforcement is intended merely to highlight the misbehavior, and that if a child happens to be enjoying his time-out, that is okay. After getting to know the child and the family for six to twelve months or longer, the therapist may suggest that the parents prepare to do a trauma reality sandtray with their child. (See Case Study, p. 277.) This combines the sad and painful facts of a child's life with the happy and resourceful times in his life. She gives the parents a "blank book" and invites them to create the story in book form prior to the family therapy session at which the family will recreate the story in the sandtray using miniature figures. The reality tray allows the parents to communicate the truth, as it is appropriate to the child's developmental age, in an honest, direct format. Deciding when to do this is a serious clinical decision. Generally, it requires that enough trust has been developed among the child, the parents, and the therapist. Sometimes, it is helpful to involve the whole family, and, at other times, it may seem better to reserve this process specifically for the MC child. Another experience that helps with bonding is viewing family photographs and maybe a video of the time when the child joined the family. It was quite meaningful, at one Talk Time, to view the video of an eleven-year-old foster girl's first birthday party with her now-deceased mother.

Play therapy: The child may take readily to spontaneous play, sandplay, and art therapies, and if he does, it is very helpful for his treatment, because these modalities allow him to more readily drop his defenses. He can begin to build the trust necessary to heal the hurts that may lie underneath a non-chalant façade.

Because the abuse or neglect was early in life, the child may tend to do a lot of play therapy that expresses these experiences. His body–mind may connect to implicit memories during the deeper awareness stage of the play, healing what his conscious memory has blocked. It is important to know that even though he may sometimes have no words for his difficult past experiences, this child has suffered trauma. Through the deeper awareness stage of play therapy, he can give direct, healing expression to multiple losses, feelings of alienation, inner conflicts about loving various family members, and negative projections about himself and his own life. Depending on the child's history, his play themes may include abandonment, neglect, giving or receiving harm, manipulation, rage, or feeling overpowered or helpless.

The play of a child who has experienced early loss is usually quite moving. Through imaginative play and metaphors, he finds ways to express his deeper inner self. This experience allows him to connect to his core identity. He may use groupings of animal families, dollhouse figures, or lots of babies to express his feelings of loss, death, neglect, and abuse. For example, he may select toys that indicate feeling alienated, like a stranded survivor who is assigned to live with a new family.

For a child who has entered the home through adoption or foster care, one goal is for him to become able, through play therapy and family therapy, to care about both his birth parents and the parents who are now raising him. If he is presently living in a loving and stable home, play therapy can allow him to rework and heal, from the inside, the insecurities and hurts left behind by his multiple losses. In the play, he finds age-appropriate resolutions for his unique history, often revealing through play what he cannot express with words. A very verbal child benefits from this experience as much as one who is less verbal. Ideally and usually very gradually, the process allows a child of any age to bond more deeply with those who love him.

In working with attachment issues, the play therapy often begins with the parent in the room, generally using spontaneous play if the child is not too oppositional. The first goal is to create an environment that encourages the child to bond with his parents. The therapist also hopes that, in time, the child will bond with her. If the child is connecting to the parent using spontaneous play, then it is most effective to allow space for it to continue, since this play goes directly to the heart of the healing.

When a child is able to do only half of the session in spontaneous play, then the therapist can use a more directive approach for the rest of the session. This combination works best with many children with attachment issues. The therapist may set up a structure for the child and parent to play together and suggest ideas and themes for them. This can be quite challenging when the child is oppositional. Sometimes, more family therapy and family play therapy are necessary before moving into the playroom. When there is extensive opposition in the parent–child relationship, the therapist may see the child alone for some sessions and build trust this way, even though she soon wants to attend to the connection between the parent and child.

The therapist needs to think clinically when making decisions and not give too much power to the child, who may have been given too much power by the family. It is important to avoid battles of will. At the same time, this is a child who has felt his life has been out of his control. Play therapy themes of gaining control can help to heal the harsher facts of his life.

The therapist assesses the needs of the siblings, who may be witnessing and engaging chronic problems. Perhaps some of the siblings have their own attachment issues. Family therapy sessions are recommended, especially in the early part of treatment. Then family sessions can be held as needed throughout the course of the MC child's therapy. A sibling may need to have therapy as well. A team approach can be beneficial, with two different therapists seeing the two children.

Therapy for attachment problems is generally long term. The prognosis is very good when the parents and therapist trust each other and work well together, and particularly when parents are willing to open up and understand their own attachment and trauma histories.

Parent education: It is essential that the parents be involved in regularly scheduled meetings without the child present; without this component, a positive, enduring outcome may be impossible to achieve. The therapist needs to understand the scope and intensity of the attachment issues unique to this child and family. Is the child on the lower end of the continuum, with a few minor problems? Or is the child exhibiting many of the serious symptoms mentioned above? Or is he somewhere in the middle? In all cases, how are the parents handling the situation, and how is it affecting any other children? It is helpful for the therapist to communicate her assessment to the parents.

On the lower end of the continuum, when entrenched major opposition is not already present, the therapy may not be very different from the play-family therapy of children with many other issues. Although the therapy is very important, the main focus may be on prevention of future problems; it may touch lightly on areas associated more with families further along the continuum.

When attachment issues occur in an older child who has entered the family through adoption or foster care, the child may be quite oppositional and may offer the therapist significant challenges. On one hand, the child will feel safe when parents offer firm but kind responses to the child's inappropriate behavior. On the other hand, the child often desperately wants to control his world. Parents do well to let him, when appropriate, by giving reasonable, limited choices. It is not helpful for the parent to banter at the child's level.

There are several concepts in Contextual Family Therapy that may be important to weave into parenting meetings (see chapter 6). For instance, split loyalty may create in the child an inner voice that says, "If I love this mom and dad who are taking care of me and wanting to love me, I will be disloyal to my birth parents." Frequently, a child is unconsciously carrying this split, which is exacerbated if the parents do not find a way to hold the birth parent in a positive yet realistic light. Split loyalty can also be present even when the parents believe they have handled this issue most optimally. Another split may be, "I can love one parent but not both."

Another Contextual Family Therapy concept relevant to treating an oppositional child is destructive entitlement. When children have been victims of adult mistakes, they begin to feel destructively entitled rather than constructively entitled. To increase constructive entitlement, it is important to develop the child's narrative in such a way that it acknowledges the failings of all of the adults. This includes how the institutions and the people in the institutions have not met this child's needs. Understanding the facts and acknowledging the injustices in a deep, personal, and intimate way can allow everyone to begin to wake up to healing. It is highly recommended to create a life book for the child. Using a scrapbook and various art materials, magazine pictures, and photographs, the parents and child chronologically track the child's life events—both positive and negative life experiences.

Exoneration is an important Contextual Therapy concept. It is complex. A child's sense of feeling that he is bad inside can be alleviated by the acknowledgment that his challenging behaviors are rooted in a history that is not his fault. Paradoxically, when a child realizes this and can forgive himself, he is more likely to be accountable and responsible for his actions. This includes, at the right time, the complex journey of exonerating—not necessarily forgiving—his parents.

At parent education meetings, therapist and parents discuss issues that have come up in Talk Time, as well as how the play therapy and sandplay therapy are progressing. Because the child's trust has been broken in the past, the therapy needs to be trust based, even while shifting the power back from the child to the parent. Initial sessions are spent coaching the parents to take charge in the face of the child's oppositional or passive-aggressive behaviors. This can be a long, intense experience, and things usually get worse before they get better. Parents need to drop sarcasm and their negative predictions when addressing their child. They can replace this with "reframing," which encourages responses that are affirming and acknowledging without using flattery. For example, "Your body language is letting me know that you are mad. I'm glad you are telling me that." The coaching is done in a way that helps parents to understand the dynamic underlying the problem so that they can apply their understanding of that dynamic to the next challenging situation. This level of challenge is often not what parents expected in adoption or in offering foster care. Part of the reverberation is that the child seems to know exactly which buttons to push to upset his parents, and their own personal deeper issues come to the foreground on a regular basis. Parents should not take the situation personally. Understanding the brain research can help with this goal. It is important that they realize that early abuse, neglect, or trauma may be a large part of why the attachment difficulties exist. Because the child needs compassionate and optimal responses, parents are challenged to regard their own reactive impulses as teachers. The therapist invites parents to do their own inner work through the practice of mindful parenting.

Adult therapy: There is high intensity in working with children who have had early abuse, neglect, and serious trauma early in life, and who did not have the opportunity for residual trust to develop during the extremely vulnerable first years of life. Parents can have high motivation to rework issues and to help trustful and loving feelings to develop and flourish; however, the chronic, defended, negative behaviors of the child with attachment disorders are challenging to even the most loving, patient, competent parent. The experience of caring for this child tends to open up every wound of the parents, often on a daily basis. They need the therapist's compassionate affirmation for the heroic task they are undertaking. The parents may think, "This is not what we signed up for." Perhaps their vision was that love would melt the heart of the child. And indeed, between the challenges, love can flow, and the child's defenses can gradually fall away, but the parents' feelings of competence and self-esteem may suffer along the way.

Perhaps it is because the label "attachment disorder" seems to apply to the child alone, or perhaps it is the alienating quality of the child's chronic difficult behaviors, or that the child's biological roots are often not the same as those of the parents who are raising him. Whatever the reason, it is not uncommon for parents to be resistant to the suggestion that they explore, in therapy, the deep emotional issues that are aroused by their experience with their child. The best healing will come when they are willing to get in touch with the vulnerabilities that are buried in the old ground of their own childhood situations. It is particularly healing for their child if they honestly confront their own issues of closeness and distance, trust and mistrust, as well as bring light to the sources of their reactivity in their relationships with their own parents, family members, and friends, and with each other.

As parents grow in self-knowledge and self-acceptance, they respond more constructively to their child's behavior. They learn the most optimal responses if they are willing to delve deeper into their own pain. It can be quite healing for parents to be in couple therapy and to share these issues with each other, if there is a foundation of trust where this can happen. Some parents do best with a combination of individual and couple therapy.

9

A Mindfulness-Based Play-Family Therapy Case Study

Introduction to the Caruso-Harris Family

THIS CASE STUDY is a composite of about a half dozen families I have worked with in Mindfulness-Based Play-Family Therapy (MBPFT) over many years. Identifying biographical information has been changed to protect the privacy of the families. Otherwise, the accounts generally stay true to the thematic content of the actual sessions, and many of the dialogues of therapy sessions are verbatim transcriptions. While the sample family has its particular cultural, economic, and emotional circumstances, MBPFT is adaptable to most situations and can be integrated with many kinds of play therapy and family therapy. The "Caruso-Harris" family has been constructed with a wide range of issues to demonstrate various parts of the theory. Both parents are involved with the children despite varying work schedules that can be hard to manage, and they have grandparents and siblings who can be helpful with the children. The parents' relationship is strained, but they are respectful of each other and of the differences in how they perceive the problems. Both show relief that they have taken the step of seeking help.

Four-Segment Evaluation—Segment I: Therapist and Parents Meet and Oumar's Developmental History

The family is middle class and multiracial, with two parents and three children, all living together. The oldest child is a girl, Linda, age nine. Six-year-old Oumar, the middle child, is the child for whom the parents have the

226

most concern (MC). The youngest child, two-and-a-half-year-old Maya, entered the family when she was adopted at the age of nine months from Guatemala. The family experienced the traumatic death of Arnold Jr., who died of SIDS (sudden infant death syndrome) when he was two months old. He seemed to be healthy and developing normally but died in his crib. Just three months later Oumar was conceived. Sharon and Arnie, the parents, hold hands as they tearfully share this information with me. I provide compassion and silence. It is important to slow down content involving loss, and to take the parent's cues as to how much or how little they may want to talk about painful life narratives, especially at such an early meeting.

Sharon is 39, Arnie 41. Sharon is European American with Irish and Italian heritage. She grew up in Mt. Airy, a peaceful and popular neighborhood in Philadelphia, Pennsylvania, that consciously chose racial integration during the unrest of the 1960s. Her maternal grandparents were both born in Ireland, her paternal grandparents in Italy. Both sets of grandparents emigrated from their respective countries. Arnie was born and grew up in Park Slope, a neighborhood in Brooklyn, New York. He is African American. His maternal grandparents were born in Tennessee, his paternal grandparents in Georgia. His parents were raised in Brooklyn, where they met. Sharon and Arnie have known each other since college and have been married for ten years. Sharon works part time as a nurse-midwife at a local hospital. Her retired parents live nearby and occasionally help take care of their grandchildren. Arnie is an airplane pilot based in New York City. He and his father, brothers, uncles, and cousins share a hunting lodge in upstate New York, where they hunt each autumn. The families vacation there during the summer.

The parents have requested therapy because of Oumar's hallucinations and nightmares. These began three months ago and are getting progressively more intense, despite a visit to the doctor and help from a family friend. Sharon's brother, who attends postgraduate classes at the Family & Play Therapy Center, referred the family for play-family therapy. When Oumar was six months old, he had a heart operation. Although he is healthy and not limited in his activities, he does need a yearly medical checkup. His most recent annual physical for his heart was just three months ago, the same time that his emotional symptoms began. Although the parents report that everything was unremarkable during the examination, I notice the amount of anxiety both parents exhibit when talking to me about it in person at this first session.

Like many families seen in private practice settings, the Caruso-Harris family has many strengths and resources. Yet they are struggling with some challenging problems and are open to receiving help. Oumar had separation anxiety when he began a five-morning-a-week preschool program at age three, but later on he adjusted well. He is having an extra kindergarten year, which seems to be helping his self-esteem. Oumar is presently healthy and has excellent gross motor control. Despite the heart disability, his parents have not restricted his normal activities. He has playmates at home and at school, although he has recently refused to visit their homes. With a history of temper tantrums from three years to five-and-a-half, Oumar acts out his anger more often than expressing it in a constructive manner. His parents attempt to talk him out of his feelings, rather than trying to really "hear" him.

The parents' present concerns are that Oumar is extremely anxious, both at home and at school. He is having auditory and visual hallucinations that are scary to him. During the day, he sees people who talk to him and fighting animals that come through the walls. He also has frightening nightmares, which jolt him from his sleep most nights. Aware of his fears, his parents are compassionate and take turns going in to comfort him. Sometimes, Oumar wakes up and comes to their room. They feel sleep deprived and also note that occasionally one of their daughters wakes up and is frightened, too. Oumar is a verbal child and is articulate about his nightmares and hallucinations, especially with his mother. However, he needs help talking about his feelings.

In addition to the medical trauma and some separation anxiety, the parents note that Oumar's adjustment to Maya's entry into their family was more difficult than they had expected. He was just under five years old when Maya, then nine months old, joined the family. He had a difficult time with the separation from Sharon when she was in Guatemala. Sharon describes this as traumatic. Maya was clingy and cried a lot at first. This was very hard for Oumar, who was having a lot of tantrums.

The parents add that it has often seemed traumatic for Oumar that his father's work schedule takes him away a lot, and he has complained about this since he was two. Oumar has frequently told his father that he does not think his father loves him because he is not home. It is a strength that both parents are involved with the children despite varying work schedules that can be hard to manage. After I have gathered information about the past (see the Developmental and Social History Questionnaire in Appendix A), parents Arnie and Sharon describe his present behaviors. Unless otherwise noted, they agree to the response.

Temper tantrums = moderate to low problem now (severe in the past)

Aggression = moderate (dad); serious (mom); occasionally hits mom or his sisters when he does not get his way

Anxiety = very serious

Disobedience = moderate (he does not listen and he nags)

Fighting = moderate (he can instigate squabbles with his sisters)

Eating = low (can be fussy)

Fine motor = moderate

Quick mood changes = moderate (dad); serious (mom)

Accident prone = low

Easily frustrated = serious

Attention span = low (dad); moderate (mom)

Fears = serious (he is particularly afraid of his hallucinations and his parents' reactions to them)

Interrupting adults = moderate (dad); serious (mom)

Self-esteem = low to moderate (has been better this past year)

Sleeping = serious because he is being awakened by nightmares

Restlessness = moderate

Initial Clinical Impressions

I begin to realize, with compassion, that from the beginning to the present, both parents have worried intensely about their son, Oumar. He was conceived consciously not long after the tragic SIDS death of their baby Arnie. I note the medical trauma, a serious operation at six months due to a congenital malformation of the heart. Both parents describe feeling anxious about their son *all of his life*. Their anxieties are renewed each year at the time of Oumar's yearly heart checkup, and the recent hallucinations seem to have begun just about the time of his last appointment.

A bout of colic each evening for two months certainly caused stress in the family, even though they report dealing well enough with their frustrations. They received help in soothing Oumar from grandparents and a close friend. I wonder how this impacted early bonding.

Despite the heart abnormality, Oumar's early physical development progressed normally. I am concerned about affect regulation because of his extended temper tantrum period. He skipped having tantrums when he was two, partly because his parents were afraid to upset him. They gave him his way or distracted him too much. I explained to them that during this rapprochement stage parents often feel happy if the child does not have tantrums. However, this often means that the child may be skipping an important developmental achievement. Because this developmental milestone was missed, Oumar may not have learned sufficient tolerance of frustration. I respond compassionately to their description of strong temper tantrums when Oumar was three and four, until more recently. Sharon remembers that they started when she went from occasional weekends working at the hospital to working three full day shifts every week. It seems that the circumstances surrounding the arrival of Maya prolonged Oumar's rapprochement stage. I write a note to remind myself to invite a discussion about this in more detail at a parent feedback meeting and to track how the parents are handling Maya's tantrums.

I wonder about the parents' experiences of anger. I notice that the initial separation anxiety when Oumar started preschool was handled well, and that he was able to visit friends' homes until recently.

The parents report that Oumar's connection to each of them is good. Given the described factors, I consider the possibility of an anxious attachment. I am concerned that the parents may not have grieved the death of Arnold Jr. and the medical problems of Oumar. I wonder how their anxiety has been affecting Oumar all these years.

They are in relative accord with regard to Oumar's current behaviors but are individuated enough to express differences in perception. It is not uncommon for the parent who is with the child more to have more concern. However, both parents see Oumar's tendency to quick frustration, his difficulty in modulating his affect, the anxiety that is manifesting in his nightmares, and finally his difficulty with separation. They make only a little connection between these symptoms and his early history. Sharon and Arnie have tried to help Oumar themselves, but they also know when to seek help. This is a sign of healthy parenting.

I want to better understand Sharon's emphasizing that she has always had difficulty saying no to her children, and that they pester her endlessly. She wants to work on it, yet feels afraid of hurting her children's feelings.

Arnie has no problem saying no, but then he feels like the "bad guy." I wonder about this, and especially about what might make it difficult for Sharon to extend appropriate firmness to her children. I later learn that this was rooted in a similar style of parenting of Sharon's mother and father.

Although it is unusual, I ask the family to commit to two sessions a week for the next four weeks, one for Oumar's Talk Time and play therapy and one to meet with both parents. I hope that this might bring some symptom relief for Oumar's almost daily nightmares. The parents look at each other, nod in joint assent, and seem relieved. Sharon suggests that, when it would be good timing, they might work on their couple relationship. I assure them that this is an option as well and will most certainly help the children. I look forward to next week's meeting.

Segment II: The First Family Meeting

Family Discussion: The Strengths and the Problems

Although this is a family meeting, two-and-a-half-year-old Maya is not present, in accordance with my recommendation. It is generally best that children between the crawling stage and three years old not attend this session.

After introductions, I ask how the children, Linda, age 9, and Oumar, age 6, were told about coming here today. Linda refers to getting help for Oumar's nightmares. Oumar sheepishly shares that they are scary. Sharon elaborates, describing the ghosts that Oumar sees, and the purple and green animals, and the people that talk to him and say scary things. She ends by saying that she and Arnie hope I can help them.

ARNIE: I told the children that their mom and I need help with Oumar's nightmares, and that we are coming for ourselves, too.

The therapist can coach parents in advance that it is good to mention, at the first meeting, that they are asking for help, and to frame the problem as a family concern. When one child in the family is hurting, it is important that the siblings understand that their parents are requesting help.

THERAPIST [looking directly at Oumar, invites him to elaborate about his hallucinations]: Do you want to say anything about your nightmares and about the things you are seeing that other people aren't seeing?

Oumar puts his pillow in front of his face.

THERAPIST: Okay. We don't need to talk any more about this now. Maybe later.

At this session, it is important that the MC, the child of most concern, be aware of why the parents are concerned, though it is not essential that the child talk about it. In fact, often children do not want to open up yet, especially when the therapist is a stranger.

I initiate a shift by asking the parents to say three things that they like about each of their children—even Maya, who is not present today. Arnie starts with Linda and elaborates on all the animals she likes. Oumar says that Linda wants to let them out of their cages. Sharon highlights Linda's ways of helping with Maya. She says that Linda is artistic and does lots of art projects and she is a good soccer player. She continues with Oumar, saying that he likes to give good hugs. She likes that he tells her when he is afraid of things, because she can help him. She adds that he is also good at soccer, and has courage because he tries things even when they are difficult.

Arnie says that Oumar is good with sports and that he can climb very well. He learned how to ride his two-wheeler bike when he was five. Arnie adds that Oumar is affectionate. I ask if Arnold can tell Oumar what he means by "affectionate." The process slows down and Arnie explains this to Oumar by giving him a hug.

THERAPIST: Now I'd like each of you [parents] to tell Linda and Oumar two things each that you'd like them to work on that may be a problem. Something that could be different, say, by the summertime. (*I usually specify a time period or holiday that is about three or four months away.*)

SHARON: Well, I'd like to start with Oumar. I need him to listen better when I ask him to do things. And he nags me when he doesn't get his way.

THERAPIST: Can you give him an example?

SHARON: Yes. When it is time for dinner or to go to bed, if he is watching TV or playing, it is hard for him to stop what he is doing and come. Then he begs me endlessly until I give in.

THERAPIST: Okay, Oumar do you hear what your mom is saying? [I repeat the mom's statement, and Oumar nods.] (*I am thinking that this is a mindful parenting issue for the mom to work on—not to give in when Oumar nags her.*)

SHARON: Also, Oumar has a lot of things he's afraid of, and it is difficult for him to try new things, and to separate from me. He can go to school, but he can't go to his friend's house or to birthday parties, and he hates it when we have a babysitter.

THERAPIST: So, pretty soon, you want Oumar to be more comfortable with going places without you, like a birthday party. Or having him be comfortable when you go out.

SHARON: Yes. It seems to be harder now than it was even, say, four months ago.

THERAPIST: So, Oumar, it sounds like sometimes you don't want to leave your mom to go to a birthday party. Whose birthday party did you miss?

OUMAR: I didn't miss it; my mom went with me.

ARNIE: And I want him to work on not getting angry so much. He isn't having as many tantrums as last year, but now he gets angry and screams and sometimes hits.

THERAPIST: So you want Oumar to work on not getting so angry. Oumar, I think you know what your dad means. [Arnie turns toward Oumar and says it directly to him.]

OUMAR: Yeah. (*I decide not to discuss this, as there are lots of things for him to work on, and the goal of this meeting is merely to begin to identify a broad range of reasons for the family to seek treatment.*)

ARNIE: Another thing is that I want to help him, because he has scary dreams and he even sees things that scare him, things that I can't see. I want him to tell me about these things that are scaring him. He tells his mom more than me, and I want him to know he can tell me, too.

THERAPIST [making eye contact with Oumar]: Oumar, I hear your dad wants to help you with the scary things that your mom and dad told me about last week. I hear your dad wants you to let him know when you see these scary things.

OUMAR: Yeah.

THERAPIST: Can you tell me more about them?

Oumar hesitates.

SHARON: It's okay to tell Ms. Dottie about them. She is going to help us.

OUMAR: Well, I see scary bears. Two. One is green and one is purple and they are fighting.

THERAPIST: So do you see the bears in your dreams?

OUMAR: No, like coming out of the closet. Sometimes I see them when I go to the bathroom upstairs.

THERAPIST: Well, I'm really glad that you can tell your mom and dad and me about them. It must be scary.

OUMAR: Yeah, it is.

THERAPIST [continuing to make good eye contact with Oumar]: That is just what to do . . . and you know to do it—to tell your mom and dad!

SHARON: Well, he has different things happen. Sometimes he tells me and sometimes he just cries and shakes.

Oumar puts a pillow over his head, giving the message that he doesn't want to talk anymore.

THERAPIST: Maybe we can help so that you can sleep better at night and stop seeing the scary things during the day. Would you like that?

OUMAR [peeking from behind his pillow]: Yes, I would!

THERAPIST: Well, I am hoping that together, your mom and dad and I and *you* can help you to get these scary things to go away. I can tell you that I do know other kids who were having these problems, and they were able to have them go away. Then they were much happier. I think it will be helpful for you to come here and play. (*It is important that the child knows very clearly that the therapist knows what the problem is, and that she offers hope—without promising the desired results—that together we can help.*)

THERAPIST [to Linda]: Do you worry about Oumar, Linda?

LINDA: No. He's okay.

THERAPIST: If you did worry, would you be able to talk to your mom and dad about it?

LINDA: Maybe. [She climbs into her mom's lap.]

THERAPIST: Do you wake up when Oumar screams from a nightmare?

LINDA: Sometimes I hear him screaming, but usually I don't wake up at night. Well, I guess I worry about him then.

THERAPIST: Oh, so it does worry you when you hear him scream?

LINDA: Well, yeah, especially when he screams and runs around the house. Then Mommy or Daddy go into his room, or sometimes he goes into their bed.

THERAPIST: I'm glad your mom and dad go in to help your brother, so you know that you don't have to take care of your brother by yourself.

Siblings often begin to take on the problem and feel that they need to solve it. Using this much energy can be harmful to their own growth and development. It is an important part of thinking systemically that the therapist keep track of how the other children are responding to family problems, especially when there is one child carrying the most distress, and therefore receiving more attention through the play therapy.

LINDA: Yeah, but I don't want to talk about it anymore.

THERAPIST: Okay, I'm glad that you told me that. I can stop talking about it with you now.

LINDA: Yeah.

Arnie asserts that he will talk about some things for Linda to work on by summertime. He says that he wants her to listen better the first time he calls her and to be kinder to Oumar. Arnie also indicates that he wants Linda to stop being fearful, even around the house. She is now afraid to go upstairs or to the basement family room alone. Linda says that she gets scared sometimes when her dad gets angry.

Sharon notes that Arnold's yelling does scare both of the kids. At the same time, she shares Arnie's frustration. Sharon elaborates that Linda cannot take no for an answer. She says that Linda nags and bugs her—the same thing she said about Oumar—"but Linda does it especially when we are at a store and she wants something." Sharon acknowledges that this is her own biggest problem: She can't say no. Arnold chimes in that he hopes Sharon can get help with this too. Linda's body language is telling us that she does not want to talk about it. At this point, what is important is that she knows that I know about her fear.

THERAPIST: Linda's fears are interesting. It is common for children her age to have these fears arise suddenly, just as you describe. I wonder how her fears are complicated by Oumar's fears? We can certainly address this as part of working with your family.

The parents show me a picture of Maya. They say three things that they like about her, and we discuss what she can work on. Just as we are about to go into the other room, Linda blurts out, "And I worry that Daddy's plane will crash, and Mommy worries when he goes hunting." I realize that I have a self-assigned "cotherapist" in Linda. I decide that it would be valuable to build in more family therapy sessions to help her get unburdened from these worries.

THERAPIST: Thank you, Linda, it's very helpful for me to know your thoughts about the hunting and the possibility of an airplane crashing.

Depending on the time boundary, I may ask more now or I may just acknowledge the concerns and file them for the future.

The Caruso-Harris Family Sand Story

THERAPIST: Now we are going to go to the playroom to play the sand game. This is how you play: Each person gets a basket and you select any three objects to put into your basket. It is in pretend, so you don't pick, for example, a dog named Hector, since that is your dog's name. You would need to pick a pretend animal with a pretend name. So you can pick objects, people, and animals, three of whatever you want, using your imagination. Just keep your pieces in your own basket, and come sit on the stools around the sandbox when you're ready.

Sometimes I say, "If possible, try to do it quietly, but if you have a question you can ask me."

Today, Oumar selects the moist sandtray. He wants to put his piece in the tray first. He selects a large pirate holding a gun and puts it in the middle of the sandtray so that the sand covers its feet. I motion to Linda that she is next, going clockwise, as if they are playing a game. Linda places a unicorn near the corner where she is sitting. Arnie places a small plane. Sharon places two Amish children in black, the girl a little older than the boy. Oumar places a larger airplane next to his dad's. Linda places an ambulance. Arnie places an American Indian hunter, with bow and arrow pointing out of the tray. Sharon places a black angel in a purple dress, with arms up, facing the pirate. Oumar places a dragon, a large dinosaurlike creature with two red heads. Linda places a large dog with two puppies. Arnie places a pair of large praying hands. Sharon places a brown-complexioned girl in a green dress holding a yellow cat with brown stripes. (See figures 9.1 and 9.2.)

THERAPIST: Now the storytelling part of the game begins. You are all going to work together to tell one story. It needs to be a pretend story. It has a beginning, a middle, and an end. You will take turns, just like when you put in the pieces. I will tell you when it is your turn. The story begins with "Once upon a time." (*I find that this age-old phrase helps adults tap into imagination.*) Who would like to start?

LINDA: Once upon a time, the unicorn wants to have an adventure, but she gets lost and she asks the mother dog to help her.

FIGURE 9.1. The Caruso-Harris family sandtray.

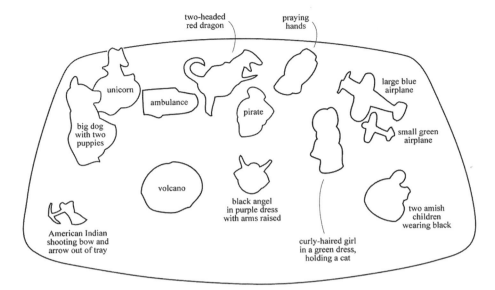

FIGURE 9.2.   Diagram of the Caruso-Harris family sandtray.

Arnie continues that they are in a country where they speak Spanish and that there is a scary, two-headed dragon somewhere. Sharon says that there are two children who see a girl holding a kitten, and they ask if she wants to play. I signal to the mom that she can move the children closer together if she wants to, following the story content. I summarize the story up to this point and invite Oumar to continue.

OUMAR: The pirate gets on the big airplane and flies it into the volcano [he reaches for a volcano on the shelf and adds it], and the pirate dies, and his ghost flies up to the helicopter, and he floats around watching everything. (*He imagines the helicopter, and I do not want to interrupt his story at this time to invite him to get a miniature helicopter. I also want to allow Oumar to include things that we cannot see.*) And the ambulance comes and helps people who are having a heart attack or are dead. (*I notice that Oumar's body is very anxious as he tells the story quickly. He has a worried expression, knitting his brow, and his breathing is stilted.*)

THERAPIST: Wow, a lot happened!

I purposely slow down the story and repeat what he said. Slowing down an anxiously told story is a technique I will continue to use in our other sessions. "The pirate gets on this plane and flies it into the volcano. The pirate dies and his ghost flies up to the helicopter . . . and then the ambulance comes and helps the people who are having a heart attack or are dead." A quiet moment follows.

The story continues. The children express themes of fear and danger, the parents themes of safety and reassurance. Each person has a final turn.

LINDA: So the unicorn [moving the unicorn over to the children] was happy because she felt safe with the angel and the children and the praying hands, and she asked the angel to help her find her way home so she could tell her mom and dad about her adventures. But she didn't think they would believe her. The end.

THERAPIST: That was your own idea for an ending. [Nods and smiles to Linda.] Hmmm. Unicorn didn't think that her mom and dad would believe her . . . [Brief pause.] Okay, Arnie, this is your last turn.

ARNIE: This airplane [the smaller one] decided to fly off and report the problem to the president and to the newspapers, and so someone came out and took their picture. [He gets all the pieces that are left in the tray and lines them up for the photo. The Indian has not been mentioned in the story. Arnie now places it in the front middle of the photo.]

OUMAR: The pirate comes back from the dead to take the picture.

SHARON: I like Arnie's ending. And then the angel helps the unicorn to get home, and she goes with her to tell the parents that the unicorn's story is true.

THERAPIST: So the parents might believe the unicorn if the angel helps tell the story?

SHARON: Yup.

THERAPIST: Okay, Oumar, your words will be the very end of the story. How do you want it to end?

OUMAR: The people that got died came back to life, and then the two-headed dragon blew fire on them and scared them. The end. (*When there is time at the end of this storytelling, I often ask for each person to give a title and we process what each person liked or did not like about the story.*)

Initial Reflections on the Sand Story

Much of what is happening in this family's story is communicated by their choice of symbols, images, and colors; the expressive energy of the objects and their placement, and the metaphors that the family members created. This sand story is rich in metaphors. Here I will point out metaphoric elements that are visible to an observer. I am not interpreting them. In fact, the selected miniatures and the story may have multiple interpretations. Further significance reveals itself as I get to know a family more.

There is notable multicultural symbolism, and the colors of the figures are expressive. The mother's selections included an African angel wearing a turquoise gown, a pair of white children (a protective older sister with a younger brother in black Amish clothing), and a brown girl in a green dress holding a kitten (I notice that she is the largest of all the human figures in the tray). Three of the pieces that Oumar picked have prominent red color: the pirate, the bright red heads of the dragon, and the volcano. The other red piece is the ambulance selected by Linda. Besides that, Linda chose a mostly-white-with-yellow unicorn and the dog and puppies that are mostly brown with a mixture of tan. The father's pieces include the small green airplane, an American Indian hunter in a tan cloth (which is the smallest human figure), and the large white praying hands.

After all of the pieces have been put in the tray, how are they arranged? Have the family members simply set their own pieces down in clusters, in front of themselves, or have they placed each piece in relation to other members' pieces some of the time? In the storytelling, when does the sequence of the story continue with the next person? When does it abruptly change? Notice how the participants use the pieces when they tell their stories. Do they refer only to their own pieces, or do they include others' as well?

I ask myself, how might the images of the ghost floating up to the imaginary helicopter relate to Oumar's hallucinations? As with the questions above, it is important that the therapist keep an open mind when asking questions, and avoid getting locked into her own interpretation.

When the father places the story into a setting where a different language is spoken, I wonder how this might be a way of including Maya, who was adopted from Guatemala, into the sandtray story. It might also be a reference to this family's appreciation of ethnic differences.

I notice that the hunter pointing his bow and arrow outside the tray is not brought into the verbal part of the story, yet he is placed center front by the father at the end of the story. Sometimes the pieces that are not used are important for future sand stories, and indeed, this figure becomes important in Oumar's sand stories later.

Linda's theme of fearing that the unicorn will not be believed reflects a common issue for children at her stage of development, as they begin experimenting with lying. This issue comes up later in therapy.

At the age of six, a child's development equips him to begin to better understand the permanence of death. I already knew some important factors: the anxiety about Oumar's heart that has been part of his history since birth and about his annual cardiology appointments. Now, Linda has just told us her perception that her mother is afraid of "Daddy being in an airplane crash." This simple sand game has helped me to better understand some of the presenting problems.

We return to the waiting room. Sharon explains to the children that she and Oumar will be coming back next week. Linda complains about this and is told that Oumar will be coming every week and that later on she may have some turns too. I shake hands good-bye, making eye contact with each person.

Segment III: Introduction of Oumar to Play Therapy

Talk Time

Oumar is accompanied to the session by his mother, who comes into the playroom with him and me. The waiting room is being used by other clients, so Talk Time takes place in the playroom. Only a few toys are available for Oumar to use during this part of the session so that he can also attend to the dialogue.

I ask Sharon and Oumar about their week. Oumar is quiet. His mother lets me know that he just started karate class, although he insisted that she stay. Oumar chimes in that he made a new friend in his class and that his mother let him play with Jake on the tire swing at the playground. Sharon acknowledges that Oumar did well in karate class. I engage Oumar regarding his playground experience, before moving on to discussion of problems.

THERAPIST [addressing Sharon]:   How did the symptoms go this week?

SHARON: It was a hard week. Maybe a little better, but still up a lot at night, and seeing things coming through the wall. [To Oumar] Do you remember your bad dream last night, Oumar? Can you tell Dottie about it?

OUMAR: No, you tell it.

THERAPIST: I am glad you can let me know that you'd rather your mom tell me what happened.

SHARON: Yes, he had a dream a couple of nights ago that a swordsman cut him in half. And a dinosaur tried to eat him.

THERAPIST [looking at Oumar as though he had told her himself]:   Well, that *is* scary!

OUMAR: Yeah.

SHARON: Last night Oumar saw a ghost come out of his closet in the playroom. No one else saw it. And the ghost was holding a little boy's hand and then the ghost said it would take Oumar's heart out.

THERAPIST [to Oumar]:   Oh my, the ghost said it would take your heart out. That *is* scary. [The therapist's voice expresses some feeling but is also somewhat neutral.] I'm so glad that you could tell your mom. It is helpful to tell your mom. What did the ghost look like?

Oumar looks up at his mom, and she reassures him that it is okay to talk to Miss Dottie.

OUMAR: Like a Halloween ghost, of course.

THERAPIST: Oh, yeah, of course, the ghost looks like a Halloween ghost. (*The therapist has been coaching the parents to stay calm, and to credit Oumar when he tells them about his hallucinations.*) Good, Oumar. Telling your mom will help the scary things to go away.

Talk Time continues. "Today we are going to play a game to help you to get the scary dreams to go away." Because of the nature of Oumar's terrifying symptoms, I decide to teach him a game that has helped many children begin to get symptom relief. Parents often help by taking a part in the role play. I find that, when children are having this much anxiety, they feel more grounded and safe if the parent stays in the room. Parents can then help the child play the game at home before bedtime. I invite Sharon to stay in the room and be part of a game to help scary things go away.

Scary Dream Empowerment Game and Application

The game that I suggest we play prior to his first play therapy session is aimed at helping Oumar be more empowered toward his nightmares.

OUMAR: Good. How do we play the scaring-dreams-away game?

THERAPIST: First, pick out some toys that are scary and put them together.

OUMAR: Okay.

He selects two big rats, one black and one white; the dinosaur dragon with two red heads that he used in the family play session; a huge, hairy spider; two large snakes; and a scary green dragon puppet with a red tongue. I get a foam sword, a pillow, and a silk blanket.

THERAPIST: Now, the way the game goes is that you lie down and pretend that this is your bed—but I'll show you first. [I lie down.] (*I have learned that most kids want me to demonstrate this role first.*) You pick one of the scary things. [I pretend I am sleeping and then get scared.] But, the next time you scare me I will have my sword and I will tell you to go away.

OUMAR: I don't want to play.

This happens a lot, so we desensitize the situation by inviting the parent to play the role of scaring the sleeping person. Sharon agrees to be part of the role play. I pretend to have the scary dream, and Sharon picks the dragon to scare me. She shakes the dragon, saying, "I'm gonna get you." I turn my head over and see it and scream, "I'm scared, I'm scared. Go away." I stay lying down and get more scared. Oumar watches.

Now I say that we are going to do it differently. I go to sleep, and this time the mom uses the scary puppet. I repeatedly close my eyes and snore a bit. Then the mom comes closer, makes noises, and says, "I'm gonna get you." This time I take my sword, sit up, and swing the sword toward the puppet. With a much more empowered voice, I say, "Go away, monster; you can't scare me!" This time the puppet backs away.

Next I have the mom go to sleep. I scare the mom with the spider and again with a rat. The repetition is important. Usually, by this time, the child will want a turn, and Oumar is ready now. I have him do the scaring first, and then role play the one being scared. We play this game for about 10 minutes while Sharon, Oumar, and I repeatedly change roles. This game is a helpful aid in the gradual reduction of symptoms. There is usually some degree of relief by the next session.

I suggest that Oumar keep a foam sword or bat in bed to use when there is a scary dream, or that he come up with his own ideas of how to scare away the fearful image. I also explain to Sharon that there are hidden anxieties involved, and that symptom relief alone will not get at the root issues. I tell her that it is important to continue therapy, explaining that the symptoms may diminish over the next four to six weeks but then, after a while, when Oumar gets into deeper work, reappear with great intensity before finally stopping. We hope they will go away permanently, but I cannot promise. I explain that in my experience, when families have worked at the deeper level, the child will eventually have only an occasional scary dream like any typical child.

Oumar's Spontaneous, Nondirected Play

Next, I invite Oumar to play with anything in the playroom he would like. I ask his mother to sit quietly and observe, joining in only at Oumar's request. I want to see whether he is able to play spontaneously and how he uses the playroom. With very little introduction, spontaneous play allows children to move toward their own healing, so I have a bias toward spontaneous play when it matches a given child's style of playing. Otherwise, I may shift to a more directed approach. I set the timer. Oumar chooses to explore the room quietly. I notice that he hugs his mom once in a while, but he doesn't involve her in the play. He examines the medical cart first and quietly tries the stethoscope. He puts the X-rays of the head and chest into the miniature X-ray machine. Then he picks up different things from the shelf, especially the skeletons, tombstones, ghosts, the volcano, spiders, bugs, and so forth. He looks at them and then replaces them. Because it is the first session, I ask him if he would like to put some of the miniatures into one of the sandboxes. He turns around and nods yes. I give him a basket like the one he was given the week before as the family was creating their sand story. He goes back and gathers many of the toys he just examined. He piles them into the basket, then makes a chaotic-looking picture in the wet sand. He pours in all of the water from one of the containers. I stay near him, at his level, and give him lots of space to create his sandtray.

Occasionally, I nod and make eye contact, enough to feel connected. I trust that the silence contains a constructive process, since he is very present and is initiating his play with self-confidence. Finally I ask, "What's happening?"

OUMAR: The spider is drowning.

THERAPIST [quietly, matching his tone]: Hmmm . . . the spider is drowning . . .

When the timer beeps, Oumar has just found the clear shoebox with a lid, and he opens this and sees different kinds of guns and knives and daggers. He lights up with interest.

OUMAR: These are cool!

THERAPIST: You like them, and you found them just as the beeper was going off. Remember that means that we have just a few more minutes to play.

He tries shooting the guns, then flips the dagger with surprising ability for a six-year-old. Then he quickly puts the guns and knives back in the box and turns to make sure his mom is there. She has been quiet but is writing away on the pad of paper I have given her to jot down any questions that come up during the session. I notice that she has more questions than most parents. I tell Oumar, "Now we can look around the room and clean up together." (*I find it very valuable to have the child help clean up, especially during the exploratory stage of play.*)

Oumar runs over and embraces his mom with an anxious hug. He says he would like to come back and play next week. I am about to explain that it is his parents' turn to come next week, for the family history session, but then I remember that the parents agreed with my recommendation to see Oumar weekly and them weekly for the first month. I ask Sharon if it is possible for Oumar's dad to bring him next week. I suggest that, if possible, the accompanying parent stay in the play therapy room for a while as Oumar gets more comfortable. This means that someone needs to take care of Maya at home, since she cannot be in the playroom with the parent.

This ends Oumar's first play session. Although it seemed important to Oumar that his mother was present, he seemed to do very well playing independently in the room. I answer one of Sharon's questions. However, since I will meet with the parents in two days, I tell her I will respond to her other concerns then.

I let Oumar know that I enjoyed playing today. I remind him to get a sword or bat to leave next to his bed in case he has a scary dream. I also recommend that Sharon and Oumar demonstrate the game to Arnie, who may also want to play. Besides the benefit of including Oumar's dad, this repetition helps reduce symptoms. I mention that it is fine if Linda and Maya want to watch or play, too. I say good-bye, shaking hands and making eye contact, tell Oumar that I will see him next week.

Reflection on First Play Session

Oumar responded quite typically to the structured game during Talk Time, as well as to his first play therapy session. In the game, he chose initially to watch more. Then he joined in to scare away the "bad dream." For the pretend play session, he was curious and even a little excited. He seemed quite anxious as was reflected in his chaotic sand picture. However, he was able to separate from his mom and to play while she stayed in the room. My sense is that he will need a parent in the room for at least a little while. He initiated spontaneous play, and let me know that he can use this healing way of playing. He seemed to trust me and was able to play creatively with his mother witnessing. Oumar was happy to find the aggressive toys at the end of the session. He was able to play with them for just a few minutes, and then was able to follow the directive to stop for cleanup. Sharon was patient watching his play. She wrote down her comments or questions as I had suggested.

Segment IV: Family History—Parents Attend

Arnie's History: The Smith-Harris Family

ARNIE: I have two brothers and two sisters. I am the second oldest. I just turned 41. [Therapist notes the names and ages of his siblings, placing them in age order.] My brother Harry is two years older than me, and he was supposed to carry on the family shoemaking business that our father, Harry Sr., learned from his father, Arnold, my grandfather. The story goes that my grandfather didn't want to stay on the tobacco plantation, in Tennessee; some family members trace back to living there when slaves were freed. Grandfather's older sister, Rennette, was living in Brooklyn, and she knew this old Italian shoemaker, Joe, who needed an apprentice. The shoemaker's only son wanted to be a surgeon, and somehow he became one. So Arnold, my grandfather that I am named after, happily left plantation life against his parents' wishes. Pop-Pop apprenticed with Joe and then worked with him for 10 years until Joe died. My dad, Harry Sr., says he started working for the shoe business as a young child, about 12 years old. He had the talent and didn't really consider another option. Eventually Dad really wanted my brother, Harry Jr., to join him, and so Harry Jr. reluctantly learned the trade. He was good at it but his heart was never in it.

The business was changing, and so my brother Harry and my father were doing custom-made shoes mostly with orthotics. So after a few years of working with my dad, Harry wanted to expand to commercially made shoes, but my father wouldn't have it. They never worked it out, so Harry just left one day and decided to study information technology. He got divorced in the middle of all the turmoil, about five years ago, when his kids were younger. He has a boy, 12; a girl, 10; and a boy, 8. My parents were thrown into a crisis, but my mom was more upset that he was divorcing than about the shoe business.

THERAPIST: How do you feel about all of this?

I draw in two squares for his sons and a circle for his daughter, making a double line between the couple to note his brother's divorce (see figure 9.3). I wonder about the impact of the family feud, knowing the possibility of a ripple effect.

ARNIE: I have to support Harry in his life. He did all of this when he was depressed and felt it was a stigma to go for help—well, that is how we were raised . . . but I care about him and he has his kids regularly on weekends. It's not easy but they are working it out, I guess. As for the shoe business, I really understand that he wanted to move on.

THERAPIST: How was that for your dad when he left the family business?

ARNIE: He was disappointed and depressed, but he eventually accepted it.

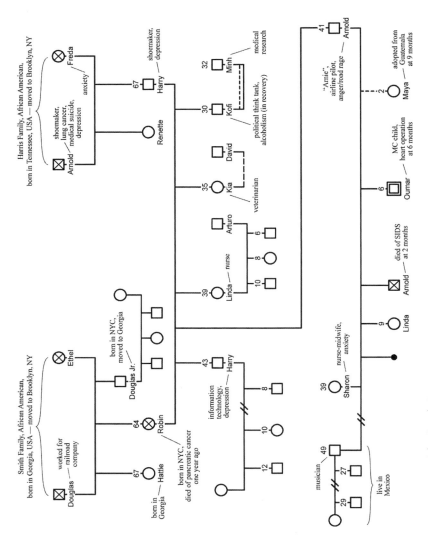

FIGURE 9.3. The Smith-Harris genogram.

248

Harry enjoys his job now, but he and my dad still suffer from depression. Well, the business fell apart and I think it is still hard between them, but they don't talk about it.

SHARON: Well, the good news is that his brother Harry has just started taking antidepressants. Arnie and I are talking to him about the benefits of therapy, and I think he just might try it.

ARNIE: Yeah, I've given up on telling Harry that therapy can help, but Sharon still discusses it with him occasionally. On the other hand, my father just gets depressed or rages, but he doesn't believe in medication. My grandfather was the same way. He worked in his early life on the tobacco plantation before moving to Brooklyn, and he seemed to enjoy the shoemaking. But then when he heard he would die of lung cancer, he ended up killing himself on the second attempt.

THERAPIST: I'm sorry . . . that was your grandfather. Did you know him well?

ARNIE: My father says he was close to him because they worked together. I could walk to their house when I got older. Grandma always had treats for us. Freda was sad because she had to leave Tennessee. Grandpa was happy—my dad says—when he was younger, and then he got more depressed.

THERAPIST: It sounds like your brother did the same thing as your grandfather: decide he didn't want to follow the family expectations about his life work. I'd like to hear more sometime about your other siblings and your parents.

Doing a genogram gives the message early on in therapy that the larger family context is important. I wonder, how is Arnie impacted by the tension between his brother and father? Did joining the Air Force and becoming a pilot help Arnie's individuation from his family of origin? And although Arnie does not suffer from a gloomy depression like his brother's, does he have an agitated depression that is impacting Oumar? Has this family grieved the grandfather's medical suicide? I wonder if Arnie's expectations for his son have something to do with Oumar's present behaviors.

Using the casual questioning format, the genogram goes on to reveal that Arnie was, and still is, closest to his younger sister Linda. Linda is married to Arturo, a professional tango dancer from Argentina. They have three children. Arnie visits them frequently in Brooklyn, especially when Sharon is working weekends at the hospital. Linda introduced Sharon to Arnie when they were roommates in nursing school. At the time, Arnie was in the Air Force training to be a pilot, so they were able to see one another only sporadically.

Sharon takes a moment to explain that during this time she became pregnant. She had an early miscarriage, and six months later the couple broke up. Arnie chimes in that they were both so young and that maybe it was good that they parted. It was a challenging and sad time. "I loved Sharon, but I couldn't be there." Sharon continues that she did not like that Arnie was away. She wanted to date other men. Sharon describes a brief two-year marriage with a musician she met who had two children living in Mexico. She is teary eyed as she briefly talks about this time. I offer a period of silence before entering the conversation again.

THERAPIST: That was a long time ago. [Silence.] Do you want to say more? It sounds like you learned a lot.

SHARON: Yes, I did, and no, that's all for now.

This exchange demonstrates that the recounting of the genogram information can meander and also trigger emotion. It is important to attend to the feelings that are in the room, even if that means the family history will not be completed that day. Sharon's speaking up also shows the value of having partners witness one another's family history. She brought it to a deeper level. Arnie shared some of his feelings in response.

ARNIE: When I heard from my sister that Sharon was divorced, I called her up because I wanted to try to get back together, and after a year or so, she was ready to date. We were cautious about reconnecting, and it had its challenges . . . but I think we have a deep love for one another, and here we are.

As the session continues, Arnie gives further details about his family history.

ARNIE: My next sister, Kia, is four years younger than Linda. Kia has always loved animals, and she's a veterinarian and a vegetarian. She's been in a serious relationship with David for the past six years. They live together and seem married. David is ambivalent about getting married because Kia isn't Jewish and doesn't want to convert. Recently, David went on our family hunting trip for the first time. Kia wasn't happy about it. I don't think he wants to go again.

I was 11 when the youngest, Kofi, was born. He was a "surprise" that divided our parents. Kofi is single, gay, and works for a political think tank in DC. He struggled with alcohol and depression, and now he's in AA. He seems to be a lot happier lately. He has a lot of friends and loves his work. I admire him. He grew up accepting himself, but my parents didn't accept him. For a long time he couldn't be open with them. Linda and I were supportive, and we encouraged him to talk to them. Though it was a difficult time, they are coming around. He is dating an Asian man, Minh, who does medical-related research. They met through their work. They are great uncles to our kids.

I ask Arnie to tell me a little about himself, noting that he is the second oldest and 41. Arnie nods and continues to say that he wanted to be a pilot for as long as he could remember. This wish seemed odd to his parents, since no one in the family had ever been in the Air Force.

ARNIE: I finished two years of college and did well in school but didn't love it like Linda and Kofi do. I joined the Air Force and trained there, but I was unhappy, and I resigned after six years. Now I prefer flying for a commercial airline and I am relatively satisfied, though it has been more stressful, of course, since 9/11—even though that was years ago.

I gather information about Arnie's connection to his younger siblings by asking relational questions. The family hunting tradition is mentioned frequently—who attends and who does not. Arnie notes that it is a ritual passed down through the generations. It bonds the men together and even the women, who sometimes participate. Sharon frowns and says that she is not used to the idea of men going hunting. She worries that someone will get killed, although she does enjoy eating the deer meat. "Either he'll die from an airplane crash or from hunting!" Arnie claims that flying a plane is safer than driving a car and that he has a high degree of job satisfaction. There is a bit of discussion about these fears.

Moving up to the parent generation, I ask about Arnie's mother Robin, who died in the past year, at age 64, of pancreatic cancer. She was seemingly healthy and then, within a couple of months, she was dead. Everyone is still grieving.

THERAPIST: I am sorry. This is a recent death of your mom. I didn't realize she had died. The first year can be particularly challenging.

ARNIE: Yes, challenging! My mom was mostly "at home" in the house adjoining the shoe shop. It had a door that connected to our kitchen. She helped my dad with the bookkeeping and the customers. She was smart! She liked the babies and was warm and loving, but she was more distant as we grew up. [He describes his mom as generally stricter than his dad.] My older brother and I gave her a hard time, too. She really pushed the children to do well in school, whereas my dad didn't seem to care. She had a good sense of humor and laughed a lot. I enjoyed her singing spirituals. I miss that now. . . . [It is hard for Arnie to remember what he didn't like about his mom, and then he notes that she could be stubborn.] She wouldn't let us do things as kids that our friends could do—like go into the city on the metro when we were 13. We would sneak off and go anyway, of course. We just learned not to tell them what we were up to. Other stuff—like joining the local baseball team. Our parents were isolated, so we weren't connected enough to seek out being on a team. (*Bowen's work on the hidden "after shocks" in a family's reaction to death [2004] provides a very valuable framework for understanding the symptoms that this family is having.*)

THERAPIST: Yeah, that sounds isolating. Did your dad have an opinion about these things?

ARNIE: He didn't care. He worked a lot. He was hard working, and he was kind.

I ask next about Arnie's dad's health. Harry Sr. is described as healthy now and mostly retired. He still makes shoes for some of his old customers. He had a heart attack and double bypass surgery seven years ago. Sharon chimes in that that was just after baby Arnie died. Harry seemed to have a quick recovery. Then Oumar was conceived just a few months later. Arnie mentions that he wasn't so sure he wanted a boy, but now he's "happy to have a boy, to have Oumar."

THERAPIST: I'm sorry for all of these painful events happening so close together. I'm beginning to see just how much has happened in a short period of time.

Although I am curious about Arnie's last comment, I decide to wait and ask more about this later, given the time constraints. Arnie and Sharon look at each other and nod.

SHARON: Sometimes I wonder how we got through it all. Maybe we are still in it?

THERAPIST: That's a good question. How do you think you get through life's challenges?

Arnie says he thinks that they have a strong relationship. Sharon adds that, although they grieved differently, they had some bereavement counseling that helped them not to blame each other.

SHARON: Sometimes meditation helps, even 10 minutes. I'd like to talk more about that time. It can still haunt me.

ARNIE: Yeah, that was a crazy time. It would be good sometime to come in together and talk more about all of this.

THERAPIST: [nodding with compassion]: We can do that.

Arnie continues to say that his dad loved to listen to jazz. He learned the saxophone when Arnie was a teenager and seemed to have natural talent.

ARNIE: He was good with his hands and could make anything, so he continued working for some years in the shoe business with his own dad. When my grandfather retired, Dad built a shop on the side of our house and moved the business there. My mom became more involved then.

THERAPIST: So it sounds like he was home a lot, then?

ARNIE: Yes, he was, but he also worked a lot. Sometimes I would hear him working in the night to get a job done when he was busy. But he ate lunch and dinner with us—never breakfast. He always took a nap after lunch, like his dad, a good habit that Pop-Pop learned from the Italian shoemaker. It's funny—sometimes he could be distant, but he also had a very warm side to him. He could hug and cry.

SHARON: You told me that he could also hit you as kids.

ARNIE: Yeah, that's true. Mostly he'd spank us on the tush with his hand or a belt, but once when he was really mad, he hit me with a switch. I was about 10 years old. I swore I would never hit my kid with a belt or a switch—I'd never do that to my kids—and I didn't!

THERAPIST: That's quite a story. This young boy made a promise to himself about his own kids when he was only 10 years old, and has kept it!

ARNIE: Yeah, I never forgot. [Continuing about his father.] My father was devastated when his dad, Pop-Pop, had cancer and killed himself a few years after Grandma Freda died. In some ways, my father felt guilty because his father didn't come live with us. Pop-Pop wouldn't sell the house they grew up in. After the kids left, he made it into condominiums, and he lived alone on the first floor of his brownstone. My dad wishes that he had insisted that Pop-Pop live with us when he got the lung cancer.

THERAPIST: Sounds like your dad may be blaming himself?

ARNIE: We don't talk about it.

SHARON: Like you—distant but warm.

ARNIE: I guess I am like that too—and I can hug and cry.

THERAPIST: I am beginning to get a feel for your relationship with your dad. This will be helpful for me in working with Oumar.

Arnie continues to talk about his grandparents and the history of depression and rage in his family. When I ask Arnie about his own anger, he says that he can "lose it" and get angry, but that he *never* hits the kids. He admits having road rage in driving a car.

ARNIE: It scares Sharon. I have been working on it, but I could use help.

THERAPIST: What do you think, Sharon?

SHARON: He does need help. And it's a big problem when it happens, though, as he said, he has never hit me or the kids. Also, I think that's right—[to Arnie] You don't get brooding like your father and brother, but you do get mad at other cars and it scares the kids and me, too. [To the therapist] He has been working on it this past year—finally.

THERAPIST: Arnie, I appreciate your bringing up the road rage. Yes, it is something we can work on. A while ago, you suggested that the two of you could come in for your own work. Maybe you will want some couple sessions parallel to Oumar's play therapy and the parent meetings. I think I see a pattern in the men of your family having sadness and rage, plus your grandmother Freda was sad that she had to leave her family and friends in Tennessee. We can try to understand what all of this might have to do with Oumar's and Linda's lives and even Maya's. In doing this work, you may help Oumar not need to follow this part of the legacy.

ARNIE: Yeah, I guess so. I never thought about it that way before, but when you write it all down there like a map, depression and anger light up. And I would like to know how it connects to our kids.

THERAPIST: Yes, we can try to understand the intergenerational impact. That leaves your mother Robin's parents.

ARNIE: My mother's parents were Ethel and Douglas. They've both passed. They lived a few blocks away, so I saw them a lot too. My grandfather was a local bus driver, and he had never left Georgia. He had a high school buddy who had moved to New York and worked for the railroad. He helped my grandfather get a job with the railroad, so my grandparents moved up to Brooklyn. It was hard for my grandmother because she didn't know anybody. They had a two-year-old girl, my Aunt Hattie, and they were expecting my mom. So, my mom was born in Brooklyn. I've heard it was a hard adjustment for my grandmother, but after a while, she really enjoyed being close to the big city. Grandpop's job with the railroad offered the family more stability. Their youngest, my Uncle Doug Jr., worked on the family tobacco plantation in high school. Then he settled back in Georgia years later. He and his wife have three children, two boys and a girl; they are all grown up. We still have the tradition of visiting the South in the summer, and both families have reunions every few years. There is an interesting family history about slavery. I should start telling our kids their history!

THERAPIST: Yes, that would be good for all three of them. And when we have more time, I would like to hear some of the stories as well.

ARNIE: Gramps died right after he retired. I was in high school. My grandmother moved in with Hattie, who never married.

Time constraints usually allow me to gather only a little information about the grandparents' history. I can come back to this later when it becomes important to the present therapy. Families become acclimated to share their personal stories in the future because of this experience of sharing their family history early on.

THERAPIST: Is there anything else important in your family history that I haven't asked about? Depression? Anxiety? Other abuse?

ARNIE: Besides being hit by Dad, nothing I can think of. Well, of course he was hit by his father too. At the time parents hit their kids, not that it makes it right. Now, of course, you can't do that. No criminal history that I know of. I mentioned my father's and brother's depression.

I have more questions about intergenerational anger, rage, and abuse, but I decide that for now the information I have will suffice. In making the transition to Sharon's genogram process, I ask if there are any spiritual or religious connections. They each describe how they were raised, and say that at present they have decided to go to Quaker meetings. They are not sure about their commitment, but both appreciate the quiet meetings and nonjudgmental atmosphere.

While making the transition from Arnie's to Sharon's genogram, I also ask about the couple relationship—how would they assess their own commitment? I inquire whether they get along with each other's families and if their families are concerned about their being a mixed-race couple.

ARNIE: This process of the last four sessions is helping me to see how much we have been dealing with in the short period of time since my mother died a year ago. Honestly, I feel somewhat distant now from you, Sharon . . . but I think it is my fault, and I don't question our love. My job flying makes some distance, but I want to be closer when I'm home. As far as our families, you mean, was there prejudice? Well, if so I think it was more covert than overt. My family knew Sharon as Linda's friend first. I do remember being annoyed with my sister Ki, when she said, "There goes another black man not available to black women." I understood what she meant by it—that with the high mortality rate in young black men, her friends were having trouble meeting available black guys. But my parents never said anything negative to me. I don't know; what do you think, Sharon?

SHARON: Arnie, I don't think you ever told me that Kia said that; I don't remember. Hmmm . . . she seemed to be the least happy about us at the time, but now she's great. I think she has her own issues now—ironically, David is white, and also because she isn't Jewish. I've had some good conversations about religion, race, et cetera with her recently. Your parents have been good to me. I think there was more resistance in my family, I am ashamed to admit. It was subtle, but when I realized that I wanted to date you again, I addressed my parents feelings directly. I think they are generally accepting of my life decisions now, and embrace Arnie. In this case, they saw me as divorced, and worried that I was making a decision again too quickly. My parents have consciously chosen to live in a racially mixed middle-class neighborhood rather than their respective Irish and Italian white neighborhoods where they grew up. My mom has said that both of my parents' families would have been happier if they had each married within their Irish and Italian culture. I think it was her way of understanding. People thought that way more at that time than they do nowadays. I think as long as we don't ignore subtleties we do okay.

ARNIE: Yeah, her parents are good to me, and her brothers and sisters, I think, really love me—believe me, we have our differences, but I love them. I actually enjoy family parties.

SHARON: It's nice to hear you say that. Also, I want to address the first question, too. I agree with you that you have seemed more distant this past year—but I also think our schedule hasn't helped. Maybe I need to stop arranging my schedule so that I'm working on your days off. Now that the children are getting older, maybe my parents can help a little more, or we can hire someone for after school. I want more closeness too. But looking at our lives this way gives me compassion for how well we are doing! And I feel like it's not only that Oumar will get help for his hallucinations, anxiety, and nightmares—we can all benefit from being here.

Sharon's History: The O'Ryan-Caruso Family

I begin a new genogram template as I start to ask Sharon her family history (see figure 9.4).

THERAPIST: How many siblings do you have?

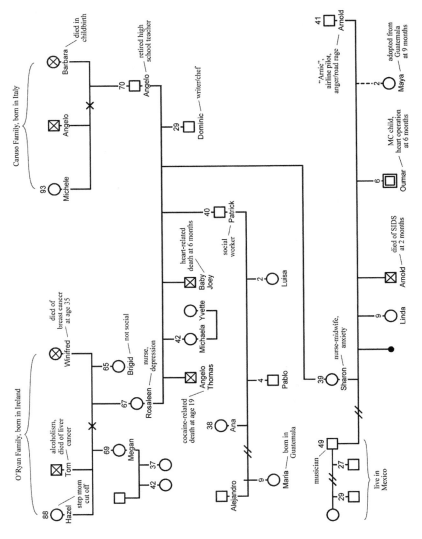

FIGURE 9.4.   The O'Ryan-Caruso genogram.

SHARON: Five. Well, there were six of us altogether—four brothers and two sisters. I am the second youngest. I just turned thirty-nine.

Sharon gives me the names and ages of her siblings, indicating whether they are married or in a committed relationship; she also provides the sexes and ages of their children. I add Sharon's first husband and his children to the genogram, including baby Arnold, who died of SIDS. Then, Sharon tells me about her siblings, beginning with the oldest.

SHARON: Angelo was nineteen when he died. I'll tell you more about that. Michaela is forty-two; baby Joey died at six months. I've mentioned him to you before. You know Patrick; he's forty. I'm next, thirty-nine, and Dominic is twenty-nine years old. Baby Joey is the one who had a congenital heart problem, like Oumar. The doctors didn't know as much about it back then. That was before I was born, so I never met him, but everybody talked about him, and we had a picture of him in the living room holding a zebra. Patrick's the fourth child. He was born only a year after Joey died. I'm number five and Dom's the youngest. He's ten years younger than me.

Sharon describes how her brother, Angelo, died while experimenting with cocaine during his first year of college. She was just 13 at the time and recalls the story of the phone call her family received. When Sharon apologizes for her tears, I warmly assure her that tears are fine here. Arnie leans over and comforts his wife. We have a moment of silence. "What a tragedy for you and your family," I gently respond.

Sharon goes on to tell us that his death made her never want to use any drugs. It was at this time that she decided to become a nurse. "I wish I could have saved him. My mother was too overwhelmed in her own grief; Micaela and I comforted one another."

THERAPIST: It's good that you and Michaela had one another. I am noticing that you learned from this experience for your own life. You decided not to use drugs, and you began to formulate a life direction that cares about other people.

SHARON: Well, I never thought about it like that until now, but yes, his death really did impact my life! It probably does have to do with my choosing to be a nurse.

Sharon describes details of growing up close to her sister Michaela, who now teaches in the south of France. She has dual citizenship through her mother's father, who was born in Ireland. This enables her to work legally in the European Union. She and her partner, Yvette, met at the university and will come home this summer for a visit. Sometimes when Arnie isn't home, Sharon and the kids have dinner with Michaela through videoconferencing. Sharon also tells me a little about her parents' response to her sister's coming out. It was hard for them, but in time they came to accept it.

THERAPIST: How about Patrick? He is forty, and I know he is a social worker.

SHARON: Yes, he takes classes here in play therapy and family therapy with you. He's the one who referred us to you. As you know, he works with a foster care agency.

THERAPIST: Let me take this opportunity to say that I know your brother, since he studies here, and he is a fine person. I want to mention that the confidentiality guidelines are very strict. As far as I am concerned, *nothing* will be said to him by me. Of course, you are allowed to say anything to him about your therapy, but I can't say anything to him, and that's how it should be. [To Arnie and Sharon] I want to be sure that you both understand that.

SHARON: I do. Patrick explained it to me, and as a nurse, confidentiality issues are familiar to me.

ARNIE: Sharon mentioned this to me before she made the appointment. I get how it works.

Sharon recounts that Patrick lived in Guatemala, where he met his wife, Ana, and stepdaughter, Maria. After a marriage and an immigration nightmare, they moved back to the United States and live nearby. There are two more children now: Pablo is four and Luisa is two. Sharon feels closest to Patrick now, as the families are supportive of each other. Arnie adds that their daughter, Linda, and Maria are the same age and both go to a Spanish immersion school in Philadelphia. Linda and Maria are now able to have some simple conversations in Spanish.

ARNIE: They're really great, supportive, and Sharon helps them out a lot when she can. It was Ana and Patrick that let us know about the adoption connection in Guatemala where we met Maya.

Sharon explains that she and Patrick lived in the shadow of baby Joey's death.

SHARON: As a result, Mom was anxious and fearful that we would get hurt. We were healthy, but they still worried. I think that's why I worry a lot, too. They also loved one another and didn't argue, like we do.

THERAPIST: So it seemed like when you were young, your mother worried without cause. Good reason, but no cause?

SHARON: Yeah. I used to feel so mad at my mom when I was a teenager, but I avoided telling her. Now that I'm a parent, I understand it better. They couldn't say no either—especially mom—and I don't think it helped me. I never learned to speak up to my friends, and in high school that was a problem. Also, I'm just like her, and I worry when I don't need to.

THERAPIST: I see. You trace not knowing how to say no to your children back to your parents, who couldn't say no to you either.

SHARON: Yeah. For example, *our* kids will have a curfew and I will make an attempt to know where they are. I had too much rope and I liked it then, but now I wish I had more limits set by my parents.

THERAPIST: I'm also wondering about your saying your parents didn't argue. Learning how to express healthy differences can be positive. Did they avoid disagreeing?

SHARON: I don't know; it's a good question.

THERAPIST: So Dom is also a lot younger than you.

SHARON: Yeah, nine years, but he was planned and wanted. My mom was thirty-eight, which was old for having a baby at that time. She was young having the rest of us, but she was feeling the biological clock— it's now or never—and I think she talked my father into one more child. I was nine when Dom was born, and I had bugged her about having a baby. I wanted a sister. For a couple of years, I walked around begging for a pet monkey if I couldn't have a sister. So I felt powerful when he was born, though disappointed that he wasn't a girl. So my mom liked having a baby, and it was a happy time in our lives. I helped out a lot. Looking back on it, I wouldn't let Linda have as much responsibility for a baby as I had for Dom. At first I really liked helping. But after a while, I'd hide and read a book so my mom couldn't find me.

THERAPIST: It seems like nine-year-old Sharon knew when it was too much. Tell me more about Dom.

SHARON: Dom was spoiled and difficult in his teen years. My mom asked me for advice about his problems. Now he's thirty and lives in New York City in a tiny apartment in Chinatown, and he's passionate about writing. He went to the Culinary Institute and makes a living as a chef. I have to be careful not to be like a mother and more like his sister. He lets me know when I step over the line.

THERAPIST: As you speak about your siblings, I'm getting an idea of how life was for you, but tell me more about growing up and your own teen years.

SHARON: School was my outlet. I excelled in school, and it helped me get away from the cloud in our house. Well, I do think Mom was depressed most of my life. Probably most of her life even way before I was born. But, as I mentioned, she had a happy period when Dom was a baby.

I notice that it is hard for Sharon to keep talking about herself and her own life. This may indicate how her mother's depression loomed over her. I decide to ask more about it.

THERAPIST: Do you know what that long-term depression could be about?

SHARON: I've asked her about it, but she doesn't see herself as depressed. I didn't realize it was depression until I moved back home after nursing school for a few months, while I was starting a new job. That was when I realized it. She doesn't just worry and get anxious sometimes; she has a chronic, low-grade depression. I've tried to get her to talk about it, but she denies it. It's frustrating for me—what do I do?

THERAPIST: Well, maybe with part of your work here, you will want to figure out what you can and can't do about your mother being anxious and depressed. What are your mom's strengths?

SHARON: Even though she's depressed, she can be warm, and she can listen when I have a problem. She gives her advice but doesn't tell me what to do. She has a good work ethic—so does my dad. Long ago, she took training to be a nurse's aide, and she could always find a job. Then, when Dom was in junior high, my mom decided to get her RN. I respect her for that. She still works at the same nursing home, but now she has more administrative responsibilities. People there love her, and I think that helps her depression. So, on the negative side, she holds things in and has a hard time making decisions.

THERAPIST: For example?

SHARON: Everything. I think it is her anxiety. Like what to have for dinner—small decisions—and should she and my dad visit my sister for her birthday? She'll call and feel torn about whatever is happening. I don't want to be like that.

ARNIE: Sometimes the apple doesn't fall far from the tree.

SHARON: Come on, Arnie, I know I worry, but I hope I'm not that bad! [They laugh.]

ARNIE: No, you're not!

I ask Sharon specific questions about how she and her siblings were parented at a young age. She describes a split in her family where her mother would make decisions for the girls and her father for the boys. She also describes her academic and social life in high school. She was a good student and has a few friends from high school that she is still close to. However, she describes a period where she found herself unable to stand up to peer pressure and feels that her parents let her do too much of what she wanted. At the time, she liked getting her way, but she wishes they had been more strict about her curfew or insisted she go to family events. "I got into more trouble than was good for me." (*I know this is important and connects with Sharon's not being able to say no to her own children.*)

As I continue to ask questions, Sharon tells me that her parents met in a pub at a celebration of her mother's friend's birthday and that her mother said, that night, that she would marry her dad.

THERAPIST: So that is how your parents met! And what a bold realization for someone who has a hard time making decisions.

SHARON: Yeah, but it was a rocky relationship for three years. Mom had a dream about being an actress, but was afraid to live in New York City. I guess it was on-again, off-again. They didn't tell us until we were teens that Angelo was conceived before they were married. Dad seemed clear, but my mom's indecision turned the corner when she got pregnant.

THERAPIST: How were their two families feeling then about the courtship?

SHARON: I'm not sure. My dad was twenty-seven when they were married. And after three years back and forth, and a baby on the way, I think everyone was OK with the Irish–Italian union. My mother's father had been sick with liver cancer.

I am curious about what isn't being said here, but will ask another time. I want to better understand how this family would be considered "open" and how it would be considered "closed."

THERAPIST: I'd like to hear more about your family's reactions at another meeting.

SHARON: My folks liked Philadelphia, so they stayed here and raised their family. Dad grew up in South Philadelphia near the Italian Market, and she grew up in Manayunk. He taught history most of his life at an agricultural high school located on the edge of the city. He is seventy and is retired now, but he really liked teaching. He is healthy and he takes long walks every day, mostly in Fairmount Park. My mom always liked the Mt. Airy neighborhood, so that's how we came to live here. I like it, too. I love the miles of woods and trails that are in walking distance from our house. It's like being in a city and living in the country at the same time.

THERAPIST: Well, there are a lot of strengths in your life, and there were happy times besides the challenges. How's your mom's health now?

SHARON: My mom, Rosaleen, is sixty-seven and healthy. Her mother, Winifred, immigrated from Ireland at eighteen. She died of breast cancer when she was only thirty-five years old. My Aunt Megan was twelve, my mom was ten, and Aunt Brigid was eight. They went to live with different relatives. As my mom puts it, their lives changed a lot. Grandpa Tom was an alcoholic, and that got worse when his wife died. The three girls always had family around to make meals and look after them, but Mom never felt she belonged anywhere. Four years later, her father married Hazel, who was ten years younger, and none of the three sisters ever liked their stepmother. My mom said she was mean and unhappy. Looking back now, my mom has more compassion for someone joining a man with three teenage daughters. It's sad, but none of the sisters stayed connected to her. She is close to ninety and lives alone. I'd like to see her again. I only met her a long time ago at somebody's funeral.

I know it's hard for my mother to express sadness about her mother dying—I've never seen her cry about it. She'll say she's sad, but she has an attitude of just picking up and moving on—you do what you've gotta do. I guess that's how she's survived. Grandpa Tom died of liver cancer just after my mother was married. He never met my brother Angelo Thomas, who was named after him.

THERAPIST: Your mother's had a lot of loss—her mother when she was only ten, her father just before Angelo was born, then baby Joey, and then Angelo's tragic death at age nineteen.

SHARON: Yeah, I should understand why she's always depressed. I wish I could help her feel better. She never realized her dream to be an actress, but she does still go to all the Broadway shows in Philadelphia and New York with her sisters, Aunt Megan and Aunt Brigid, and I must say they laugh a lot together! In fact, it's the only time I've see Brigid laugh. Maybe it's because she was the youngest when their mother died, but she's basically very unhappy and lives alone. She doesn't socialize or join us for family events.

In Contextual Family Therapy, this information is like discovering a gold mine. This is an enormous amount of loss. It helps me to understand Rosaleen's chronic depression. I wonder how Sharon's sensitivity to her mother's depression is impacting her own relationship to her own losses and to her children and husband. Will Sharon choose to work on the relationships with her parents after Oumar's crisis is healing? Will Sharon reach out to her mother's stepmother?

THERAPIST: How was your parents' relationship with each other?

SHARON: Basically good, I think. I rarely saw them argue. Sometimes I idealize their marriage. Once they had a big fight—it was unusual. I worried that they would divorce. I think they respected one another a lot, and went through a lot together that brought them closer. After Dad retired, they traveled. Now they go to exotic places with senior groups.

Later, when Sharon's parents come in for a therapy session with Sharon, her mother sheds light on her parents' relationship by admitting that both of her parents had a style that avoided confrontation. This, in turn, helps Sharon begin to understand a root level issue: why it is so hard for her to say "no" to her children. She doesn't like confrontation either!

THERAPIST: It sounds like an interesting family to me! How about your father's side?

SHARON: My dad, Angelo. He was first generation, raised near the Italian Market in South Philly. Dad says he was mischievous in high school and had trouble learning, but that's why he wanted to be a teacher, and people say he's a really good teacher. Angelo's mother died in child-birth, and his father married his mother's best friend, Michelle. She loved the baby like he was her own. And sadly it turned out that Michelle could never have children, so my father didn't have any siblings. Michelle is ninety-three and lives at Mom's nursing home.

When I look at how I was parented . . . I don't want to worry as much as my mom. I want to be happier with my life than she was. I don't want to split the children up on how we raise them. I'd like to feel closer to my kids than I do to my dad. I like my dad, but he's distant. Maybe there's still time for me to get closer to him. I want to be a good listener like my mom, but less anxious than she is.

THERAPIST: I think that now you may be able to get closer to your dad. And that will also help you in your relationships with your children. What do you think?

SHARON: Is that how it works? I'd also like help with our different parenting styles—with Arnie's temper and my anxiety.

THERAPIST: Is there anyone on your genogram that you haven't mentioned who has a history of any abuse, drug or alcohol abuse, depression, anxiety, criminal history, other issues of concern?

Sharon cannot think of anything more to add at this time, so we review and highlight what she has already said. I show the parents the colorful mandala that outlines the stages of play therapy and briefly explains how the play therapy happens. We discuss continuing to help Oumar with his nightmares and separation anxiety, and to start looking at some of the underlying reasons for his symptoms. Next week will begin Oumar's weekly sessions of play therapy. I emphasize that is is important for both parents to take turns bringing Oumar for his sessions. Sharon addresses Oumar's therapy schedule, which is on her day off. I ask Arnie if he can make at least one of the four sessions and then, of course, the parent meetings. Arnie says that that is workable.

THERAPIST: Since we're out of time for today, I'll ask each of you to think about insights from your past and how you were raised that may help with the present situation. I'll give you a little more feedback at our next parent meeting about my reflections. Some of the intergenerational information may not be relevant for awhile, but it's very helpful for me to have it.

Reflection on the Family Histories

A primary goal of the genogram process is to gain an understanding of the manner in which the parents were themselves parented over earlier generations. It is the beginning of formulating a narrative history—important to develop when working with families. What are the circumstances of their lives, the resources and the pains that inform their current situation? In this particular case, the history of depression, including a medically related suicide, is noteworthy. This genogram session reveals the recent loss of Arnie's mother, Robin, who died suddenly of pancreatic cancer just a year ago. It reveals clues about the roots of attachment in the feelings expressed about parents and grandparents. Sharon was raised by a mother whose mother died when she and her sisters were children. She is now cut off from her stepmother. Arnie was raised by a father whose mother died in childbirth. How did this loss impact how Arnie was raised? What was the impact of immigration experiences, from Ireland and Italy, on relationships within Sharon's family? What history related to slavery might be influencing Arnie's family narrative, and what is the significance of the fact that his father's family is still living on the plantation where their ancestors were once slaves? What about Arnie's grandparents' move from the South? Are there topics regarding race and class that are relevant but being avoided? Will the couple have their own therapy to get to root-level issues, or will they choose to help their son only with his present anxieties? Contextual Family Therapy is valuable for exploring all these questions. This process lays a foundation for the practice of Mindful Parenting by helping the parents become consciously aware of the influence that their own histories bring to bear on their style of parenting and of being a couple.

Oumar's First MBPFT Session
Following Evaluation

The following segment takes place after the four-segment evaluation is completed. We have decided to continue to have two meetings a week for the next month: the mindful parenting meetings, which only the parents will attend, and Oumar's play-family therapy sessions. Once there has been enough alleviation of Oumar's scary symptoms and his parents' anxieties have lightened, we have the option of moving to the typical pattern of four sessions of play-family therapy followed by one parent meeting.

I have suggested to the family that the therapy may take about a year unless difficulties arise that the family or I am currently unaware of. I have welcomed the parents to have their own couple therapy to address issues they are struggling with in their marriage and within their families of origin. After the first month, they agree to continue coming every other week so that they can do both parenting and couple work.

Talk Time

Sharon has managed to be more compassionate about Oumar's intense anxiety. At this meeting, she confides that she worries that it could mean that he is mentally ill. At first he was having these scary nightmares every night, and he doesn't remember most of them. Although they are already less frequent than they were, they are just as intense. I comment to Sharon that I understand her worry and that we need to talk about this—her fear of Oumar's being mentally ill—later when Oumar is not here. (*Helping parents with boundaries of what is appropriate and not appropriate to talk about is important.*) Although I cannot promise anything because every child and family is different, I repeat that, based on my experience with this problem in other children, I believe that the symptoms will decrease gradually within the next month or two and that the best we can do now is to help the whole family to cope. I am compassionate about how challenging it is and how well the family has done in trying to help Oumar. I again advise the parents to try to contain him in his room at night rather than letting him run around the house.

This week, the scary dream that Oumar told his mom concerns the sunlight. Oumar asks his mom to describe it to me.

SHARON: The sunlight befriends the little boy, but then the boy dies from the sunlight.

THERAPIST [looking at Oumar as though he had spoken himself]:   It is very good that you can tell your mom these scary dreams. It sounds like the sun was like a friend, and then the boy dies from the sun.

OUMAR: Yeah, it started to burn me up.

THERAPIST [nodding]:   Wow. [Pause.] It sounds scary to almost burn up.

OUMAR: Yeah, but I didn't.

THERAPIST: No, you didn't burn up in the dream.

OUMAR: No. Mommy was there, and she hugged me, and she let me go back to her room. Daddy was at work. I am mad Daddy isn't there too.

THERAPIST: Mommy came in and hugged you, and you went back to her room. But you are mad that your daddy isn't there too. Right now you are right here with your mom and me, and you are okay. Do you think if your daddy were home that he could stop the nightmares?

OUMAR [nodding his head]:   Yeah.

THERAPIST [quietly nodding]:   Hmmm . . . you think if your dad were home you wouldn't have these nightmares. No wonder you're mad at your dad. You think if he were home you wouldn't have them. (*It is important to model for parents to take a child's fears seriously—to "get it"—even if it does not match adult logic.*)

Later, I ask, "So when Dad is home and not flying his airplane, do you have the nightmares?"

OUMAR: Sometimes. But I feel better.

We go on to discuss this and plan to talk more to his dad about this next week. Sharon then encourages Oumar to tell me about the people who come out of the wall. He looks scared again, his brow tensing. He looks me in the eye. Then he covers his face with a pillow. I can tell this is going to be difficult. Oumar asks his mom to tell me.

SHARON: The other night when we were upstairs getting ready for bed, he told me about the visitors that come. They are a family with parents and grandparents, and there are some children in the family. They are dressed in old-fashioned clothes. The parents talk to him and say that he is to come to them. That we—his dad and I—are not his real parents and that they are his real parents.

Oumar moves the pillow away from his face and looks at me.

THERAPIST: How brave it is that you can tell your mom. I can really understand why you feel scared. These people are telling you that your mom and dad are not your real parents, and yet they are. [Pause.] That must be scary and confusing.

OUMAR [with a dead serious and scared expression]:   Yeah.

It is clear that, although he has had fewer dreams and fewer hallucinations in the past week, his experiences have been very intense. It is important that he is able to externalize the experiences by telling his mom, and that she then tells me as he listens. He is also quite able to express his feelings in play therapy, and this encourages me to believe that he will continue to get relief.

Reenacting Oumar's Scary Dream

During the remainder of the Talk Time, we create a big yellow sun using construction paper. For the next five minutes, we enact Oumar's sun dream and use the sword to scare it away, playing the scary dream empowerment game as we did last week.

Play Therapy Session

This is Oumar's third time in the playroom. I already know from the four-segment evaluation that Oumar is comfortable with spontaneous, imaginary play and that he has some anxiety about being in the playroom without a parent. This time, expecting his resistance, I invite him to come into the playroom with just me. When possible, I like to have a session alone with the child. I am not surprised when he looks scared and says he'd like his mom to come too. I have asked her to leave Maya home until Oumar can feel comfortable with me in the playroom, and now my intuition is confirmed. Having Oumar get to know and trust me is a priority. I tell Oumar, "Well, I am glad you can tell me that you want to have your mom with you in the playroom. And next week your dad will be bringing you to play, and he can come in too. So let's have your mom or dad in the playroom for a while." (*Children can suggest what they want, but since this is a clinical decision, I find it best that the child understands that the therapist makes the decision.*) I ask the parent to sit quietly while the child plays, and only to engage the child if invited, and then to keep it in imaginative play. I coach the parent a bit so that the responses are reflective. I give Sharon a tablet of paper and invite her to write down any thoughts or questions. I will address these briefly at that end of the session or more fully at the Parent Education and Feedback Meetings that are built into the process.

At the beginning of the play session, I set the timer as Oumar goes directly to the dry sand and plays with it for a few minutes. He sifts it through his hands. He then takes a large stone heart from the shelf and buries it in the sand. He buries and unburies the heart a few times, looking up at me and back, then leaves the heart buried when he sees a toy ride-on train with a bell. He tries riding the train, but his six-year-old body is too big for it. He tumbles and laughs. I remind him that when the timer beeps it will be time for cleanup—and that we have lots of time.

Oumar continues to play with the ride-around train, putting a large, brown boy doll/puppet on it. He then engages me, and I use a dog puppet to respond, keeping the play in pretend. He instructs the dog to be naughty and at first the dog does not go to his room when told. Taking the cue, I enact this. Next, Oumar selects three big dinosaurs and has them play aggressively with one another—each biting the next one's tail before they all kill one another. Then quickly he says, "Now they are all friends." (*A child's play themes do not have to make logical sense to us. With this approach, it is better not to ask, for example, "If they are friends, why do they kill one another?" This would bring the child to his explicit, left-brain thinking mind and pull him away from the imaginative, more implicit state of mind, where there is greater access to healing trauma.*)

OUMAR: Now this one cuts him open and pulls out his heart.

The two-headed dragon pulls out the heart of the brontosaurus.

THERAPIST: Cuts him open and pulls out his heart . . .

Oumar is quiet for a minute, then leaves and looks in the closet. He finds a peanut ball and rolls on it with his whole body.

OUMAR: Can I do that?

THERAPIST: Sure.

Oumar then tries something dangerous with his body on the peanut ball.

THERAPIST: I need you to be safe on that. It is important for me to keep the room safe for you.

I witness quietly as Oumar plays safely on the peanut ball, rolling around with his whole body for a little longer, and then goes back to the sandtray. He quietly buries and unburies a small red plastic heart, and then he gets the large white and black rats and two Ninja Turtles with swords, two airplanes and fire engines, an ambulance, dump trucks, a back hoe, snakes, a big purple frog, spiders, more snakes, and army men. He layers the sandtray anxiously with many toys. He puts the brontosaurus and T-rex from the floor into the sandtray.

OUMAR: The Ninja Turtle is taking cover.

THERAPIST: Taking cover.

OUMAR: He hears him [meaning the white rat], he sees him. The two rats try to kill the Ninja Turtle.

Oumar fixes the sword more tightly in Ninja's hand. The rats try to kill the Ninja Turtle, and he protects his heart with a shield. After intense playing, the Ninja "slices off the white rat's head and makes him dead." He takes out the heart and buries it in the corner of the sandbox.

Following this extended play, Oumar goes over to the timer and asks if the time is up. I let him know we have two more minutes. He goes back to the dog puppet who is waiting and invites his mother, who has been sitting patiently, to join in the play.

OUMAR: Doggy come out now. Mommy, you be the doggy. [I coach Sharon to get her cues by whispering as they play this for a few minutes.]

SHARON [as doggy]:   Does doggy come out?

OUMAR: Yeah, you come out now.

The session ends in playing bubbles.

As the beeper sounds, he takes the large red binoculars and asks if he can keep them. I reflect that he wants to keep them and explain that all the toys have to stay in the playroom. I reflect his disappointment as he learns the playroom expectations. Once the beeper sounds and we are cleaning up, we are now in reality, not pretend. This five minutes helps the child to come back from the world of imagination and to feel grounded in reality before leaving the room.

After my explanation, Oumar charges toward the peanut ball and throws his body on it. I say, "Once the beeper sounds, it's time for cleanup. Here, put the ball into the closet," and he cooperates. "Here, you put the dinosaurs away, and I'll start to put the toys in here away." Sharon also helps. (*I have developed an end-of-session ritual for just before opening the door. I hold the child's hands and our eyes connect and then we both stomp our feet. The purpose is to connect and to transition from pretend to reality.*)

Reflection on Play Therapy Session

This is a very typical early play session. Oumar explores several areas, then plays for a longer time in two areas, exhibiting themes that reflect his anxiety. He expresses fear about having his head cut off, which is actually happening in his nightmares. Sometimes, the early sessions get right to the heart of the matter. In some ways, this is a preview of what is ahead, possibly developing themes that will expand later on. His play of burying and unburying the large stone heart is interesting, and he continues this play in later sessions. I notice that after engaging in a theme with strong energy, he moves away from the play.

Toward the end of the session, he invites his mom into the puppet play. I am surprised that he does not play more with her today, but he does seem to feel comforted that she is present. Then Oumar chooses the bubbles, which is interesting, because we find that children use bubbles to help with separation. Frequently bubbles provide a good transition at the beginning of the session, in separating from the parent; Oumar uses them to transition with his mom away from the playroom and the therapist.

The Exploratory and Limit Setting Stages

When the family is cooperating with therapy and the child feels safe in his parental relationships, there is often an early reduction of both the initial symptoms and the family stress and anxiety. Oumar's therapy process during the next four to six weeks follows this pattern, with a gradual decrease in the frequency and intensity of his nightmares and hallucinations. The themes remain similar: A green and a red buffalo may be fighting and a skull may appear in a dream. Sometimes the family in his hallucinations is kind and friendly, and he enjoys them. I coach the parents to tell Oumar that it is fine to enjoy them when they are friendly, but, "It's confusing for these people to say scary things to you, like that you should join them, or that your parents are not your real mom and dad. Your mom and dad will help you so this can stop."

Oumar's weekly play therapy sessions are going well. His parents are taking turns bringing him, and they are starting to help him stay in his bedroom at night. Sharon notices she lets him come into their bedroom more often when Arnie is flying. He is learning to sleep on the floor mattress. Sharon is generally sympathetic about Oumar's nightmares, though she has my compassion for feeling sleep deprived. We discuss the sleep issues at our parent meetings.

Talk Time

Honest Dialogue: Oumar With His Dad

When Arnie comes to Talk Time with Oumar, I can see that Oumar has been telling his father more about his experiences, as his dad requested. Oumar is very direct in saying that his dad is not home enough and that he does not like it. "You're not there to help me with my monsters!" Oumar shouted at him one day. "And this week you're going hunting and you won't be home again!"

ARNIE: When you're older you can go hunting with me.

OUMAR: But I don't want you to go!

ARNIE: I am going, and your mom will be home to take care of you, and granny too.

I have recommended the book *How to Talk So Kids Will Listen & Listen So Kids Will Talk* to Arnie and Sharon. Although Arnie admits that he has read only the first chapter, we have been practicing active listening in our parent meetings. I decide to take this opportunity to coach Arnie in the moment and interrupt their talking.

THERAPIST: Oumar sounds really angry at you, and as we have been discussing at our parent meetings, it's good for him to be able to tell you his feelings. It's an important part of having his symptoms go away.

ARNIE [looking his son in the eye]: I'm glad that you can tell me how mad you are. It's hard for you that I'm not home a lot when you have these scary dreams.

OUMAR [in an angry voice]: Nightmares!

ARNIE: Yeah, nightmares. I'm your dad, but I'm not able to make your dreams, nightmares, or the things you see in the daytime go away.

OUMAR [still mad]: Right! And I want you to stay home and not go hunting.

ARNIE: I hear how mad you are, and that you want me to stay home, but I have to work, and I *am* going hunting with Gramps and Uncle Harry and the others. When you're older, you can come.

Arnie is especially motivated because he understands that when Oumar expresses these things, he is not keeping them in his body. The father-son dialogue, in addition to encouraging an authentic relationship, is also part of the strategy to reduce anxiety and ultimately eliminate the hallucinations. Oumar has an opportunity to express his feelings and to be heard by his father. This is often the best a parent can do, and it teaches children to accept what they cannot change. Later, we discuss this topic again at a family meeting.

Play Therapy: A Summary of Early Sessions

In Oumar's early play sessions, his themes have alternated between chaotic sandtrays and stories about hunting. In creating the sandplay stories, Oumar is very anxious and uses mostly large toys. He often uses the three dinosaurs, the two big rats, the hunter with the bow and arrow, dump trucks, backhoes, fire engines, the large pirate with the gun, ambulances, Ninja Turtles, two unicorns, dolphins, sharks and whales, and a Superman who at first is powerless and later becomes more powerful. During the exploratory and limit setting stages, he dumps more toys into the sandtray than seem to fit. Gradually, he uses fewer pieces and his stories become more coherent. Most of his first sandplay is done with me and either his mom or dad as observers.

After a couple of months, when Oumar is less anxious, I recommend that his accompanying parent stay in the waiting room during his playtime, letting Oumar have his session alone with me. Sharon's response lets me observe that she, too, is less anxious. Arnie understands that Oumar's play is less self-conscious when they are not there.

Generally, he moves back and forth, within one room, between using the sand table and playing in the play area with props and pretend stories. He opens the clear shoebox with the handguns, knives, daggers, binoculars, sheriff's badge, police gun, handcuffs, and so forth. He shows his competence with spinning the plastic dagger, and then he usually creates a hunting story. As the sessions go on and we are alone in the playroom, he invites me to be a part of the play themes. He is often the hunter and I the deer, pig, or buck. Sometimes he changes our roles, and I am the hunter shooting the prey. (*Shifting roles in play therapy is common, as it allows the child to experience the feelings of being both victim and victimizer.*) We use props— felt antlers, a pig nose—that I put on when he assigns these animal roles to me. He has discovered the red cylindrical tunnel that pops open. He crawls in and hides his weapons in there. After the first few sessions, he seems to understand how the play works, and he does not push many limits. He readily stays in pretend most of the time. He is learning to be safe and to respond to me when I speak up for safety.

The trust between Oumar and me is growing. In fact, I notice that he starts to use the guns and rifle more when his mom is not in the playroom, expressing his aggression more freely. I notice that the play is gradually transitioning out of the limit setting and exploration stages and just beginning to enter the deeper awareness stage of healing.

Family Meeting

Even after he speaks up to his father in Talk Time about wanting him to be home more, Oumar continues to express his frustration. I suggest that we have a family meeting about his father's airline schedule and his mother's schedule at the hospital. I also want to better understand the involvement of the multiple caregivers in the family context, including grandparents, aunts, and babysitters. I recommend that Linda, Oumar's older sister, come to this meeting and share her thoughts.

At this meeting, Oumar repeats his angry message to his father, and an interaction follows that is similar to what occurred during Talk Time a few weeks prior. This time, Oumar's mother, his sister, and I served as witnesses as his father reflects and really tries to hear Oumar's feelings. Then Linda speaks up about not liking it when her mother has to work on weekends. She says that she is more used to her father's hours. Oumar agrees with Linda that he "hates it" when his mother has to work weekends. Although both parents start out in a defensive mode about their schedules, with some coaching they are able to stop and hear their children's feelings. They follow this by explaining again to the children the necessary realities of their scheduled lives.

In Contextual Family Therapy, an honest dialogue may not alter the facts of their lives, but it is very beneficial for children to be heard and to be able to discuss challenging topics with their parents. I noticed that the parents respond well to some suggestions that could bring improvements within the limits of their schedules.

Trauma Reality Sandtrays

Trauma reality sandtrays are based on the parent participation that is crucial in MBPFT. Over the course of several sessions with the therapist, the parents—without the child present—compose the child's story within the family context. They also work on the life book at home between sessions. The completed book includes a recounting of both the happy times and the challenging times throughout the child's life. When the book is ready, family sessions are held in which the parents create sandtrays that tell the child's life story using sandtray miniatures, with the book as a guide. Although I only occasionally do a trauma reality sandtray before 6 to 12 months into treatment, the acute nature of Oumar's symptoms is an important factor in deciding to start this process after only two months. Trust, both in me and in the safety of the environment, has been well established, which is essential.

The parents write Oumar's story with the central goal of addressing his anxiety about his early medical trauma. Our objective is to ease his and the family's immediate stress, and to alleviate his nightmares and hallucinations. Then the family will be able to confront the underlying anxieties and move toward deeper healing.

Preparation to Create the Trauma Reality Sandtrays

As the parents make sandtrays during our preparatory meetings, it is poignant to hear Sharon and Arnie describe their still-raw feelings about getting the news that Oumar had a heart defect, the pain of watching their little baby suffer medical intrusion, and their fears attached to the knowledge that he would need another operation as a teenager. This is an opportunity for them, without their children present, to safely express to each other their painful feelings about the threat to their child's life. Long-held anxieties gradually begin to be neutralized. The anniversary of baby Arnold's death comes up during this time, and I suggest they make a sand picture about him. Their feelings about Oumar and baby Arnold have tended to be conflated. It is deeply moving to see them differentiate the experiences.

I further recommend that they each choose trusted family members or friends with whom they can discuss their worries and their healing process. The internal shifts that are occurring in the parents will have a positive influence on the whole family situation. Combined with the effects of Talk Time, family sessions, and play therapy, these efforts are a crucial contribution to Oumar's and the family's continued healing.

During the period of weekly preparatory meetings, Sharon requests sessions for herself alone. Sharon brings the book to our meetings and works through her fear-filled feelings. One day she tells me about her brother Angelo's death. She tells me a dream that she had, foretelling his death, that she has never before shared with anyone. A month later, she decides to make a sandtray of this dream and let Arnie witness it.

In compiling their book of Oumar's history, Sharon and Arnie decide to start their story with a happy theme: their marriage. The children know that their parents met earlier in life and then broke up, and they know that Sharon was married before. At one point, they even met her stepchildren. However, they do not know about the miscarriage that occurred in their early dating years. We discuss this and decide to keep it private for now. However, we agree that it might be suitable to tell Linda the following year.

Part of the therapist's responsibility is to know enough about child development and family dynamics that she can comfortably make such recommendations.

The following dialogue is part of the discussion about how to present Oumar's birth and medical complications when the whole family comes to work on the trauma reality sandtray.

THERAPIST: When it comes to talking about his heart defect when he was born, you want to tell the children the simple truth and progress toward the operation. You may want to remind Linda that she was just three years old. Tell the truth, but don't overwhelm the children with details. You can speak frankly to him about the intrusive nature of the medical interventions that he had to undergo as a newborn baby. Mention why they were helpful, though difficult.

Noticing Sharon's tears, I wait to allow her to express her feelings. She wonders if it is suitable for the parents to allow their feelings to show while telling the story to their children. I assure her that it is fine for children to see a parent weep. I explain that prolonged crying, where a child feels like she has to take care of the grownup, is not helpful for children.

THERAPIST: Let what is true be your guide. For example, you may say that you were worried about Oumar's operation, but the doctor did tell you that other babies have had this heart operation, and he believed that everything would be okay. Maybe admit that Mommy and Daddy were still worried, but not as much, when they saw that the doctor wasn't so worried. You can say this, if it is true. Only say what is true.

At the part where you make the sand picture of little baby Oumar on an operating table, it would be helpful to find a way to express your fears. Are you ready to do that?

SHARON: You mean to say that he could die?

THERAPIST: Yes. His play is full of themes showing that everyone was worried and is still worried about the possibility that he may die. Finding a poignant way to say it honestly and simply will help neutralize the fear energies, maybe sooner, maybe later.

ARNIE [turning toward Sharon]: Well, I think that is what we have been preparing to do, and I'm ready. You know what I mean, Sharon. What do you think?

SHARON: It still feels heavy to me. I can better understand how, by avoiding talking about this—not only to family members but to one another—it created like a pressure cooker for our fears. I am realizing that we each have fears and anxieties that go back to our own childhoods, and they may be part of the dam we've built, even between us. So it feels like one big step we can take: to begin to unload all these things we don't even realize we are carrying. Yes, I am ready too.

Oumar's parents had not yet told him that during his teenage years, he would need another heart operation. I suggested that we do this at a different session during the integration stage of the play-family therapy.

Children do better when they hear the truth about their lives directly from their parents, starting with the basic facts and expanding a little at a time as they grow up. Waiting too long to tell a child runs the risk of having him overhear important facts about his life, or of having a relative or friend unwittingly reveal the "secret." The withholding of loaded truths seems to be part of the buildup of anxieties that lead to acute symptoms.

The First Trauma Reality Sandtray

We schedule an hour and a half for the reality tray, and I make sure that I have a half hour free afterward in case more time is needed. It is hard to predict how a reality sandtray session will go, and I want to leave ample time to address whatever might come up this first time. The children seem excited as they watch their parents pick out figures to tell a story. Although they help select pieces to represent themselves and their grandparents, they are aware that today's picture is being made by their parents. Oumar also puts the two-headed dragon into the tray, and Linda puts a big spider in. Seeing them as symbols of their fears, I suggest to the parents that they let the pieces stay for now.

On this first day, the story is about the parents' marriage, Linda's birth story, and moving to their new house. Although a little out of sequence, the tray includes a scary story about the "Jersey Devil" that Grandpa told the children just before Oumar's nightmares began. We have discussed this story a few times during Talk Time meetings, and I have recommended including it in the tray with the idea that externalizing the story might help to neutralize it. We end the tray for today on the day of Oumar's birth.

Sharon leaves me a voicemail a few days after the session. She says that she and Arnie are surprised at how involved the children were, and how well they listened. Sharon has noticed that Linda has seemed more relaxed at home since the sandtray. She says that she and Arnie feel ready to talk about the core events of Oumar's birth and the operation, including their fears that he could die, and so we schedule the next trauma reality tray session for three weeks later.

Talk Time—Following the First Reality Tray

Facing Into the Dream

After discussing some fun events during the past week, Arnie says, "There were no nightmares until last night." At first Oumar wants his dad to tell me his dream, but Arnie encourages him to tell me himself. He does so, with notable anxiety

OUMAR: There is a door monster and a Yeti monster. I open the door monster and inside it I see the Yeti monster.

THERAPIST: The Yeti monster.

OUMAR: Yeah—like in the video game. And then the monster eats me.

THERAPIST: How does he eat you? All of you or some of you?

OUMAR: He eats me by the feet, that's all. [His facial expression shows concern.]

THERAPIST: What are you wearing?

OUMAR: Regular clothes.

THERAPIST: I can see this would be very scary.

OUMAR [looking therapist in the eye]: Yeah, I couldn't even walk if I didn't have feet.

THERAPIST: Right, without feet you couldn't even walk. Good thing you told your dad about your dream.

OUMAR: And I told my mom, too.

THERAPIST: What does the Yeti monster look like?

OUMAR: He's white with bloody teeth.

As part of our family therapy Talk Time, I invite Oumar to make a picture of his dream using sand miniatures. His father's witnessing presence helps him feel safe. (*This process is an adaptation of Eugene Gendlin's work, as described in* Let Your Body Interpret Your Dreams *[1986]. Notice that it is very different from when a child makes a spontaneous sandtray. The therapist encourages the child to tell the dream using sand miniatures. The dream is more the reality of his world than pretend, so I generally keep a parent present when a young child tells a dream.*)

Oumar selects a purple door as the "door monster"; a soft, woolly lamb lying on its side with a red streak of blood across its abdomen to represent the Yeti Monster; a bed; and a little boy with a red cap on. He places the boy outside the door in his bed. The lamb is on the other side of the door.

THERAPIST [pointing to the boy with the red cap and speaking in third person]:   He's lying in bed, and he realizes he's having a dream. What happens?

OUMAR [taking the boy out of bed]:   He opens the door—and it is hard to open—so he karate chops the door—and he sees it right away. And he eats his feet. [He has the lamb eat the boy's feet, and then without words he has the boy run back to his bed.]

THERAPIST: Then what?

OUMAR: He karate chops the door again, and this time the boy says to the sheep, "I'm going to make you dead."

THERAPIST: The boy is going to make the sheep dead. (Maybe it would have been better form to repeat exactly, "I'm going to make you dead.")

OUMAR: No, no! Because the sheep comes back alive and he goes back to bed. [He puts the boy in the bed and the "sheep" behind the purple door.] Then mommy comes in. [He moves the sandtray figure of mommy and pauses.]

THERAPIST: What happens?

OUMAR: He's crying, and tells his mom he had a dream about the door monster . . . Then I go back to bed [moving the toy figure of the boy] and lie down—and then I get up. [He walks the boy to the door.] This time he [the boy] says he is going to make him [the sheep, Yeti monster] dead!

THERAPIST [matching Oumar's tone]:   This time he is going to make him dead!

OUMAR: He opens the door and takes the boy and puts his arm out and he knocks down the sheep and says, "I'm going to make you dead!"—but he's not dead yet. [He puts the boy back into bed.] Now he thinks I'm dead, but I'm not—and then I knock him down and he dies.

THERAPIST: He dies.

OUMAR: Yeah, forever.

THERAPIST: He dies forever.

OUMAR: Then I go back to sleep, and I don't need Mommy to come in—'cause he died.

THERAPIST: You don't need Mommy to come in because the monster died, forever.

OUMAR: Yeah, and I go to sleep.

This dream occurred one week after the first trauma reality tray. He had not had any scary dreams or hallucinations until about a week later, the night before coming to this session. One can see in the metaphors that Oumar's mind is connecting to his fear of dying and slowly moving toward a more empowered stance. After telling us his dream, he moves directly into his half-hour play session, and his play continues to dip into the deeper awareness stage. Arnie waits in the waiting room.

The Second Trauma Reality Sandtray

Three weeks after the first reality tray, all five family members come to the second reality tray meeting, again with their book of Oumar's life. Linda is quite excited and Maya, now closer to three years old, is patient and interested. Oumar seems anxious. The parents begin taking turns telling the story from where we finished last time: Oumar's birth. They slow down the details and are doing a wonderful job: "And when you were born, you were a little bit blue in color, so the doctors had to take you fast to make sure you were okay. We worried a little bit, but then they brought you back. The next day, they told us that we would need to bring you back to the hospital for a heart operation when you were six months old. It was a serious operation, but it would help you to live. The doctor told us he expected everything to be fine. Grandma Rosaleen took care of you that day, Linda, and Maya, you weren't born yet, not even in Guatemala."

They describe the transition to the operating table and how Oumar would be asleep for the operation. They are coming to the the part where it is important to tell Oumar that they worried that he could die. Then there is a long pause. I wait quietly and think, "Uh-oh, you are missing your cue." The pause grows longer . . . and then Linda says, rather matter-of-factly, "And we thought you might die!" Her statement catches all three grown-ups off guard, but then both parents chime in and support Linda's assertion of what everyone has spent years avoiding saying.

There is a section in the tray about Oumar going to his yearly cardiology appointment to have his lungs tested. Sharon explains in simple language why he has a yearly checkup. "It's to be sure that there is enough blood in your lungs, and if there isn't you need another operation. But every year your heart is just fine." Arnie interjects, "We have to take special care of you." The parents have pasted the ultrasound of Oumar's heart into the book. He is quite proud of it.

The book of Oumar's six-year life narrative continues with family photos: Oumar's first birthday; Halloween; Oumar's second birthday party with his cousins; Oumar riding a fire engine; Linda and Oumar in a sandbox with their grandpop Harry, who built it; Oumar's first nursery school experience, including pictures of him playing at the playground with his best friends; the arrival of Maya, adopted when she was nine months old, when Linda was seven and Oumar was four; Oumar's prekindergarten schoolmates; and Oumar going off to full-day kindergarten. The family reflects on how uspet Oumar was when his mother went to Guatelmala to get Maya and how challenging Maya's first months were. This, in turn, increased Oumar's stress.

The book includes a combination of magazine pictures, simple drawings, and photographs, including one of Arnie's whole family at a reunion in

Georgia. With humor, Sharon and Arnie have put at the end a drawing of an old man, which they have labeled "Oumar"; they say they think he will live to be very old. Oumar asks if his mom or dad will die. (We have discussed this question at our parent meetings, because most six-year-olds ask it.) His mother answers, addressing all of the children, "Everyone dies. We just don't know when. And I expect to live to be very, very old." Arnie says, "Maybe I will live to be a hundred because I am very healthy, but as Mom said we never know when we will die." Linda says, "That is, if you don't crash in an airplane"—and everybody laughs except Maya. The parents seems very comfortable. They have done a really wonderful job. In the play therapy room, Oumar's play has continued to go steadily into the deeper awareness stage. There has indeed been a major reduction in the frequency of nightmares, though when they have happened, they have been intense. However, the family has developed more skill in managing them.

The Deeper Awareness Stage

Soon after the family's two trauma reality sandtray experiences, which have taken place three weeks apart, Oumar's play therapy has started to enter the deeper awareness stage. He is doing well in the playroom without a parent, and his play seems less self-conscious. Week after week, he plays out themes that gradually come closer and closer to reworking the trauma. From the seventh month to the ninth month, his play is consistently deeper.

His anxiety has subsided, and Oumar and his family are getting some symptom relief. I have explained to the parents that, until the play reveals that he is facing into the powerlessness of the trauma, we will not have root-level healing. As the seventh month begins, his nightmares and hallucinations revive a bit, as predicted. The parents remember my warning that the initial symptoms can come back more intensely in this deeper awareness stage: "Things can seem to get worse while they are actually getting better."

The Zen of Play Therapy

During the play therapy, Oumar gradually builds up his theme of hunting and the deeper play extends over the next few months. Today, it starts to feel more serious. In hindsight, I realize that his next few sessions are a turning point in his play therapy. He usually uses the red tunnel, placing the box of guns, knives, and swords inside. He may be quiet in there for five minutes, handling and examining the objects. He may put on the sheriff's badge that is in the box and also look through the binoculars.

I stand quietly at the other end of the tunnel, glancing in to keep connected and waiting for his cues. He is very engaged in his solitary play. He starts to tuck a gun and a knife into his pants. This kind of buildup can signal to the observant therapist that a child may be preparing to do trauma play. We have continued for many sessions to play the hunter-hunted themes, taking turns being rabbits, bears, deer. Gradually the energy gets more quiet.

Oumar asks me about the timer. "Yes," I tell him, "I have set it and we have plenty of time." (*I have seen lots of children check about the time when they are about to move into deeper awareness. The encouragement to stay in pretend pays off, as Oumar enters the deeper awareness in his play.*)

OUMAR: Where's that big gun [meaning the rifle]? I can't find it. [He puts on an animal nose.]

THERAPIST: Hmmm . . . where is it? (*In this stage I will help him find props, whereas in the exploratory stage I would wait for him to find things.*)

OUMAR [using the handgun]: We are going to shoot the . . . ?

I don't understand, and I don't ask, because he is involved. He aims across the room, shoots the gun, and walks around quietly looking for the rifle. "Oh, there it is." He puts a jagged hunting knife into a sheath and tucks it into his pants. He takes a small gun from his pants, drops to the floor with the rifle too, and shoots with the smaller gun. "I'm gonna shoot you," he says to me. I realize I did not hear his cue.

THERAPIST [whispering]: What do I pretend to be? (*It is important that the child not think he is shooting the actual therapist. Staying in pretend avoids any confusion.*)

OUMAR: An elk with antlers.

I look around for the soft felt antlers we have been using, but can't find them. I see a broken top of a stethoscope that looks like antlers and hold it up.

THERAPIST [whispering]: Antlers. [Getting her script from the hunter] Does elk look at you or not see you?

OUMAR: No, don't see me. He doesn't know I'm here.

In past play, knowing this cue has seemed important—sometimes the animal sees him and sometimes he does not. Oumar directs the elk to walk on the other side of the room. He goes into the tunnel and crawls to the other end and leans out, with half of his body in and half out. "I need binoculars." He crawls back into the tunnel to get them. He comes back and looks at the elk through the binoculars. I notice that his play is very purposeful and self-directed; he is breathing deeply. It also feels very serious and quiet in the room. It is important to respect the sacred ambiance that he is creating.

The "elk" crawls innocently on hands and knees, quietly looking around, holding the antlers to its head but not making eye contact with the hunter.

OUMAR: Now you see me.

Elk makes eye contact.

OUMAR [shooting the rifle]: You're dead.

THERAPIST [falling over and whispering]: Elk is dead.

Elk lies very still. (*I think that being still without the reflection may have been better—especially because he is clear we are in pretend. It is not good for a child to think he has killed the therapist.*) The hunter goes to the tunnel and gets the weapon box and brings it over to the elk. He takes his jagged-edged knife and cuts off the antlers. He shoots the elk in the head and then cuts around the elk's heart, pretends to remove it, and puts it on the floor. Then he quietly plays with the things in the weapon box. He tries to put on the sheriff's badge and cannot, so he drops it to the floor. He takes another gun, points it away from us, and shoots. We stay there quietly for a few minutes. Suddenly, without my understanding what is happening, the hunter shouts, "Lie down!" to himself. It seems that he is now enacting the animal that was shot. He makes a noise. He now experiences being the victim.

After a few long minutes of silence, in which the two animals lie dead, Oumar changes the scene. He moves to another part of the room and addresses me: "What's this? Is it an arrow?"

THERAPIST: You can pretend it's an arrow.

OUMAR: Where's the bow?

THERAPIST: You can pretend a bow.

OUMAR: I have a bow at home.

I am quiet because his comment is leaving the pretend.

OUMAR: Here, I'll use this.

He sings into a toy microphone. I can see that this is meaningful, intentioned play, and it seems to offer him a way, in metaphor, to step away from the intensity of the play. I just follow him, feeling a little confused.

OUMAR: Here, say something. [He hands me the toy microphone.]

THERAPIST [whispering]: What should I say?

OUMAR: You shot a buck and a deer.

THERAPIST [using the microphone and a deep voice]: I shot a buck and a deer.

OUMAR: Say you shot two bucks and one rabbit.

THERAPIST: I shot two bucks and one rabbit.

OUMAR: The answer is yes.

He goes over and pours a whole pitcher of water into the sand. He takes the big stone heart and buries it in the middle of the tray. I am quiet and present.

OUMAR: Now you go over there and be a rabbit, and you go to bed. It's dark and now I become a pig tomorrow. We go to sleep. [We lie quietly, sleeping for a minute.] It's time to wake up. It's sunny out.

THERAPIST [whispering]: Does rabbit wake up too?

OUMAR: Yeah. You see pig. [He has the nose on.]

THERAPIST: Hi, pig. I'm rabbit.

OUMAR: Now you be the pig [giving me the nose]. Go to sleep, pig. I'll be a few minutes. [Therapist with pig nose goes to sleep. Oumar picks up a bucket and goes to the shelf. He puts the mic in the bucket, then a trumpet, then goes to the sandbox and unburies the heart and puts the heart in the bucket.] Now I'm a boy, and I'm going to a party. [Removing my nose and putting it on himself] I can scare everyone. Okay, here we are at the party, I must scare the people. I scare you.

THERAPIST: What am I?

OUMAR: A boy.

THERAPIST [not understanding and used to being an animal]: A bull?

OUMAR: No, you are scared. You are a boy without a heart.

THERAPIST [putting a baseball cap backward on my head]: I'm a scared boy without a heart. [Whispering] What do I say or do?

OUMAR: You run away.

He has me alternate being scared of him and running away, and then not being scared, saying, "I'm not scared of you." He still has the pig nose on.

OUMAR: You get your gun and shoot me.

THERAPIST [as the boy with the cap, getting his gun]: The boy is going to shoot you.

Instead, Oumar shoots the boy with the cap on and knocks him over.

THERAPIST [in a boy voice]: You got me. [Falling over] You got the boy.

OUMAR: And now the mom and dad look and say, "Son . . . Son . . . I think he's dead."

THERAPIST [lying still and dead, whispering]: The mom and dad think their son is dead.

Oumar takes the knife out of the sheath and cuts out the boy's heart.

THERAPIST: Is it bloody?

OUMAR: Yeah, it's all bloody.

We are both quiet for a minute.

OUMAR: Can I be done now?

THERAPIST: Yeah, you can be done.

His expression is strained. (*I notice the sequence of his saying that he wants to be done now immediately after I ask if it is bloody. I am annoyed at my unmindful comment. It affirms how important it is not to insert our own agenda. I sense that he has stopped the play prematurely, although the bell was about to ring.*) Oumar goes over to the large brown boy puppet and puts it on the small train to ride it around. This is the first time I remember him doing that since our earliest sessions. He seems to use this as a way of moving away from the power of the trauma theme. At the next session, he plays the same theme, and when he cuts out the boy's heart, I remain quietly present. He solemnly buries the heart in the sand. He reverses roles and I am the hunter and he is the boy.

THERAPIST [whispering]:   What does the hunter do with the heart?

OUMAR: He buries it in the sand.

The hunter buries the big stone heart in the sand. We are both quiet for about a minute.

OUMAR: Now you are the doctor and you take the stethoscope and listen to the heart. [The doctor quietly follows instructions and waits.] The heart is strong; it can go back into the boy.

THERAPIST [putting the heart back in the chest]:   The heart is strong.

OUMAR: Now I am alive again. Forever.

THERAPIST: Now the boy is alive again. Forever.

Oumar smiles and looks at me very directly, and I smile. He gets the toy train and rides the boy puppet around the room, ringing the bell and singing, "I've been working on the railroad." The bell rings to end our playtime. I put away the toys today. Usually, after a session that is this intense I do the cleanup myself. Since I am cleaning up, I want to find another way to bring him back to reality, so I ask him what he'll be doing after he leaves today with his mom. I have him hold my hands and stomp his feet a bit before leaving the room.

In the deeper awareness session above, the therapist follows the child. The play is kept in imagination. The therapist asks for most cues from the child so that it is the child's projections (and not the therapist's) that unfold. Even when the therapist could not quite see a logic to the play, she gave reflective responses and Oumar generated what needed to happen. Oumar faced the core of his trauma when he cut out the heart and created the story that allowed him to have his character say, "And now the mom and dad look and say, 'Son . . . Son . . . I think he's dead.'" These are his exact words in the play and it was very poignant for me to be with him and to say back to him that the parents think their son is dead. I needed to say it with the same neutral voice that he said it. For much of trauma play, children may not make eye contact with the therapist. Yet eye contact is sometimes sought by the child during certain moments of trauma play, as noted in the example above. In this intimate connection, we stay in the metaphor, yet the child feels that you really get the core of his trauma. This exchange promotes healing. It is understandably hard for a parent to repeat those words and to keep their equilibrium in deep play eight months into the child's playtime. The gift is that the play therapist can mirror the child's responses in the heart of the trauma as he faces into the powerlessness and creates metaphoric stories so the healing can happen.

For the next month, Oumar's play themes are similar, but there is a shift in intensity, and I realize that the deeper awareness stage is gradually moving into the integration stage. Oumar's nightmares have stopped and he has not been hallucinating for quite a while now. His aggressive behaviors have shifted into speaking up more directly at home and finding ways to say what he feels and thinks. He is happy to go to school and is not exhibiting separation anxiety. He is able to go on play dates but does not want to sleep over at his cousin's house yet.

The Integration Stage

At a play session in the month following the above sessions, Oumar starts out with a hunting scene and then goes over to the easel and asks if he can paint. Using one color at a time, he makes a collage of bright colors. Each color is contained, with a little blending at the borders. He enjoys how his painting looks as he fills the whole page. He is breathing freely and even hums some of the time.

At the next session, he goes back to the dinosaur play, but there is less fighting and aggression as he moves the scenes from the floor to the sandtray and tells stories with a beginning, middle, and end. His themes include problem solving and more powerful Superman figures than he used in his earlier play.

We have another family session to check in with everybody and to talk about the operation Oumar will need when he is a teenager. Maya, who is now three years old, joins us for the discussion. Oumar and Linda ask questions about the operation, and nobody seems overly anxious talking about it. There is an evident decrease in the current level of family anxiety that has resulted from the parents' couple therapy, in which they have processed past family anxieties.

Family Therapy: Oumar Confronts Dad

In his hunting play, Oumar stops using the red tunnel and instead builds a lookout post with the large blocks and the futon. The intensity of this play never reaches the level it did in the sessions described above. Then, one day during cleanup after the hunting play, as I am thinking about suggesting closure to the parents, Oumar tells me that he doesn't want to be a hunter when he grows up. "Yeah, I don't want to kill animals."

I gulp, then say, "You don't want to be a hunter and kill animals when you grow up."

I have had some in-depth conversations with Arnie about the significance of hunting in this family—especially for the boys. I know Oumar's father will be *very* disappointed. Hunting is an intergenerational legacy that bonds the men and develops important life skills to provide food. I say to Oumar, "Maybe we should talk to your mom and tell her?"

"No!" he tells me firmly.

It can be tricky when a child tells you something and then does not want you to tell his parent. I find that most of the time when I say, "Well, we'll talk about this at the end with your mom," the child does not object. I make my best clinical decision, and if it is important to tell the parent, then I let the child know it is my responsibility. However, this agenda can wait, so I honor Oumar's request.

The parents are scheduled to come in for a parent meeting the following week. I tell Oumar that I think it is important for him to be able to tell his dad, and that it would be brave of him. Oumar says, "*I* want to tell my dad, but I'm scared." I say I would be glad to help him do that. I suggest that he can come with his parents next week and tell his dad then, realizing that it is really important to him to be the one to tell his dad first. At the end of the session, with Oumar present, I ask Sharon if it would be possible for her and Arnie to bring Oumar to the already scheduled parent meeting. I say that he has something important to tell his parents, especially his dad, and I emphasize that I think that her presence is important. I say I think he wants to wait until that meeting, and I look at Oumar to see if that is correct. "Yes, *I* want to tell Dad," he says to his mom rather anxiously. "Dottie will help me."

You can be sure that my countertransference is rising. I want to prepare the dad so he will have time to work out his feelings and be as understanding as possible, but I choose to let this unfold. The following week, I receive a phone message from Sharon a few hours before the meeting, saying that something unexpected came up and that she will not be able to attend. She says that Oumar and his father will be there. I wonder if I should postpone the meeting, as I think it best for both parents to be present. I realize that perhaps I have been counting on the mom to soften the blow. Then I think about the challenge for Oumar of holding the news and decide to see what will happen.

Father and son come into the playroom, where we are to have our meeting. They usually sit next to each other on the futon. Oumar asks for a chair. I place a folding chair next to his dad as I sit about 8 feet away. Oumar picks up the chair and places it next to me. Wow, I think, this is going to be a man-to-man talk, and he wants my support.

I open the meeting by saying that Oumar has requested this meeting because he wants to tell his parents something very important. I say that it is something that might be hard, especially for his father, to hear, but that I hope he will understand how important it is to hear his son's honest feelings. I hope that Arnie will realize that it is hard for Oumar to say what he wants to say. Arnie looks curious and apprehensive. I turn and say, "Oumar, are you ready to tell your dad this hard thing?" In a rather serious but very nervous way, the little boy says, "Dad, I decided that I don't want to be a hunter when I grow up." Silence. I see the color go out of Arnie's face, but he keeps his composure.

ARNIE: You don't want to hunt when you grow up? Why wouldn't you want to hunt?

OUMAR: I don't want to kill the animals.

Arnie starts to defend this, and I interrupt and say that what is really important now is that Arnie can hear what his son is feeling. "Oumar is almost seven years old, and right now he is feeling like he doesn't want to hunt and kill animals. This was his own idea, and he told me last week. He said he was afraid but that *he* wanted to tell his dad. I said I thought it was important and brave of him to want to tell you. I think you want to hear your son's honest thoughts, even though it may be disappointing to you."

Silence.

"Yes," Arnie finally says to Oumar. "I want to hear how you really think, even though I'm disappointed. You don't want to kill animals."

After we talk about this for a little while and I notice that Oumar is breathing more regularly, I decide that I need to be multipartial now to the father's viewpoint. I think it would be too much tonight for Oumar to have his father elaborate on all the reasons he values hunting, so I choose not to ask these questions. Instead, toward the end of the family session, I ask just one question to be partial to the dad's side.

THERAPIST: Oumar, can you hear that your dad is trying to understand that you may not want to hunt when you grow up?

OUMAR: Yeah.

THERAPIST: So right now you don't think that you want to hunt when you grow up, and your dad hears this. It's okay for you to say that—for you to not want to hunt. But let me ask you a question. When you get older, if you change your mind and decide you want to hunt, will you let your dad know that?

OUMAR: Yeah, but I don't think I'll change my mind.

THERAPIST: OK. You don't think you'll change your mind.

I feel that this has honored the differences and has allowed me to be mulitpartial to the dad's side. I want to give the very disappointed dad a perspective that what Oumar is saying at seven years old may not be what he thinks later—although it may be.

Reflection on Father-Son Dialogue

There is not one correct way to work with a problem. We need to have an underlying framework for both play therapy and family therapy. In my countertransference I realize that I just want Arnie to say, "Yes, of course, I really want you to tell me how you feel and it is totally okay for you to never go hunting if you don't want to." I was considering preparing the father in advance so that it would be gentler, and he would have an opportunity to process his feelings, rather than allowing Oumar to see his dad's face reveal his fresh disappointment. I wanted the mom there because I thought I could count on her to be generously accepting of his wish not to hunt. However—right or wrong—I decided to support Oumar's wish to be the one to tell his dad that night and to trust his courage despite nonoptimal conditions because that's what happened that day. Ironically, I noticed that it was about five weeks after the play session where he had killed his last buck in the playroom.

Couple Sessions With Sharon and Arnie

The Parents Address Fairness Issues and the Give and Take of Family Life

After a few months of therapy, when the family is having symptom relief concerning Oumar's problems, Sharon and Arnie request a meeting to discuss unfairness issues in managing family life that keep surfacing in our parent meetings. In MBPFT, the same therapist can meet with the parents for couple sessions, provided it is a sound clinical decision. I first invite each of them to list what they appreciate about the other on this topic. Both are able to respond positively. Then Sharon starts when I ask her, "What is unfair?"

SHARON: It's horribly out of whack. I do as much cleaning as he does, plus everything else. I sign the kids up for things, take them to the doctor appointments, go to all the school meetings. Cook the meals.

THERAPIST: How do you want help?

ARNIE: I vacuum more than Sharon does. I go to school meetings when I can. I'm not usually home for those parent meetings, but I go if I'm home. The school doesn't call up and ask about my pilot's schedule before they give us an appointment.

THERAPIST: Sharon, you end up feeling more responsible. Do you ask for help?

SHARON: I *am* more responsible, and I don't want to have to ask for help. I want him to initiate helping. For example, when he is home, he doesn't look in the backpacks, so it's an extra job for me. I don't want to have to teach him that.

ARNIE: It's not that she has to teach me. When I do get home, it's usually later and it's all done. But I admit, she does more. She does a lot more. I am more than willing . . . Give me things, I'll do them. I know she does a lot. She puts out trash every week. She tends to do it before I do it. She likes doing it. She gets up at 5 AM even on her days off; this is her style. She works out, then takes the trash out.

SHARON [shaking her head]: No. I don't want that job. I'm afraid that you won't put it out on time and you're not in the habit of doing it, because you're not always home on Wednesdays. But when you are home, I wish you'd do it.

ARNIE: Tell me what to do; seriously, I'll do it. I mean it.

THERAPIST: How about the trash thing? It's concrete. Do you want Arnie to take over, or do you enjoy doing it?

It helps to use concrete examples as we focus on the dynamic of the relationship. As Sharon and Arnie dialogue, both become aware of their different styles regarding how and when to put out the trash. (*Slowing the process down allows them to learn from the present example how to apply the pattern to a similar situation in the future.*)

Reflection on Fairness Issues

At the end of the session, I observe that their common ground is that they agree that there *is* unfairness. I have been listening to both "sides" with what Contextual Family Therapy calls multidirected partiality. Sharon identifies that what she wants most is that he feel his own power about family things and initiate, deciding what to have for dinner and making it, initiating discussion of what sports the kids will sign up for. Sharon has the insight, for the first time, that her anxiety may be causing her to be too controlling. Arnie admits that he needs to "step up to the plate" and is quite willing to do more. However, he wants Sharon to say what he should do, whereas Sharon's main point is that she wants him to figure it out for himself. The couple continues the session and identifies some concrete ways to meet each of their needs better.

At one point or another in working with couples, issues of fairness come up, and it is important to give them attention. I recommend *Try to See It My Way: Being Fair in Love and Marriage,* by B. Janet Hibbs (2009), a Contextually informed, practical guide for couples. At this point of the work with this couple, the three of us are learning how to work together. As trust builds, more deeply sensitive issues usually open up.

Couple Therapy Using Sandtray Miniatures

Contextual Family Therapy is dedicated to helping people gain the capacity to engage one another in truthful dialogue. Compassionate hearing of each other's life narrative depends on sharing personal vulnerabilities from the past as well as the present. CFT holds that each of us carries a system of "invisible loyalties," which bind us unconsciously to the accumulated emotional residue of previous generations. Today, this might be included in what is called an epigenetic impact. Exploration of these sometimes obvious and sometimes obscure facts from our past can help us better understand the present.

The following sandtray experience takes place after the couple has been many months in therapy. At the time, Oumar's therapy work is in the integration stage. This is the first time that I invite Sharon and Arnie to make a couple sandtray together. Arnie seems a little uncomfortable at first, and he hesitates. Then he agrees to give it a try when I say that today will be easy, because for this first time they will each pick only six pieces with a specific theme. They go on to share an unusually poignant hour together. In addition to demonstrating the power of sandtray symbols, the interchange also illustrates the inclusion of awareness of the influences from the family of origin, an awareness that started with the original genogram session. At the end of the hour, Sharon makes a very important observation, that leads full circle to further intergenerational inquiry that will, in turn, help shift some long-entrenched family issues.

To start, I give them each a large basket. The directions are simple: "You divide your tray into two parts. Then you each pick three objects that represent positive parts of yourself, parts that you really like. Then you each pick three objects that represents parts of yourself that are ugly, nasty—what you don't like about yourself" (see Boik & Goodwin, 2000).

Sharon begins to choose pieces; Arnie hesitates for a while. Sharon tells Arnie she is picking the things she *likes* first. I suggest that he not think too hard. He agrees and begins to pick his six pieces. Arnie draws a line down the middle of the tray. After having quietly placed their six pieces on their own half of the tray, each looks at the other's side of the tray. Sharon laughs: "Look, mine are white (family of 4, boy and girl with parents) and yours are black (man with puppets playing with two boys). We quietly view the tray together. Arnie asks if he did it right. I say that it's hard to do it wrong. In reviewing the video later on, I will notice an expression of deep feeling on Arnie's face, as he turns with meaning and the couple look at one another. Arnie smiles. Sharon holds her face in her hands and continues to look at him. At the time, I did not notice the poignancy of this moment of connection.

Arnie starts right in, saying that he likes that he is family oriented, pointing to two latency-aged brown children hanging out with their dad, playing with puppets. He says that he likes that he does not smoke cigarettes any more. Arnie is not sure his money represents something positive or negative. On the positive side, he likes that he wants to see himself as financially stable; but he lacks the money now, so is that negative? They discuss this for a while.

Sharon introduces her positive pieces. She identifies a Buddha figure as her spiritual guide. The purple bowl with a smiley face sun is her love of nature, and the books represent her wanting to grow and learn. Sharon then picks up her family grouping: two parents and two kids in winter clothes. She takes a little brown girl in a pink dress with her arms out and places her up against the family of four. "And I love my family." She points to the same in Arnie's tray. I acknowledge that they are both family people, and they comment positively about each other's selection.

Next, Arnie begins to discuss the pieces that are about parts of himself that he doesn't like. He picks up the skeleton man with red jeweled eyes, riding a motorcycle, to tell Sharon how much he worries (see figure 9.7). "I've never told you this before." He gives her examples and says that he sometimes has so much anxiety that his heart races. I ask questions to differentiate his response from typical anxiety.

ARNIE: Oh, yeah, the heart starts racing. [He demonstrates with noises and his hand pounding his heart.] Sharon, you don't know that I al-

FIGURE 9.5.   Sharon and Arnie's couple sandtray.

ways tend to think the worst. I'm having a panic attack, but I act calm with you and the kids." [Sharon is quiet.]

THERAPIST: I think it is actually good you are saying that here tonight.

ARNIE: And she never knew that.

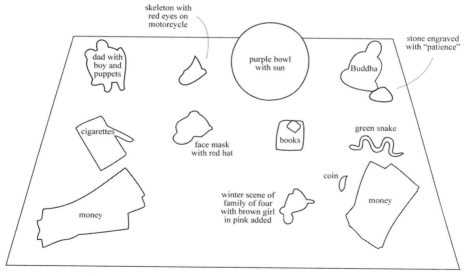

FIGURE 9.6.   Diagram of Sharon and Arnie's couple sandtray.

FIGURE 9.7.   Arnie's skeleton on a motorcycle.

THERAPIST [to Sharon]:   What is it like for you to hear this part of Arnie that you never knew?

SHARON: Um . . . I'm surprised and confused. You present more positively to me.

ARNIE: That's true, I do. But I am anxious all the time about everything. [He folds his arms for the first time in this discussion.] It's a lot of things. I think about stuff happening . . . to my kids . . . it's a lot of things.

THERAPIST [pointing to the skeleton man on the motorcycle]:   This piece is symbolic of a lot of things, not just the skeleton?

ARNIE: A lot of things, like worrying about getting stopped by a cop . . . worrying about being wrongly accused . . . to something horrible happening to one of my kids. I don' t know, I can't explain it . . I think about stuff that I shouldn't think about. [Silence.] You know what I mean?

THERAPIST: You can't control it?

ARNIE: Exactly.

THERAPIST: You can't stop it, once it starts . . .

ARNIE: Right. It's like, goddammit . . . [He unfolds his arm to gesture to his head] I try to shake it off . . . It's like, come on, come on . . . It's not happening, like, constantly, constantly, throughout the day.

THERAPIST: I understand it's not constantly throughout the day, but once it comes you can't control it. There may be a reason it gets sparked . . . but then it's hard to stop.

ARNIE: Right, right . . . and then when I stop it, it stops.

THERAPIST: Your heart beats, and you have physical responses to it like an anxiety attack.

ARNIE: Yeah, it's almost like that.

Sharon continues to be a quiet, perplexed witness. Arnie continues. Selecting his next object from the tray, a distorted face with a red hat, he says, "I don't know if that is the right face for it . . ." He picks up the face and puts it back down. "Another thing I don't like about myself is that I feel a lot of times, when I holler, I make people feel like this." He chuckles uncomfortably as he picks it up again and waves it toward me.

THERAPIST: You make the *other* people feel like that?

ARNIE: My family, my wife.

The face symbolizes how he makes others feel when he hollers. He expresses empathy and regret for others when he makes them feel sad, and for himself. I reflect that he does not like others to feel that way. Sharon is deeply moved, placing her hand over her heart as she says, looking directly at Arnie, that she is deeply moved because she did not know he felt this way. Her eyes begin to tear.

THERAPIST: I'm hearing, Sharon, that you are moved.

Sharon gives a full nod.

ARNIE: I try to show this macho role, but when I'm alone I feel badly. I need to learn how to say what's true, what's really happening.

THERAPIST [addressing Sharon in a soft voice]:   I think it is also honest of you to share that you didn't realize that Arnie was also feeling badly when his actions make everybody feel terrible. You were more aware of yourself and the kids, but you weren't aware that he feels that way. And that it means a lot to you to have him say that.

SHARON: It means a lot.

The energy in the room shifts. I say humorously, "And this is the game you didn't want to play?" We all laugh.

Sharon, speaking in her turn, points to the small snake on her side of the tray. "I struggle with being firm. I don't like that about myself. I wish I could be more firm and assertive, and it feels flimsy and weak to me." She also talks about feeling envious of others who have money, and finally she says that she has been more impatient lately and wants more patience. "I don't like being so angry. I can feel this anger in me." She moves her hand up the core of her body. "And I never had that before."

THERAPIST: You feel it more in your body than you did before. So whether it is anger at the kids or anger at Arnie or your mother, you feel it more in your body."

SHARON: Mm-hmm.

THERAPIST [speaking slowly and quietly]:   The good news might be that by feeling it in your body, we could work with it more. It may have been in your body before, and you didn't feel it. Feeling the anger could be a positive thing.

Sharon nods. Arnie is relaxed, looking at Sharon.

THERAPIST: It's a body cue, and you start to listen to that feeling in your body. Like asking where does it start in your body.

Sharon indicates her stomach and moves her open hand up to her throat.

THERAPIST: Up to your throat. From your stomach to your throat.

Sharon moves her hands up and indicates kissing her two hands and extending them out. "It comes out." She smiles and looks happy as she says that.

THERAPIST [surprised]:   It comes out? It doesn't all get stuck in your throat?

ARNIE: Yeah, she is starting to holler more.

Sharon nods heartily.

ARNIE: Yeah, she tends to raise her voice up—like me.

THERAPIST [to Sharon]:   And you aren't used to that.

ARNIE: I see what she's talking about. I totally see what she's talking about.

SHARON: And I *hate* that about myself! My parents did not do that to me, and I don't want to do that to my kids.

ARNIE [scratching his arm]:   Am I teaching her that?

THERAPIST [with humor]:   I didn't say that! [We all laugh.]

ARNIE: No, it's a question. Could I be teaching her that and not consciously knowing she is picking that up from me?

THERAPIST [addressing Sharon]:   What do you think?

SHARON: I think in a way it could be like a habit, and maybe that's part of it. It's like yelling is part of our house, whereas before yelling wasn't part of our house. We didn't do that, and maybe now it's just part of the house. More like I don't know what else to do.

THERAPIST: Oh . . . you don't know what else to do . . .

SHARON [leaning over and picking up the small green snake in her tray]: Which, I think, has to do with this . . .

THERAPIST: Say more about that.

SHARON: If I could be more firm, maybe I wouldn't get to the yelling stage. I'm starting to put this all together. You must be thinking we're all anxious, not just Oumar! Like anxiety is the theme of our family or something.

This leads to a discussion about intergenerational anxiety and its impact on children. Arnie describes both of his parents as anxious and wonders whether either of them had uncontrollable thoughts like his.

ARNIE: I usually think of my father as depressed, but today, when I describe out loud what happens to me, I think he suffered from this too, and didn't tell anybody.

THERAPIST: Yes, you may have picked it up early. And now you have the opportunity to stop this legacy by helping Oumar. In fact, your work will benefit Linda and Maya as well.

Sharon describes her mother as more anxious than herself. She says that maybe she is willing to do some family therapy with her mother, if that would help reduce the whole family's anxiety. She acknowledges what Arnie has shared with her today and lets him know that it helps her to feel closer to him.

Ending the session, I tell them, "You have both shared a lot today. Our time is up now, but we can come back to some of the topics that were raised. It will be helpful for you *and* your children for us to explore the interconnections, on both sides of the family, regarding the legacy of anxiety and fears. By working on these themes as they impact your present life, a lot of healing can happen. This process that you are in will help your children, as it already has, to reduce their anxieties and to live more peaceful lives. Good night!"

Linda's Sandtray Work

After seeing Oumar for a year of therapy, I begin working with another of the Caruso-Harris children, nine-year-old Linda, who is having more anxiety than is typical for someone her age. Linda seems to have picked up her mom's anxiety about her dad's job as a pilot for a commercial airline. She has also witnessed her brother's terrifying nightmares and daytime hallucinations. I have recommended to the parents that Linda have about 10 play sessions for herself, each preceded by our regular 20-minute Talk Time with the parents.

Every week, Linda comes into the playroom quite excited and ready to get to work. Week after week, she gives all her time and attention to making sandtrays. During her first two sessions, she creates lovely pictures that let me know the strengths of her life. They depict scenes of families doing interesting things together and portray an orderly life. I remain quiet and mindfully attentive, feeling that she is fully present. I notice that she seems to have a comfortable awareness of my presence and is feeling quite safe to work. She occasionally asks for a certain object, but she stays very focused on her creation throughout the duration of the session. When she seems to have finished, I ask merely, "What's happening?" and she says just a bit about her picture.

As I sit quietly for Linda's third picture, she takes 25 minutes to build a beautiful town of houses, lampposts, bridges, trees, and all kinds of people and pets. Then she goes over to the shelf and, after looking for about three quiet minutes, comes back with a basket of magnetic marbles of various colors. She tosses one marble at a time at all different areas of her picture, and then she individually adds a second marble, magnetically touching each of the first marbles. Ten sets of marbles are spread throughout the town. She looks up at me, for the first time seeming satisfied with her picture. During this whole time, I have paid complete attention to her but never said a word. Now I merely ask, "What's happening?"

LINDA [pointing to the miniatures]: This is a town and it is Halloween and everyone is dressed up in costumes, and these [pointing to the groups of two marbles stuck together] are bombs.

She indicates that she is finished, so I decide to ask a question, staying in metaphor.

THERAPIST: Hmmm . . . do the Halloweeners know that the bombs are there?

LINDA: No.

THERAPIST: Hmmm, they don't know that the bombs are there.

She offers no more words. I leave it at that, respecting that she has been able to externalize her feelings through her metaphor and has already said a lot! Linda chooses to make sandtray pictures with occasional art work for most of her sessions. This, combined with productive Talk Time sessions with each parent allows her to work through her present anxieties and to be more comfortable in her world.

Conclusion

Sharon and Arnie continued to work on their issues every other week for a year after Oumar stopped coming for therapy. In couple therapy, Sharon continued to work on her difficulty in saying no to the children. Arnie had experienced and witnessed racial profiling with his father when he was a little boy, and getting in touch with these feelings felt to him like the beginning of a healing process. Arnie also became more sensitive to the impact of his anger on Sharon and the children, motivating him to get control of his reactivity. The road rage began to diminish.

Sharon chose to do individual therapy to better understand why she was so stuck in being unable to restrain herself when her children asked for things that were unreasonable. Sometimes she talked about her history and pain, she did Focusing and created sandtrays to express herself. Sharon still felt guilty about asking her parents to come in to discuss the problem. It was confusing that she described her parents as having the "ideal marriage." They loved one another and rarely argued. Sharon wished that she and Arnie would not argue! On the other hand she was just beginning to feel frustrated, even angry that her parents had not put more limits on her. "Of course I liked getting my way all the time when I was younger." Looking back, she saw the consequences of this as especially harmful during her high school years. She found herself unable to meet peer pressure and would go along with things that she did not really want to do, but had no skill in confronting others and standing up for herself. Sharon shared her present worries about her children as they were getting closer to teen years and her struggle to say "no" to them when she knew she should. After a number of sessions preparing, Sharon decided to invite her parents to join her for a session. Her primary motivation was for her own children, as she did not like confronting her parents about her own problems.

We scheduled the family therapy session for an hour and a half. Sharon's parents, Rosaleen and Angelo arrived. They were a little anxious at first, but Rosaleen shared that they had also had family therapy with their other daughter, and they soon became comfortable. I invited Sharon to share what she appreciated about her parents and assured them that our motivation was not to have them here to blame them, but to better understand how the past is impacting the present. Sharon explained to her parents the difficulty that she had always had with her children. She told her parents that she had begun to see that she has been repeating the same thing with her children that she had learned from them. Sharon admitted having severe difficulty setting appropriate limits because she was afraid of hurting everyone's feelings. She felt vulnerable when her children talked back to her and vulnerable to ask her parents for their help.

Sharon's parents also shared concern about some of the impolite and sometimes arrogant behaviors that they saw in their grandchildren. "They never talk to me that way," Rosaleen reported. About a half hour into the session, as I was asking for more details about a marriage that both of them attested to as being quite good, Sharon's mother said, "Well, I think our relationship was so good because I *hated* conflict. I would do anything to avoid it."

"Ah," I said, "So it was rooted in avoiding conflict." Angelo admitted that he too would do what he could to avoid conflict. In each respective family of origin, they identified their roles as "peacekeeper." Rosaleen said she had always just done what her father told her to do, so there was no conflict. "That was how I learned to survive, especially after my mother died." She expected her children to do the same. Angelo said that he just did what he wanted and avoided conflict by making sure his parents did not find out.

This was discussed for the rest of the session, and Sharon left understanding a whole new piece of her life narrative. She began to see that it was not so bad that she and Arnie argued. They needed to learn to argue when the kids were not hearing all the details. and to listen better to one another. Sharon said, "I never realized that what was at the root of this problem that I've had, like forever, was that both of my parents avoided conflict. I never learned how to 'do conflict'!"

Sharon worked on this issue for over a year, and I am happy to report that she began to make a major shift. When Arnie saw the changes in Sharon after several meetings with her family, he decided to consider how it might help him to have a meeting with his father and possibly his brother. Arnie admitted worrying about his grandfather's medical suicide and his father's tendency to get depressed. Should he and Sharon invite Harry to live with them? Arnie wanted Sharon to be part of these discussions.

At the time of this writing, Oumar is no longer coming to therapy. His parents report that he almost never has nightmares, and when he does they feel able to help him. He seems happier and lighter than they have ever seen him. He was even at ease about his last annual checkup. Linda is doing better all around. The fears that are typical for her age are subsiding, and she seems to understand that lying is not acceptable. Maya is doing well, having tantrums that her family is helping her to get through. She is enjoying her first year at preschool and is doing well making friends. Arnie and Sharon report greatly reduced anxiety. They both notice a big difference—they no longer carry daily angst about the possibility of Oumar dying.

Not long ago, the family requested a meeting. Everyone attended, and although it raised their anxiety, both parents conveyed a primarily neutral energy. The family knows that life will continue to have its challenges as Linda enters junior high, as Oumar faces the possibility of heart surgery as a teenager, and as Maya begins to wonder about her history and how she came to join her family.

Appendix A:
Sample Forms and Questionnaires

Developmental and Social History Questionnaire   Date: /   /

Family Name:_____   Child of Most Concern (MC):_____   Age:____   Date of Birth: /   /

Early History
A. Conception: Was it a conscious decision?   ☐ Yes ☐ No
B. Pregnancy: Were there and problems with the health of the mother?   ☐ Yes ☐ No
C. Delivery: Apgar score of health of baby (1–10): _____
D. Infancy (Please comment on the following issues.)

    1. Baby at birth?   2.First 3 months?

    3.Feeding problems?   4. Nursed? Age weaned? Process of weaning?

    5. Excessive vomiting?   6.Excessive crying?

    7.Colic? Describe.   8. Other problems or illness of baby during first year? Second year?

E. Any physical problems of parents in child's first year? Second year?

F. Post partum depression?

G. Has the child, a sibling, or a parent had a serious illness, surgery, or hospitalization since child's birth?
    Date: /   /   Details: _____

Developmental Milestones
Please write the ages at which the following milestones were reached.
    A. Crawled: _____   B. Walked alone: _____
    C. Knew ten words: _____   D. Talked in sentences: _____
    E. Completed toilet training: _____
    F. Is there any history of problems concerning toilet training?   ☐ Yes ☐ No
    _____

    G. Temper tantrums: At what age(s)? _____   How frequent? _____
    How intense? _____   How were they handled by parents/adults?
    _____

Medical History
A. Please check the appropriate boxes to indicate the child's medical history at any age.
    ☐ Illness   ☐ Allergies
    ☐ Head Injury   ☐ Chronic Ear Infection
    ☐ Eye Problems   ☐ Convulsions/Seizures
    ☐ Frequent Colds   ☐ Asthma
    ☐ Other: _____
    Comments: _____

B. Is the child taking medication now?   ☐ Yes ☐ No   If so, what medication? _____
C. Trauma: Has the child experienced any kind of trauma (deaths of relatives, friends, pets; medical interventions;
    Physical, emotional, or sexual abuse; etc.)?
    _____

FIGURE A.1.   Developmental and Social History Questionnaire.

309

Child Care & Early School History

A. Age of infant when both parents were back to work: _____

B. Who took care of the child? Describe setting. Were you pleased?

_____

_____

C. List care of child until preschool setting.

_____

_____

D. Preschool
    1. Name of school/child care: _____
    2. Describe setting:
    3. How did the child do...   socially/behaviorally?
                                     emotionally?
                                     cooperatively?

E. Kindergarten
    1. Name of school/child care: _____
    2. Describe setting:
    3. How did the child do...   socially/behaviorally?
                                       emotionally?
                                     cooperatively?

F. Grades 1–3
    1. Name of school/child care: _____
    2. Describe setting:
    3. How did the child do...   socially/behaviorally?
                                       emotionally?
                                     cooperatively?

G. Has the child had any extended separation from parents? ☐ Yes ☐ No   If so, please describe:

_____

Habits

A. Please rate problems on the following scale: (No Problem | Low | Moderate | Serious)

(N | L | M| S) temper tantrums   (N | L | M| S) easily frustrated ·
(N | L | M| S) aggression   (N | L | M| S) attention span
(N | L | M| S) memory   (N | L | M| S) fears
(N | L | M| S) anxiety   (N | L | M| S) interrupts adults
(N | L | M| S) disobedience   (N | L | M| S) clumsiness
(N | L | M| S) stealing   (N | L | M| S) awareness of danger/safety issues
(N | L | M| S) fighting   (N | L | M| S) self-esteem
(N | L | M| S) eating   (N | L | M| S) sleeping
(N | L | M| S) fine motor control   (N | L | M| S) gross motor control
(N | L | M| S) quick mood changes   (N | L | M| S) disturbs children at school
(N | L | M| S) accident prone   (N | L | M| S) restless/overactive
(N | L | M| S) language (lisp,stuttering,articulation,etc.) (N | L | M| S) attachment

B. Describe a typical day in the child's life. How much TV, videos, and electronic games does the child watch each day?

_____

C. Does the child have two or three close friends in the present class setting? Do they visit one another's homes? How often?

_____

FIGURE A.1.   Continued.

Older Children and Adolescents
SUPPLEMENT TO DEVELOPMENTAL AND SOCIAL HISTORY QUESTIONNAIRE

Date: / /

Family Name:_____ Child of Most Concern (MC):_____ Age:____ Date of Birth: / /

Middle School (4-6)

1. Name of school:

2. Describe setting:

3. How did the child do...   academically?

socially/behaviorally?

emotionally?

Junior High (7–8)

1. Name of school:

2. Describe setting:

3. How did the child do...   academically?

socially/behaviorally?

emotionally?

High School (9–12)

1. Name of school:

2. Describe setting:

3. How did the child do...   academically?

socially/behaviorally?

emotionally?

Does the student have a job?

What are the students hobbies or interests?

FIGURE A.2.   Older Children and Adolescents Supplement.

Adoption

SUPPLEMENT TO DEVELOPMENTAL AND SOCIAL HISTORY QUESTIONNAIRE

Date: /   /

Family Name:_____   Child of Most Concern (MC):_____   Age:____   Date of Birth: /   /

Adoption Information

1. Was the adoption open or closed?

2. What was the age of the child at adoption?

3. Was the child from outside the United States?

4. What information is known about the birth mother?

5. What information is known about the birth father?

6. What information is known about environments and extended families of the birth parents?

7. Additional Information: Include, if available, ages, medical information, reasons for adoption, life circumstances of the child prior to adoption (e.g., Was the child in foster care or an orphanage? What is known about this time?).

8. How did the child do with attachment to adoptive parents, siblings, and other family members and friends?

Open Adoption

1. How was the relationship with the birth parent(s) prior to having the baby join your family?

2. How much time did the baby spend with the birth parent(s)? How was the quality of this time?

3. Did anyone else take care of the baby?

4. What is the present agreement for communication with the birth family?

Artificial Insemination Information

FIGURE A.3.   Adoption Supplement.

Foster Care

SUPPLEMENT TO DEVELOPMENTAL AND SOCIAL HISTORY QUESTIONNAIRE

Date: / /

Family Name:_____   Child of Most Concern (MC):_____   Age:____   Date of Birth: / /

Foster Care Information

1. Date child joined your family: / /

2. What were the circumstances of the child's life just prior to coming to your home?

3. How was the transition? What has happened with attachment and bonding issues?

4. What strengths do you see in the child?

5. What problems do you see in the child?

6. Do you actively seek to engage the child in his or her cultural or ethnic background?

7. What information is known about the child's history in the birth family (e.g., mother, father, siblings, environment)?

8. What were the circumstances of the child's leaving the birth family?

9. How does the child relate to his or her parents at the present time? What has the child been told about the birth parents? Does the child discuss or fantasize about them? Who is the internal parent?

FIGURE A.4.   Foster Care Supplement.

History of Foster Care Placement

1. Family name and information:

2. Circumstances entering this family:

3. Circumstances leaving this family:

4. Strengths of this family:

5. Problems in this family:

6. What do you know about attachment and bonding issues with this family?

History of Foster Care Placement

1. Family name and information:

2. Circumstances entering this family:

3. Circumstances leaving this family:

4. Strengths of this family:

5. Problems in this family:

6. What do you know about attachment and bonding issues with this family?

History of Foster Care Placement

1. Family name and information:

2. Circumstances entering this family:

3. Circumstances leaving this family:

4. Strengths of this family:

5. Problems in this family:

6. What do you know about attachment and bonding issues with this family?

History of Foster Care Placement

1. Family name and information:

2. Circumstances entering this family:

3. Circumstances leaving this family:

4. Strengths of this family:

5. Problems in this family:

6. What do you know about attachment and bonding issues with this family?

FIGURE A.4. Continued.

Family Evaluation Session

Date: / /

Family Name:_____ Child of Most Concern (MC):_____ Age:____ Date of Birth: / /

Child's Name:	
Parent's Name:	**Parent's Name:**
What this parent likes/loves about this child...	What this parent likes/loves about this child...
What this parent wants this child to work on or change in the next 3 months...	What this parent wants this child to work on or change in the next 3 months...

Child's Name:	
Parent's Name:	**Parent's Name:**
What this parent likes/loves about this child...	What this parent likes/loves about this child...
What this parent wants this child to work on or change in the next 3 months...	What this parent wants this child to work on or change in the next 3 months...

FIGURE A.5. Family Evaluation Session form.

Monthly Talk Time Notes

Family Name: _____ Child of Most Concern (MC): _____

Week 1	Date: / /
Talk Time	
Significance of Play Themes	
Mindful Parenting Issues	
Misc.	

Week 2	Date: / /
Talk Time	
Significance of Play Themes	
Mindful Parenting Issues	
Misc.	

Week 3	Date: / /
Talk Time	
Significance of Play Themes	
Mindful Parenting Issues	
Misc.	

Week 4	Date: / /
Talk Time	
Significance of Play Themes	
Mindful Parenting Issues	
Misc.	

FIGURE A.6.   Monthly Talk Time Notes form.

Parent Dialogue Meeting Agenda

Date: / /

Family Name: _____ Child of Most Concern (MC): _____

Therapist's Agenda

Review weekly notes from Monthly Talk Time Notes form.	
Summary of strengths and what is going well	
Observations of normal development	
Occasionally, check in with how the therapy relationship is going. Ask about all family members as needed.	

Parents' Agenda (Prepare at the start of the meeting.)

Topics	Comments	Priority
Summary of strengths and what is going well		
Relevant developmental history information. How are the symptoms?		
Relevant genogram information		
Child at home?		
Child at school?		
Friendships?		

Summary of Meeting (Follow-up?)

FIGURE A.7. Parent Dialogue Meeting Agenda form.

Appendix B:
Training and Supervision at the
Family & Play Therapy Center*

OUR COMPREHENSIVE POSTGRADUATE program offers training and supervision in Mindfulness-Based Play-Family Therapy and the related modalities of Mindfulness-Based Sandtray Therapy and Contextual Family Therapy. Our training program and individual and group supervision are available both onsite in Philadelphia and live online around the world. In addition to our core courses, which either follow the academic year or take place over the course of a week, we also offer occasional one-day seminars and multiday conferences by nationally recognized authors of books in the field. Following are lists of our certificate programs and core courses. Please see our website (www.fptcenter.com) for extensive information about these programs and courses, as well as individual supervision, group supervision, seminars, and conferences.

Certificate Programs

- Mindfulness-Based Play-Family Therapy Certificate Program
- Mindfulness-Based Sandtray Therapy Certificate Program
- Contextual Family Therapy Certificate Program

Core Courses in Mindfulness-Based Play-Family Therapy

- Introduction to Mindfulness-Based Play-Family Therapy

*See http://www.fptcenter.com for additional information.

- History and Techniques of Play Therapy with a Focus on Deeper Awareness Stage of MBPFT
- Advanced Child Development Course with a Component in Mindfulness-Based Play-Family Therapy (Two-Year Course, 6 hours per month)

Core Courses in Mindfulness-Based Sandtray Therapy

- Sandtray Therapy with Children Ages 3 to 12
- Sandtray Therapy with Teens & Adults
- Relational Sandtray Applications
- Sandtray Theory & Focusing

Core Courses in Contextual Family Therapy: Sample Topics

- Introduction to Contextual Family Therapy, including Trauma Reality Tray
- A Framework Rooted in Human Relationships
- Therapeutic Methods & the Therapist in Context
- Truth, Trust, and Healing Relationships Through Dialogue
- Intergenerational Balance, Parentification, Trust, and Loyalty
- The Nuts & Bolts of Creating Genograms in a Multiethnic and Multicultural World

Bibliography

Ainsworth, M. D. S., Andry, R. G., Harlow, R. G., Lebovici, S., Mead, M., Prugh, D. G., & Wootton, B. (Eds.). (1962). *Deprivation of maternal care: A reassessment of its effects*. (p. 97–165). Geneva: World Health Organization.

Allan, J., & Hillman, J. (1988). *Inscapes of the child's world: Jungian counseling in schools and clinics*. Dallas, TX: Spring.

Amatruda, K., & Simpson, P. H. (1997). *Sandtray: The sacred healing*. Novato, CA: Authors.

Axline, V. (1964). *Dibs in search of self.* New York: Ballantine.

Axline, V. (1969). *Play therapy.* New York: Ballantine.

Badenoch, B. (2008). *Being a brain-wise therapist: A practical guide to interpersonal neurobiology*. New York: Norton.

Bettelheim, B. (1976). *The uses of enchantment.* New York: Knopf.

Boik, B. L., & Goodwin, A. (2000). *Sandplay for diverse populations*. New York: Norton.

Booth, P., & Jernberg, A. (2010). *Theraplay: Helping parents and children build better relationships through attachment-based play* (3rd ed.). San Francisco: Jossey-Bass.

Boszormenyi-Nagy, I. (1992). Interview by William Doherty with Ivan Boszormenyi-Nagy. Washington, DC: American Association for Marriage and Family Therapy.

Boszormenyi-Nagy, I., & Krasner, B. (1986). *Between give and take: A clinical guide to contextual therapy*. New York: Brunner/Mazel.

Boszormenyi-Nagy, I., & Spark, G. (1973). *Invisible loyalties: Reciprocity in intergenerational family therapy*. Hagerstown, MD: Harper & Row.

Bowen, M. (1978/2004). *Family therapy in clinical practice*. Lanham, MD: Rowman & Littlefield.

Bowlby, J. (1966). *Maternal care and mental health*. New York: Schocken Books. (Original work published 1951)

Bowlby, J. (1988). *A secure base: Parent-child attachment and healthy human development*. New York: Basic Books.

Bradshaw, J. (1995). *Family secrets: The path to self-acceptance and reunion*. New York: Bantam Books.

Brody, V. (1997). *The dialogue of touch: Developmental play therapy*. Northvale, NJ: Jason Aronson.

Brooks, D. (2012, September 27). The psych approach. *New York Times*. Retrieved from http://www.nytimes.com/2012/09/28/opinion/brooks-the-psych-approach .html?_r=0

Brown, S., with Vaughan, C. (2009). *Play: How it shapes the brain, opens the imagination, and invigorates the soul*. New York: Penguin.

Davis, N. (1996). *Therapeutic stories that teach and heal*. Burke, VA: Nancy Davis.

Deikman, A. (1982). *The observing self: Mysticism and psychotherapy*. Boston: Beacon Press.

Doidge, N. (2007). *The brain that changes itself: Stories of personal triumph from the frontiers of brain science*. New York: Penguin.

Drewes, A. (Ed.). (2009). *Blending play therapy with cognitive behavioral therapy: Evidence based and other effective treatment techniques*. Hoboken, NJ: Wiley.

Ducommun-Nagy, C. (2002). Contextual therapy. In F. Kaslow, R. Massey, & S. Massey (Eds.), *Comprehensive handbook of psychotherapy, Vol. 3: Interpersonal/ humanistic/existential*. New York: Wiley.

Ducommun-Nagy, C. (2006). *Ces loyautés qui nous liberent*. Paris: Jean-Claude Lattes.

Faber, A., & Mazlish, E. (1999). *How to talk so kids will listen & listen so kids will talk*. New York: Avon.

Felitti, V. J. (2004). The origins of addiction: Evidence from the Adverse Childhood Experiences Study. Retrieved from http://www.nijc.org/pdfs/Subject%20 Matter%20Articles/Drugs%20and%20Alc/ACE%20Study%20-%20Origins ofAddiction.pdf

Gendlin, E. (1981). *Focusing*. New York: Bantam.

Gendlin, E. (1986). *Let your body interpret your dreams*. Wilmette, IL: Chiron Publications.

Gil, E. (1991). *The healing power of play*. New York: Guilford Press.

Gil, E. (1994). *Play in family therapy*. New York: Guilford Press.

Gil, E. (1996). *Systemic treatment of families who abuse*. San Francisco: Jossey-Bass.

Gil, E. (2006). *Helping abused and traumatized children: Integrating directive and nondirective approaches*. New York: Guilford Press.

Gil, E., & Drewes, A. (Eds.). (2005). *Cultural issues in play therapy*. New York: Guilford Press.

Goldenthal, P. (1996). *Doing contextual therapy: An integrated model for working with individuals, couples, and families*. New York: Norton.

Gottlieb, D., & Claflin, E. (1991). *Family matters: Healing in the heart of the family*. New York: Dutton.

Greenspan, S. (1992). *Infancy and early childhood: The practice of clinical assessment and intervention with emotional and developmental challenges*. Madison, CT: International Universities Press.

Grosskopf, B. (1999). *Forgive your parents, heal yourself: How understanding your painful legacy can transform your life.* New York: Free Press.

Guerney, L. (1978). *Parenting: A skills training manual.* State College, PA: Pennsylvannia State University.

Hargrave, T., & Pfitzer, F. (2003). *The new contextual therapy: Guiding the power of give and take.* New York: Brunner-Routledge.

Hibbs, B. J., with Getzen, K. J. (2009). *Try to see it my way: Being fair in love and marriage.* New York: Penguin.

Higgins-Klein, D. (1983). *The impact of the birth of the first child on the family dynamics.* Unpublished master's thesis, Hahnemann University, Philadelphia.

Homeyer, L., & Sweeney, D. (2011). *Sandtray therapy: A practical manual* (2nd ed.). New York: Routledge.

Hughes, D. (2007). *Attachment-focused family therapy.* New York: Norton.

Hughes, D. (2009). *Attachment-focused parenting: Effective strategies to care for children.* New York: Norton.

James, B. (1994). *Handbook for treatment of attachment-trauma problems in children.* New York: Free Press.

Kabat-Zinn, J. (1994). *Wherever you go, there you are: Mindfulness meditation in everyday life.* New York: Hyperion.

Kabat-Zinn, M., & Kabat-Zinn, J. (1997). *Everyday blessings: The inner work of mindful parenting.* New York: Hyperion.

Kaiser Greenland, S. (2010). *The mindful child: How to help your kid manage stress and become happier, kinder, and more compassionate.* New York: Free Press.

Kalff, D. (1980). *Sandplay: A psychotherapeutic approach to the psyche.* Santa Monica, CA: Sigo Press.

Kaplan, L. (1978). *Oneness and separateness.* New York: Simon & Schuster.

Killough McGuire, D., & McGuire, D. E. (2001). *Linking parents to play therapy: A practical guide with applications, interventions, and case studies.* Philadelphia: Brunner-Routledge.

Krasner, B., & Joyce, A. (1995). *Truth, trust and relationships: Healing interventions in contextual therapy.* New York: Brunner/Mazel.

Landreth, G. (2002). *Play therapy: The art of the relationship* (2nd ed.). Muncie, IN: Accelerated Development.

Levy, T., & Orlans, M. (1998). *Attachment, trauma, and healing: Understanding and treating attachment disorder in children and families.* Washington, DC: Child Welfare League of America.

Lieberman, A., & Van Horn, P. (2008). *Psychotherapy with infants and young children: Understanding and treating attachment disorders in young children.* New York: Guilford Press.

Lowenfeld, M. (1979). *The world technique.* London: Allen & Unwin.

Lowenstein, L. (2010). *Creative family therapy techniques: Play, art, and expressive activities to engage children in family sessions*. Toronto: Champion Press.

MacLean, K. L. (2004). *Peaceful piggy meditation*. Morton Grove, IL: Albert Whitman.

MacLean, K. L. (2008). *Peaceful piggy yoga*. Morton Grove, IL: Albert Whitman.

MacLean, K. L. (2009). *Moody cow meditation*. Somerville, MA: Wisdom.

Mahler, M., Pine, F., & Bergman, A. (1975). *The psychological birth of the human infant*. New York: Basic Books.

McCarthy, D. (2007). *"If you turned into a monster": Transformation through play: A body-centered approach to play therapy*. London: Jessica Kingsley.

McGoldrick, M., Gerson, R., & Petry, S. (2008). *Genograms: Assessment and intervention* (3rd ed.). New York: Norton.

McGoldrick, M., Giordano, J., & Garcia-Preto, N. (Eds.). (2005). *Ethnicity and family therapy* (3rd ed.). New York: Guilford Press.

McGoldrick, M., & Hardy, K. (Eds.). (2008). *Re-visioning family therapy: Race, culture and gender in clinical practice*. New York: Guilford Press.

McKay, M., Fanning, P., Paleg, K., & Landis, D. (1996). *When anger hurts your kids: A parent's guide*. Oakland, CA: New Harbinger Publications.

Minuchin, S. (1974). *Families and family therapy*. Cambridge, MA: Harvard University Press.

Mitchell, R. R., & Friedman, H. (1994). *Sandplay: Past, present and future*. New York: Routledge.

Mitchell, R. R., & Friedman, H. (Eds.). (2008). *Supervision of sandplay therapy*. New York: Routledge.

Moustakas, C. (1959). *Psychotherapy with children: The living relationship*. New York: Harper & Row.

Norton, C., & Norton, B. (1997). *Reaching children through play therapy: An experiential approach*. Denver, CO: Publishing Cooperative.

O'Connor, K., & Schaefer, C. (1994). *Handbook of play therapy* (Vol. 2). New York: Wiley.

Ogden, P., Minton, K., & Pain, C. (Eds.). (2006). *Trauma and the body: A sensorimotor approach to psychotherapy*. New York: Norton.

Oppenheim, D., & Goldsmith, D. (Eds.). (2007). *Attachment theory in clinical work with children: Bridging the gap between research and practice*. New York: Guilford Press.

Panksepp, J., & Biven, L. (2012). *The archaeology of mind: Neuroevolutionary origins of human emotions*. New York: Norton.

Parens, H. (1987). *Aggression in our children: Coping with it constructively*. Northvale, NJ: Jason Aronson.

Parens, H. (2011). *Taming aggression in your child: How to avoid raising bullies, delinquents, or trouble-makers*. New York: Jason Aronson.

Perry, B., & Szalavitz, M. (2006). *The boy who was raised as a dog.* New York: Basic Books.

Phelan, T. (1996). *1-2-3 Magic.* Glen Ellwyn, IL: Parentmagic.

Prosky, P., & Keith, D. (Eds.). (2003). *Family therapy as an alternative to medication: An appraisal of pharmland.* New York: Brunner-Routledge.

Rubin, T. (1969). *The angry book: Quieting the storm within.* New York: Macmillan.

Satir, V. (1972). *Peoplemaking.* Palo Alto, CA: Science and Behavior Books.

Schaefer, C. (1993). *The therapeutic power of play.* Northvale, NJ: Aronson.

Schaefer, C., & Carey, L. (Eds.). (1997). *Family play therapy.* Northvale, NJ: Jason Aronson.

Schaefer, C., & Gilbert, J. (2012). What play therapists need to know about a child to develop an individualized treatment plan. *Play Therapy, 7*(4), 10–12.

Schore, A. (1994). *Affect regulation and the origin of the self: The neurobiology of emotional development.* Hillsdale, NJ: Erlbaum.

Schore, A. (2003a). *Affect dysregulation and the disorders of the self.* New York: Norton.

Schore, A. (2003b). *Affect regulation and the repair of the self.* New York: Norton .

Schore, A. (Speaker). (2009). *Right brain affect regulation: An essential mechanism of development, trauma, dissociation, psychology* (Audio recording). Austin, TX: EMDRIA.

Siegel, D. (2010a). *The mindful therapist: A clinician's guide to mindsight and neural integration.* New York: Norton.

Siegel, D. (2010b). *Mindsight: The new science of personal transformation.* New York: Bantam.

Siegel, D., & Bryson, T. (2011). *The whole-brain child: 12 revolutionary strategies to nurture your child's developing mind.* New York: Delacorte.

Siegel, D., & Hartzell, M. (2003). *Parenting from the inside out: How a deeper self-understanding can help you raise children who thrive.* New York: Penguin.

Stern, D. (1985). *The interpersonal world of the infant.* New York: Basic Books.

Stern, D. (2004). *The present moment in psychotherapy and everyday life.* New York: Norton.

Sunderland, M. (2006). *The science of parenting: Practical guidance on sleep, crying, play, and building emotional well-being for life.* New York: DK Adult.

Terr, L. (1990). *Too scared to cry: How trauma affects children . . . and ultimately us all.* New York: Basic Books.

Thich, N. H. (2011). *Planting seeds: Practicing mindfulness with children.* Berkeley, CA: Parallax Press.

Tolle, E. (1999). *The power of Now: A guide to spiritual enlightenment.* Novato, CA: New World Library.

Tolle, E. (Speaker). (2005). *The Findhorn retreat* (Audio Recording). Novato, CA: New World Library.

Walsh, F., & McGoldrick, M. (Eds.). (2004). *Living beyond loss: Death in the family* (2nd ed.). New York: Norton.

Webb, N., (Ed.). (1991). *Play therapy with children in crisis: A casebook for practitioners.* New York: Guilford Press.

Welwood, J. (Ed.). (1983). *Awakening the heart: East/West approaches to psychotherapy and the healing relationship.* Boulder, CO: Shambhala.

Wickes, B. (2000). Integrating attachment concepts from Western psychological and Buddhist perspectives. In T. M. Levy (Ed.), *Integrating attachment concepts from Western psychological and Buddhist perspectives.* San Diego, CA: Academic Press.

Winnicott, D. W. (1965). *The family and individual development.* London: Tavistock.

Index